Dubai Red-Tape

A Complete Step-by-Step Handbook

HADEF هـادف الظـاهـري
AL DHAHIRI وشــــركـــاؤه
& ASSOCIATES
LEGAL CONSULTANTS AND ADVOCATES

The Team

Contributing Authors	Louise Andrasevic	
	Pamela Grist	Pamela@Explorer-Publishing.com
Editors	Claire England	Claire@Explorer-Publishing.com
	David Quinn	David@Explorer-Publishing.com
	Jane Roberts	Jane@Explorer-Publishing.com
Proofer	Mariela Reagon	
Contributing Researchers	Rania Adwan	
	Shelley Gibbs	shelley@explorer publishing.com
	Yolanda Rodrigues	
Production Assistant	Mariela Stankova	Mimi@Explorer-Publishing.com
Research Manager	Tim Binks	Tim@Explorer-Publishing.com
Research Team	Helga Becker	Helga@Explorer-Publishing.com
	John Maguire	John@Explorer-Publishing.com
	Miki Binks	Miki@Explorer-Publishing.com
Sales Manager	Alena Hykes	Alena@Explorer-Publishing.com
Advertising Team	Caroline Pfenninger	Caroline@Explorer-Publishing.com
	Laura Zuffa	Laura@Explorer-Publishing.com
Corporate Sales	Sue Page	Sue @Explorer-Publishing.com
Design Manager	Pete Maloney	Pete@Explorer-Publishing.com
Design Team	Ieyad Charaf	Ieyad@Explorer-Publishing.com
	Jayde Fernandes	Jayde@Explorer-Publishing.com
	Jay Pillai	Jay@Explorer-Publishing.com
	Zainudheen Madathil	Zain@Explorer-Publishing.com
Distribution Manager	Ivan Rodrigues	Ivan@Explorer-Publishing.com
Distribution Team	Abdul Gafoor	Gafoor@Explorer-Publishing.com
	Feroze Khan	Feroze@Explorer-Publishing.com
	Mannie Lugt	Mannie@Explorer-Publishing.com
	Rafi Jamal	Rafi@Explorer-Publishing.com
Accounts & Administration Manager	Andrea Fust	Andrea@Explorer-Publishing.com
Accounts Assistant	Cherry Enriquez	Cherry@Explorer-Publishing.com
Publisher	Alistair MacKenzie	Alistair@Explorer-Publishing.com

IT

IT Manager	Ajay Krishnan R.	Ajay@Explorer-Publishing.com
Programmer	Smitha Sadanand	Smitha@Explorer-Publishing.com
Printer	Emirates Printing Press	

Explorer Publishing & Distribution

Office 51B, Zomorrodah Building
PO Box 34275, Dubai
United Arab Emirates

Phone (+971-4) 335 3520 Fax (+971-4) 335 3529
info@explorer-publishing.com
www.explorer-publishing.com

ISBN 976-8182-25-3

First published 2002

Copyright © 2002 Explorer Group Ltd

Managing Dubai's Red-Tape

Whether you've just arrived in Dubai, you've been here a while, or you're about to leave, there is always a certain amount of paperwork that needs processing. The table below gives you an overview of the red-tape you're likely to encounter and directs you to the procedure to cut through it.

Dubai Explorer

If you live in Dubai then you have to own this book, simply because it is packed with everything you need to know about finding a home, getting settled, exploring the city and beyond, and hitting the town!

UAE Off-Road

Your weekends need never be boring again with this definitive guide to off-roading. Whether you're a novice or an experienced driver this book will be right at home on your dashboard!

Underwater UAE Explorer

If you're a PADI diver, or want to be, a keen snorkeller, or wish you were, the Underwater Explorer is a must-own. Written by an expert it contains essential info about the UAE's underwater world.

Family Explorer

'We're bored! Are we there yet? I want, I want, I want' - you'll never hear these words again with the Family Explorer. From birthday parties to ball pits, it's time for Super Nanny to move over!

Street Map Dubai Explorer

It's easy to loose your way (sometimes your mind!) in Dubai – especially with roads that loop unexpectedly and lanes that suddenly merge. Fear not with Street Map in your glove compartment you'll never get lost again.

Starter Kit

You're here in Dubai and you need an NBF (New Best Friend)...look no further, the Starter Kit is perfect for the job. Three in one – Dubai Expat, Red-Tape and Street Map it's all for one and one for all!

Residents' Guides

Mini Guides

Activity Guides   **Lifestyle Guides**

Map Guides

Photography Books

Dear Reader,

We are pleased to be the co-sponsor of the Dubai Red Tape Explorer, which is a highly useful addition to the Explorer series. Although we did not prepare the text, we did review the contents and anticipate that the information provided will make your life in Dubai easier.

Coinciding with the publication of Red Tape is the 25th Anniversary of this firm providing legal services in the UAE and our Dubai office move to the World Trade Centre. Hadef Al Dhahiri & Associates is among the oldest and largest law firms in the UAE. We are a full service business law firm that is active in general corporate & commercial law, banking and finance, construction & projects, real estate, shipping, insurance and international trade, and all related dispute resolution.

As of the date of publication, our team consists of 40 lawyers who are predominately educated and have practiced in the UK, the US, Canada,

Australia, New Zealand, as well as a range of Middle Eastern jurisdictions. Our team is bilingual in English and Arabic, whilst many of our lawyers are also fluent in additional languages.

We look forward to being of continued service to the business community of the UAE.

Yours Sincerely, Sadiq Jafar, *Managing Partner*

HADEF هادف الظاهري
AL DHAHIRI وشـــركــاؤه
& ASSOCIATES
LEGAL CONSULTANTS AND ADVOCATES

Hadef Al Dhahiri & Associates, 18th Floor, Dubai World Trade Centre, Sheikh Zayed Road
P.O. Box 37172, Dubai, UAE, Tel: +971 4 332 3222, Fax: +971 4 332 3300
Email: s.jafar@hadalaw-dubai.ae, Website: www. Hadalaw.com

Red-Tape Unravelled

How To Use Dubai Red Tape

Like it or not, living and working in Dubai involves a lot of paperwork and bureaucracy. But help is at hand, because for every conceivable procedure you're likely to encounter, Dubai Red-Tape tells you – in plain and simple language – what you'll need, where you should go, what it'll cost and how long it's likely to take. From visas and licences, to housing, cars and doing business, Duabi Red-Tape gives step-by-step instructions to help make your life easier.

Each procedure is explained from beginning to end:

[1] '**Overview**' tells you what the procedure will achieve, and who it is suitable for.

[2] '**Prerequisites**', describes what you need to have already done beforehand, or what situation you must be in for this procedure to be relevant.

[3] '**What to Bring**' is fairly self-explanatory, listing all the documents and certificates you'll need, plus what the cost will be.

[4] '**Procedure**' explains where you need to go (always with a map reference and opening hours), describes what will happen at each stage of the process, and gives you an idea of how long things should take. After much deliberation, we also decided to include charges and fees to give a guideline of the costs involved, even though they are the most notorious variable. We suggest you always bring extra cash and your bank card, and be ready to run to the nearest ATM or bank selling e-Dirhams (see [p.6]).

[5] '**Related Procedures**' points you to other areas that you may also have to deal with.

So who is Dubai Red-Tape for?

1- You've just arrived, you're setting up and settling in...
You'll have lots of questions, and you may not even know everything that you should be doing. The first four chapters of the book (Visas, Housing, Communication, Driving) will come in most handy – the overview section at the beginning of each will give you the lowdown on what's involved. We suggest you read these chapters to make sure you've got everything covered.

2 – You're already here / you're about to leave...
Dubai Red-Tape isn't just for new arrivals – it covers everything you'll have to deal with during your stay, and most importantly tells you how to wrap things up before you leave. To find a specific procedure turn to the Table of Contents on [p.111], or go to the comprehensive index at the back of the book.

3 – You're in Dubai to do business...
The comprehensive Business chapter starting on [p.211] has all you need to know, covering everything from immigration and labour cards to commercial agents and free zones.

Beginning on p.269 is the handy **Directory** section. The Directory lists hundreds of useful phone numbers such as embassies, hotels, car showrooms, schools and hospitals. You'll also find the contact details, locations, and opening hours of all the government offices and departments you'll be dealing with. And throughout Dubai Red-Tape, every office or location mentioned has a map reference – these correspond to the Dubai maps starting on p.295, so you'll always be able to find your way around town.

Web Updates

While a tremendous amount of research has gone into providing you with the most up-to-date and accurate information possible even Explorer can't predict the future, and inevitable changes are sure to occur. What we can do though is keep you informed of any such changes via our website. Just visit www.Explorer-Publishing.com go to guide books and select **Red-Tape**. Any updates to the procedures in this book will be shown. In addition if you have any comments regarding any aspect of this book - the good, the bad and the ugly - we would love to have your feedback via our on-line reader response form. You may even win yourself the entire Explorer catalogue!

Info/Law/Tip Boxes

In addition to the text explaining each procedure, you'll occasionally see these little boxes – 'Info' boxes give additional information and highlight extra services, 'Tip' boxes give handy hints to make things go more smoothly, and 'Law' boxes explain any legal aspects you need to be aware of.

Essential Documents

Passport
You'll have to show your passport when carrying out many of the procedures listed throughout the book. You may also have to provide photocopies of the page showing your photo and the page with your visa, so come prepared.

Photos
For just about every licence and application, you'll need lots of colour photos. Many photo shops around Dubai will take your picture and process the prints. You should ask to keep the negatives, or a CD, for when you need new copies.

NOC – No Objection Certificate (or No Objection Letter)
For many procedures you will require a letter from your sponsor or employer, stating that they have no objection to you renting a home, applying for a licence, buying a car etc. The NOC, on company headed paper, should state your name, position and passport number, and should then be signed, and stamped with the company stamp.

Salary Certificate

To apply for certain services you will need to present proof of your earnings. Just as with a No Objection Certificate, a Salary Certificate should be on company headed paper, and must be signed and stamped to make it 'official.'

Copies

In addition to your passport, you may also be asked for photocopies of various other documents, licences and certificates. As a security measure it's worth keeping copies of all your essential documents in a safe place anyway, should you be unfortunate enough to lose the original.

Additional Documents

Depending on the procedure, you may sometimes need additional documents such as a birth certificate, marriage certificate, driving licence (or international driving licence), education certificates, school records, professional certificates, divorce papers, power of attorney – for more informatin see the table on [p.8]

What is eGovernment?

The eGovernment initiative aims to provide access to public services via the internet, allowing residents to apply for licences, pay bills, and carry out other procedures online, rather than having to visit a government office. Most websites do require you to register first, but it's worth persevering in order to avoid all that travelling and queuing! The instructions throughout Dubai Red-Tape tell you how to carry out procedures in person, but will also tell you if the same process can be achieved online.

Tip   Arabic or English

Always keep in mind that any document written in Arabic is the legally binding one; the English version isn't. Therefore many institutions require that application forms are completed in Arabic. Apart from the fact that this is an Arabic speaking country, Arabic is obligatory when information accuracy is crucial, such as with immigration and labour matters, to avoid any misunderstanding. Etisalat and some others, however, allow the customer to fill out forms in either English or Arabic.

Tip   Typed or Handwritten

In general, all institutions prefer typed forms for clarity. Some departments are more lenient on this matter than others, particularly those offering personal rather than commercial services. If typed forms are necessary, you'll usually find a typing desk or office who'll help you out for a small fee.

What are e-Dirhams?

The Dubai Government is increasingly promoting the use of e-Dirham cards in ministries and departments, in place of cash. The same size as a credit card, the pre-paid cards can be bought at participating banks and are available in denominations of Dhs.100, Dhs.200, Dhs.300, Dhs.500, Dhs.1000, Dhs.3000 and Dhs.5000. Alternatively, regular users can apply for a personalised card that can be 'topped up' at a bank whenever necessary. When it's time to pay for a service or procedure simply present your e-Dirham card, and the appropriate amount will be deducted. Some departments don't accept e-Dirhams yet, while others say they'll accept nothing but. The rules can also be different within the same department, depending on the procedure. It's best to ask as soon as you arrive what the preferred payment method is – that way you can quickly go out and buy a card if required (you'll nearly always find a bank on site or nearby), rather than face buying a card in advance and not being able to use it.

Reader Response

If you have any suggestions or comments on this book or any of the Explorer products we would love to hear from you. Our Reader Response form on our website, **www.Explorer-Publishing.com**, is quick and easy and helps us gain essential feedback on all our books – which means we can keep improving them!

Also not only will your input help us continue getting better and better you could also end up winning a holiday in the Seychelles for your troubles!

Web Update

While Dubai's government is committed to cutting back on the red-tape involved in setting up in Dubai, both for individuals and businesses, changes in rules and regulations are inevitable. Therefore, if there have been any changes or additions to the procedures included in this book they will appear on the Explorer website. Just log on to **www.Explorer-Publishing.com** and click on the **Red-Tape** link. This page will tell you if there have been any changes to specific procedures – giving you the heads up before you head off to plough through Dubai's administrative maze!

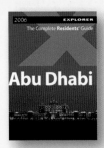

What are the different types of visas?

All tourists, prior to entry, are issued a limited term visit or tourist visa by the Immigration & Naturalisation Department. Those wanting to stay in Dubai for the long term need permission in the form of a residence permit. Unless you are joining a spouse already resident and working in Dubai, you must have a job to get a residence permit.

A new employee cannot enter the country without prior approval of a work permit by the Ministry of Labour & Social Affairs. This department is therefore closely linked with the Immigration & Naturalisation Department.

Immigration & Naturalisation Department (IND)

The Immigration Department, located in Bur Dubai, is one of the busiest offices in Dubai. Millions of visas and permits are issued here, the department at times struggling to keep up with the ever-increasing numbers of visitors and residents. The IND is one of the main authorities deciding who can enter the country. As with similar departments all over the world, you can expect long queues, many counters, unclear procedures and plenty of paperwork.

Changes in policy occur overnight, and can be reversed just as quickly. As immigration is such an important and sensitive issue, all rule and regulation changes should be monitored continually – they can suddenly make your life easier, or sadly, much more difficult.

Ministry of Labour & Social Affairs

This Ministry is a federal institution and is responsible for labour issues and approval of all labour-related permits (with the exception of some free zones). Only official representatives of companies deal directly with this Ministry. Employees will in general never have to enter the Ministry buildings and, in fact, the Ministry is very strict on who is allowed to enter the building and who is permitted to submit documents. Only an officially authorised person, such as the company owner, sponsor or PRO, may perform the labour-related procedures for each company.

All documents submitted must be in Arabic.

Web Update

While Dubai's government is committed to cutting back on the red-tape involved in setting up in Dubai, both for individuals and businesses, changes in rules and regulations are inevitable. Therefore, if there have been any changes or additions to the procedures included in this book they will appear on the Explorer website. Just log on to **www.Explorer-Publishing.com** and click on the **Red-Tape** link. This page will tell you if there have been any changes to specific procedures – giving you the heads up before you head off to plough through Dubai's administrative maze!

Entering Dubai

1 Overview

- Everyone entering Dubai needs a visa, except for citizens of GCC countries (Bahrain, Kuwait, Oman, Qatar, Saudi Arabia, UAE).
- Certain nationalities do not need to apply in advance for a visa – the visa will be given on arrival (see 18).
- All visit visas are for a limited term, and are issued by the Immigration and Naturalisation Department. You can apply for a visit visa at UAE embassies abroad (see Directory p.15).
- If you plan to live in Dubai, you will initially need a work permit (if you are taking a job) and subsequently, a residence permit.
- To get a residence permit you must have a work permit. Work permits are issued by the Ministry of Labour and Social Affairs.
- If you are accompanying a family member who has a job in Dubai, you do not need a work permit before applying for your residence permit (e.g. a wife accompanying her husband, elderly parents accompanying their children).

Sponsors › Sponsorship is an important concept for expatriates in the UAE. Rather than having financial implications, your 'sponsor' takes legal responsibility for you entering and/or living in the country. The sponsor can be a company or individual, a hotel, airline or tour operator. It is usually the sponsor who will apply for your visit visa or residence permit at the Immigration and Naturalisation Department in Dubai.

If your sponsor is your future employer, the company will take care of all charges involved with the process. Families of eligible employees are not sponsored by the company, but rather by the employee himself. In most cases, he is responsible for the entire procedure and all related costs, unless the employer agrees to also cover family members.

Sponsorship plays an important role in business as well. Most types of company require a sponsor to set up operations outside a free zone (see Business [p.211] and Appointing a Local Service Agent [p.245]).

Visiting ›
Dubai All visit visas allow only one entry into Dubai. Some nationalities can extend their visas for an additional 30 days, but once the maximum length of stay has expired, you must leave the country (see Visas [p.15]).

⚠ There is a penalty of Dhs.100 for every day that you overstay your visa.

Becoming ›
Residents Once you have arrived in Dubai, your sponsor will apply for a residence permit, submitting your passport to the Ministry of Labour. This process should be initiated as soon as you enter the country, as all processing must be complete before the entry visa expires. Once the application has been approved, you will receive a residence permit in your passport. Normally the duration of the permit is three years, during which time you may leave and enter the country as often as you wish (see Residence Permit [p.25]).

Your residence permit will be for the emirate in which your sponsor is registered. This should be the first consideration when applying for the visa.

Company sponsorship allows you to work only for the company which sponsored you.

Tip **Private vs. Public Sector Employment**

All procedures related to work visas in this chapter cover private sector employees only. Public sector (government) employees and those working in free zones are subject to different employment regulations and procedures, although there may be some similarities.

Info 'Banning'

'Banning' is a term that many new residents may not be familiar with, but you may unfortunately find yourself dealing with a 'ban' if your new job in Dubai doesn't work out how you expected. Previously with the banning law, job hopping was almost impossible for most categories of worker, but the recent relaxation in the laws has been welcomed wholeheartedly by Dubai's workforce. Even if you left your previous employer on good terms, the Ministry of Labour could stamp a six-month ban in your passport, thus preventing you from taking up any other job in Dubai for that period. Now however, as long as you leave your current job on good terms, and you get a no objection letter from your employer, you will be able to transfer your sponsorship to another employer without difficulty. Of course, your employer may refuse to give you the letter, particularly if you are leaving your current job to work for a competitor. In such cases you are likely to get a ban, although you can lodge an appeal with the ministry.

Be Prepared

Before you get behind the wheel make sure you have your wits about you. The driving in Dubai leaves rather a lot to be desired and the number of traffic accidents are quite shocking. For more information on driving habits refer to the Driving section of the Residents chapter in the *Dubai Explorer* (The Complete Residents Guide) available in all leading bookshops and supermarkets.

1 Overview

The e-Dirham card is a prepaid electronic payment tool introduced by the Ministry of Finance and Industry. E-Dirham cards replace the use of cash as payment for procedures at various federal government ministries.

The card has added security features that prevent misuse and forgery. It can be deactivated in case of loss or theft by calling the Tele e-Dirham Service (24 hours a day, 7 days a week). This service can also be used for balance enquiries, PIN changes, and many other transactions.

While it started out as revenue collection tool, the e-Dirham has gradually become the preferred payment method for many local government departments, some semi-government organisations, and even some private sector companies.

You can use your e-Dirham card to register online for federal government services. Online services now available are e-tender and e-sinaee.

There are two types of e-Dirham cards:

Fixed Value Card

• This card is non-rechargeable and is purchased at face value. You can use up to two cards to settle the fee of any one service you are applying for.

• Fixed value cards are available in denominations of Dhs.100, 200, 300, 500, 1,000, 3,000 and 5,000.

• Cards are available at e-Dirham member banks (see table on [p.272] for a list of e-Dirham banks).

• No documentation is required to buy fixed value cards.

• Cards are valid for six months, and are non-refundable.

Government Client Card

•This card is intended for frequent users of government services and can be used by both individuals and organisations.

•The card is PIN-protected and personalised, with the company name, and the name, photograph and signature of the cardholder.

•The card can be charged with any amount. You can recharge the card at any of the e-Dirham member banks.

•The funds you load onto the card are valid for six months, and are not refundable.

•To determine card balance, call 800 2243

E-Stamp While you will not have to deal with e-Stamps yourself, it is helpful to know that the Government uses this term when referring to the payment receipt, printed on completed online application forms.

2 Prerequisites

Individual > • Valid residence permit

Company > • Valid trade licence

3 What to Bring

Fixed Value Card > ☐ Cash (Dhs.100, 200, 300, 500, 1,000, 3,000, or 5,000)

Government Client Card > ☐ One passport photo

☐ Cash or bank transfer for the amount required

4 Procedure

Fixed Value Card > • Purchase the card at any e-Dirham member bank (see Directory [p.272])

Location > Ministry of Finance & Industry, Department of Revenue   Map ref 8-F1

Hours > Sat-Wed 07:30-14:30

Government Client Card > • Complete the Government Client Card application form available at the Ministry of Finance & Industry or at any e-Dirham member bank (see Directory [p.272])

• Submit the application at the Ministry of Finance & Industry

• Once the application is approved, a card will be issued and personalised the same day

• Collect the card, which will have a value of zero

• The PIN number (personal identification code) will be sent in a secure envelope to you

• Go to any e-Dirham member bank to charge the card

• Pay any amount, either with cash or through an account transfer

• To personalise and e-enable the card, enter a PIN code at the bank at the time of purchase

The e-Dirham card is then used for one of the following two options, depending on the ministry visited:

Ministry > • After following the required procedure, the counter officer will request your e-Dirham card

• The card will be inserted in the payment terminal at that counter and only the exact amount of service fee will be debited

• You may use up to two cards to settle the fee of any service (Fixed Value Card)

• A receipt will be issued in two copies; one copy is attached with the application and the other copy is returned to you along with the e-Dirham card

Typing Office > • The typing office clerk will fill in the application form with your personal details using an online 'Smart Form'

• The fee will be automatically determined

• The clerk will insert the e-Dirham card into the payment terminal and the service fee will be debited

• You may use up to two cards to settle the fee of any service

• The application form will be printed out with the e-Stamp logo and all payment details

• Submit the application form at the ministry/government department for processing

Visas

E-Dirham

Essential Documents

Documents

1 Overview

There is a lot of paperwork involved in moving to a new place, and Dubai is no exception. You can save yourself some time and frustration by having all the right documents when you arrive. If you are starting a new job, note that some employers will require you to have your education certificates certified, notarised and attested. This should be done in the country where they were issued, so if you are reading this while still in your home country, get it done before you leave! If you are already in Dubai, you can use the post or a courier service to send your documents back for attestation. (see Notarising & Attesting Documents [p.11]).

Personal > At some time during your setting up stage, you may need the following documents (where applicable):

Passport, birth certificate, marriage certificate, divorce papers, driving licence, international driving licence, education certificates, school records (to register children at schools), professional certificates, power of attorney.

Company > You should bring the following documents from the company headquarters, home country, or country of issue; as you may need to present them when setting up an office in Dubai:

Board of Director's resolution, power of attorney, parent company's memorandum of association, main company's certificate of incorporation, and the audited accounts of the parent company.

Personal Documents		
Document	**Related Procedures**	**Notarise in Country of Issue**
Passport	All procedures	No
Birth Certificate	Sponsor family members	
	Marriage	Yes
Marriage Certificate	Sponsor wife	
	Obtain a birth certificate	
	Register a new-born child	Yes
Divorce Papers	Marriage	Yes
Driving Licence	Obtain a Dubai driving licence	
	Hire a car	No
International Driving Licence	Hire a car	No
Education Certificates	Obtain a work permit	
	Set up a company	Yes
School Records etc.	Register at school	No
Professional Certificates	Obtain a work permit	
	Transfer sponsorship	
	Set up a company	Yes
Power of Attorney	Marriage	Yes

Lost Documents

1 Overview

If an important document is lost or stolen, notify the police in person. You will be asked to return to the police station two days later, to check whether the document has been recovered. If it hasn't, the police will issue a report – you will need this before you can apply for a replacement document from your embassy or any of the ministries.

If you lose documents while here on holiday, notify the police headquarters to get a report. Your document details will be entered into their database, so that nobody can travel in or out of Dubai with your documents.

2 Prerequisites

• Document has been lost or stolen

3 What to Bring

☐ Photocopy of the lost document

☐ Letter from your sponsor verifying that you work for the company and that you have lost the document

☐ Trade licence (copy)

☐ Establishment labour card, or

☐ Establishment immigration card

Fee > ☐ Dhs.50

4 Procedure

• Go to the police station in the district where the document was lost, rather than to police headquarters (see Map Ref.[10-E7] or Directory [p.289])

• Pay Dhs.50 and collect a receipt from the Police.

• Return two days later to check whether the Police have recovered the document.

• If not, they will issue a police report addressed to the concerned department(s) (Ministry of Labour, embassy, etc), confirming that the documents have indeed been misplaced or stolen.

Visas

Essential Documents

Essential Documents

Passports

[1 Overview

Validity › Passports should be valid at least six months past the date of entry and have at least three unused pages.

Procedures › It's not a bad idea to carry your passport with you for any administrative procedure. If you are applying for or cancelling a residence permit, or applying for a liquor licence, you may need to leave your passport with the authorities.

Separate Passports › It is recommended that all family members have their own passport. Note that a child on a parent's passport may not travel unaccompanied.

Lost Passport › If you lose or damage your passport (see Lost Documents [p.9]), inform the Department of Naturalisation & Immigration within three days.

Photocopies › Always bring a photocopy of your passport with you. Make sure all relevant pages with personal details are photocopied as well.

Resident Permit › If residency is required for an application, provide a copy of your residence permit together with the passport copies.

Passport Photos › Format: 4 x 6 cm, colour. Always bring extra photos!

> **Tip** Make Copies & Keep Them Within Reach
>
> Having copies of lost documents makes replacing them much easier. Keep copies of all important documents with you, and keep a set with someone else in case you need to access them while you are away.

> **Traveller's Info**
>
> To find out more about travelling to and from Dubai, such as the health requirements, travel insurance needs, travelling with children or physically challenged visitors check out the Traveller's Info section of the **Dubai Explorer** (The Complete Residents Guide) available in all leading bookshops and supermarkets.

Notarising & Attesting Documents

1 Overview

Ensure all important documents have been notarised (and attested if applicable) before moving to Dubai. It is much quicker to do it while still in your home country, than to use a courier service or the post from Dubai.

The notarisation procedures for Canada, the UK and US are listed in this section. For notarisation in other countries, contact the nearest UAE embassy for instructions regarding authentication and related costs. In all cases, a copy of the documents must be stamped by a Notary Public, then endorsed by the Ministry of Foreign Affairs and the UAE embassy in that country.

Terms & Definitions

Term	Definition	In other words...
Certified	A copy of the original document, certified by the issuing authority	The document is genuine
Notarised	A certified copy of an original document duly notarised by a Notary Public or other authorised person	The signature is genuine
Attested	A certified, notarised copy of an original document bearing the stamp of a UAE embassy abroad	The issuing institution is genuine

Tip Attestation at GCC Embassies

If necessary, documents may also be notarised at any GCC embassy abroad. Check with the embassy first.

International Courier Services

Some international courier companies (such as Aramex) will take care of attestation for a fee. Contact the courier companies for further information.

Info Attesting documents in the UAE

If you are unable to carry out document notarisation in your home country prior to arriving in the UAE, you can:

• Send the document to a Notary Public in your home country

• Have the notarised document attested by either your embassy or consulate in the UAE

• Have the document attested by the UAE Ministry of Foreign Affairs

Visas

Essential Documents

Notarising & Attesting Documents in Canada

1 Overview

For a detailed overview see p.11.

2 Prerequisites

• Documents need to be notarised

3 What to Bring

☐ All documents (originals) to be notarised

4 Procedure

Notary > Public
• Submit the original and one copy of the document and inform the Notary Public for which country the document is being notarised

• If you have several documents to be notarised, ask the Notary Public to bind the documents together, list each document on a cover page and classify all as one document (this is to avoid each document being charged separately)

• The Notary Public will stamp a copy of the entire document

Federal > Government
• Have the document authenticated by the Department of Foreign Affairs, Canada

Location > Department of Foreign Affairs (+1 800 267 8376 in Canada; +1 613 944 4000 outside of Canada)

Hours > 08:00-16:00 Mon-Fri

• Submit the original document along with a covering letter stating your request and contact details to: Foreign Affairs Canada, c/o JLAC, 125 Sussex Drive, Ottawa, Ontario, K1A 0G2, Canada

• Provide a self-addressed return envelope and arrange return courier service if submitting outside Canada

• Have the document endorsed

Location > UAE Embassy (+1 613 565 7272)

Hours > 09:00-16:00 Mon-Fri

• Submit the document to the Authentication Office

• If you send it by mail, provide a self-addressed return envelope

• The embassy will return the attested document to you

• Contact the embassy if there are any delays

Notarising & Attesting Documents in the UK

1 Overview

For a detailed overview see [p.11].

2 Prerequisites

• Documents need to be notarised

3 What to Bring

☐ All documents (originals) to be notarised

4 Procedure

Notary Public >
• Submit the documents and inform the Notary Public for which country the documents are being notarised

• If you have several documents to be notarised, ask the Notary Public to bind the documents together, list each document on a cover page and classify all as one document (this is to avoid each document being charged separately)

• The Notary Public will stamp a copy of the entire document

Location > The Foreign & Commonwealth Office (+44 207 008 1500)

Hours > Mon-Fri 09:30-12:30; 13:30-16:00

• Submit the notarised document to the Legalisation Department

• If you are sending the document by mail, attach a covering letter informing them for which country the document is being legalised. Enclose a daytime contact number as well as an envelope addressed to the UAE embassy and a postal order for the correct amount

• The Foreign & Commonwealth office will forward the document for you

• Pay £12.00 for each document (cheque or postal order)

Location > UAE Embassy (+44 207 581 1281)

Hours > Mon-Fri 09:30-13:00 (lodging applications), 13:00-14:00 (collections)

• Submit the document to the Legalisation Department to have it attested

• Pay £10.00 for each document (postal order)

• If you are sending the document by mail, the embassy will mail the document back to you. If you wish the document to be returned by registered mail, enclose a prepaid envelope.

Visas

Essential Documents

Essential Documents

Notarising & Attesting Documents in the USA

1 Overview

The US Federal Information Center (800 688 9889), open 08:00-20:00 EST, Mon-Fri, can give you advice as well as information on government office contact details for each state.

2 Prerequisites

- Documents need to be notarised

3 What to Bring

☐ All documents (originals) to be notarised

4 Procedure

Notary Public ›
- Submit a copy of the documents and inform the Notary Public for which country the documents are being notarised
- If you have several documents to be notarised, ask the Notary Public to bind the documents together, list each document on a cover page and classify all as one document (this is to avoid each document being charged separately)
- The Notary Public will stamp a copy of the entire document

County Clerk ›
- Have a County Clerk stamp the copy of the document

Secretary of State ›
- Have the Secretary of State stamp a copy of the document
- Documents must be stamped by the County Clerk or Secretary of State of the state where the certificate or document was issued

Location ›
US State Department (+1 202 647 4000)

Hours ›
07:30 – 11:00 Mon – Fri
- Submit the document to the Authentication Office
- If you want the document forwarded to the UAE Embassy, enclose an envelope with the UAE Embassy address printed clearly, together with a cheque for the right amount. Attach a covering letter requesting that the US State Department forwards the document to the UAE Embassy in the envelope provided.

Location ›
UAE Embassy (+1 202 243 4444)

Hours ›
07:30 – 11:00 Mon – Fri
- Submit the document to the UAE Embassy
- If you send it by mail, provide a self-addressed envelope
- The embassy will return the attested document to you

Visas

1 Overview

The UAE Ministry of Interior specifies that all visitors to the country must have a visa ('entry visa') to enter the country. A visa allows an individual to enter the country for a short or temporary period, as opposed to a residence permit, which allows an extended stay in the UAE.

The following visas are covered in this section:

- Visit visa (on and before arrival)
- Tourist visa
- 14 day transit visa
- 96 hour transit visa

The entry visa to be applied for depends on several factors: (see tables below for details)

- Nationality
- Sponsor
- Intended period of stay
- Purpose of visit

Nationality

Nationality	Visa Options
GCC nationals (Bahrain, Kuwait, Oman, Qatar, Saudi Arabia)	No visa necessary
33 nationalities (see **Exempt Countries** [p.18])	Visit visa upon arrival, employment or residence visa
Other nationalities	Tourist, transit, visit, employment or residence visa

Sponsor

Sponsor	Visa Options
Airline, hotel or tour operator	Tourist or transit visa
UAE-based company	Transit, visit or employment visa
UAE resident	Transit or visit visa

Intended Period of Stay

Visa	Maximum Permitted Stay in Dubai	
Transit visa	96 hours	Non-renewable
Transit ('visa for a mission')	14 days	Non-renewable
Tourist visa	30 days	Non-renewable
Visit visa	60 days	30 days renewable
Visa on arrival	60 days	30 days renewable

Purpose of Visit

Purpose of Visit	Visa Options
Tourist	Transit or tourist visa
Family or corporate visitor	Transit, tourist or visit visa
For future employment	Employment or visit visa
For residence without employment	Residence or visit visa

Timing ▶
- Visitor must arrive within 60 days of date of visa issue
- Permitted length of stay includes dates of both entry and exit into/from Dubai.
- Visas valid 60 days are valid for exactly 60 days – not two calendar months.
- Visitor must leave the country before the visa's expiry date. On departure, a fine of Dhs.100 is payable to Dubai Immigration for each day overstayed, in addition to a fixed overstayed visa fine of Dhs.100.

Granting a visa does not guarantee entry. As in other countries, entry is at the ultimate discretion of the Immigration authorities on arrival.

Visas must be issued for the port of arrival only; if you are flying in to Abu Dhabi, you will need an Abu Dhabi visa to enter the country.

Visitor's Costs

Visa Type	Application Fee	Renewal charge
96 hour transit visa	Free	Not applicable
14 day transit visa ('visa for a mission')	Dhs.120 Dhs.100 (urgent fee)	Not applicable
Tourist	Dhs.100 Dhs.50 (maximum hotel service charge) Dhs.100 (urgent fee)	Not applicable
Visit	Dhs.100 Dhs.100 (urgent fee)	Dhs.500
Visa on Arrival	Free	Dhs.500

Future Resident's Costs

Visa Type	Application Fee	Renewal charge
Employment	Dhs.100	Not applicable
Residence	Dhs.100	Not applicable

Prerequisites ▶
- Visitor holds a valid passport or a document allowing entry into Dubai and re-entry into country of residence
- Visitor's passport is valid for the maximum permitted stay in Dubai (see Intended Period of Stay table [p.15])
- If visitor needs to be sponsored (see Nationality table [p.15]), the sponsor is resident in Dubai and eligible to sponsor a visitor (see Sponsor table [p.15])
- Visitor has not been deported from the UAE
- Visitor is not banned from entering the UAE
- Visitor is not an Israeli national
- Visitor will arrive and depart from Dubai International Airport

Health > rements
- No health certificates are required for entry to the UAE, except for visitors who have been in a cholera or yellow fever infected area in the previous 14 days

Children > under 14
- Children travelling to the UAE on holiday must be accompanied by a parent
- Children may travel on their own or on their parent's passport (in which case they will be on the parent's visa)
- When children visit parents who are resident in Dubai, only the parents are permitted to sponsor the child (not friends or immediate relatives)

There is no refund under any circumstances once a visa application has been submitted.

E   Application Forms Online

Visit www.dnrd.gov.ae for application forms for the various entry visas. Once you register with the service, you may complete the forms online, then print them out and deliver them to the appropriate department.

Info   Visa or Permit?

There is some confusion between the term 'visa' and 'permit' and when going through your residency process you will no doubt hear both terms being used. With this book 'visa' refers to the permission given to enter the UAE while a 'permit' is the permission to reside in the country, be it for employment or as a dependent of a resident.

Visas

Obtaining a Visit Visa On Arrival

1 Overview

Passport holders of the following countries will be granted a visit visa on arrival in Dubai for no charge.

List of Exempt Countries		
Andorra	Hong Kong	Portugal
Australia	Iceland	San Marino
Austria	Ireland	Singapore
Belgium	Italy	South Korea
Brunei	Japan	Spain
Canada	Liechtenstein	Sweden
Denmark	Luxembourg	Switzerland
Finland	Malaysia	UK
France	Monaco	USA
Germany	Netherlands	Vatican
Greece	Norway	

2 Prerequisites

Validity >
- 60 days from date of entry; renewable for another 30 days
- Passport is from one of the countries listed above
- Visitor has no intention to do any paid or unpaid work in Dubai during the visit

3 What to Bring

☐ Passport

4 Procedure

Location > Passport Control, Dubai International Airport   Map ref 9-B9

Hours > 24 hours
- After landing at the Dubai airport, proceed directly to passport control
- A visa will be stamped into your passport

5 Related Procedures

- Renewing a Visit Visa [p.24]
- Applying for a Temporary Driving Licence [p.142]

Applying for a Tourist Visa

1 Overview

If your nationality is not listed in the table opposite and you intend to stay a maximum of 30 days in Dubai, your hotel, airline or travel agency may be able to apply for a tourist visa on your behalf.

2 Prerequisites

• Applicant will be sponsored by a hotel or tourism company

3 What to Bring

☐ Passport (copy)

Fees > ☐ Dhs.100 – visa application fee

☐ Dhs.100 – urgent charge (optional)

☐ Dhs.50 (maximum) – hotel service charge

4 Procedure

• Make the reservation with the hotel or tour company
• Send all documents and credit card details by fax or mail to the hotel or tour operator
• Up to seven days later (if you requested an urgent application, within one day), a copy of the visa will be sent to you and the original visa placed at the airport
• Upon arrival at Dubai International Airport, hand over your copy of the visa to the Immigration desk and collect the original visa

5 Related Procedures

If sponsorship is arranged by a hotel, you must stay at that hotel. The length of stay depends on the hotel's policy.

△ Visitors must have a copy of the visa to be able to board the flight to Dubai. Passports must be valid at least three months longer than the visa expiry date. This visa cannot be extended or renewed.

Visas

Applying for a Visit Visa (Before Arrival)

1 Overview

A visit visa can be applied for by either an individual or corporate sponsor, allowing the visitor to stay in Dubai for up to 90 days. It is issued to those who have an appointment to visit a company, or to those visiting a friend or relative who is resident in the UAE. Sometimes this visa is issued for tourism purposes as well.

Only those in certain job categories and family members are permitted to transfer a visit visa to a residence/employment permit (see Transferring a Visit Visa to an Employment or Residence Permit [p.30]).

2 Prerequisites

Validity >
- One entry within two months of date of issue
- 60 days from date of entry; renewable for another 30 days
- If you remain in the UAE beyond your permitted period of stay, you will have to pay a fine of Dhs.100, plus Dhs.100 for each day you have overstayed. This fine is payable before you are permitted to leave.

Family >
- Sponsor's monthly basic salary is at least Dhs.4, 000 plus housing allowance, or total salary is Dhs.5,000

GCC resident >
- Visitor is a businessman, company manager or representative, or holds a professional post

Wife of >
GCC Citizen
- The wife has a valid residence permit in her husband's GCC home country
- Her husband is residing in the UAE

3 What to Bring

☐ Visitor's passport (copy)

Fees >
☐ Dhs.100 – visa fee (e-Dirham)

☐ Dhs.10 – typing fee

☐ Dhs.100 – urgent charge (optional)

☐ Dhs.10 – visa deposit fee

Company >
Sponsor
☐ Two application forms typed in English or Arabic (forms are available from the typist or can be downloaded from www.dnrd.gov.ae)

☐ A letter stating the reason and purpose of the visit. Where applicable, proof of relationship may also be required

☐ Trade licence (copy)

☐ Immigration card (original & copy) (see Applying for an Establishment Immigration Card [p.253])

☐ Representative card (original & copy) (see Applying for Immigration & Labour Representative Cards [p.255])

individual > Sponsor

☐ The profession of the visitor as per the Immigration Department codes (found on the website or with a typist)

☐ Two application forms in English and Arabic (typed)

☐ Sponsor's employment contract (original & copy)

☐ Sponsor's tenancy contract (copy), unless accommodation is provided by the employer

☐ If sponsoring wife, marriage certificate (original & copy)

4 Procedure

- Purchase an e-Dirham card and request an 'urgent' slip (if needed)
- Go to a typing office near the Immigration Department, where the typist will fill in the application forms for you
- Pay the application and typing fees at the typing office

Location > Immigration Department   Map ref 7-B4

Hours > Sat-Wed 07:30 – 12:00 (submission); 12:00 – 14:30 (collection)

- Submit all relevant documents at the visa section of the Department of Naturalisation
- Collect a ticket
- Return after 12:00 to collect the visa (minimum two hours after submission)
- Fax the visa to the visitor and make a copy of the visa
- Deposit the original at the visa counter in the airport (next to the Arrivals hall) at least two hours before the arrival of the visitor and have the copy stamped
- Pay the visa deposit fee at the bank counter
- The visitor will exchange his/her copy of the visa for the original upon arrival at the Immigration desk in the airport

5 Related Procedures

- Renewing a Visit Visa [p.24]
- Applying for a Temporary Driving Licence [p.142]
- Transferring a Visit Visa to an Employment or Residence Visa [p.30]

1 Overview

This non-renewable visa is also known as an Entry Service Permit, as it mainly serves company visitors. It is issued to those visiting a company based in the UAE, and staying a maximum of 14 days in the country. The wife or child may accompany the applicant. GCC nationals and those from one of the 33 exempt countries (see Exempt Countries [p.18]) visiting on business do not need this visa to enter the country.

Validity › Urgent visas are valid 14 days from the date of issue, regular visas, seven days after collection

2 Prerequisites

- Visitor has a return ticket
- Visitor has a valid passport
- If a job title is mentioned in the passport, the visitor should belong to a professional job category

3 What to Bring

- ☐ Two application forms
- ☐ Trade licence (copy)
- ☐ Visitor's passport (copy)
- ☐ Transit visa card (original & copy)

Fees › ☐ Dhs.120 (e-Dirham) – visa application charge
- ☐ Dhs.100 – urgent charge (optional)
- ☐ Dhs.10 – visa deposit fee

4 Procedure

- Purchase an e-Dirham card and request an 'urgent' slip (if needed)
- Go to a typing office near the Immigration Department, where the typist will fill in the application forms for you
- Pay the application and typing fees at the typing office
- The sponsor must sign and seal the application forms before submitting them

Location › IND, Dubai Airport Free Zone   Map ref 9-D8

Hours › Sat – Wed 07:30 – 12:00 & 14:00 – 16:30 (submission); 13:30 – 18:30 (collection)

Sponsor › • Submit all relevant documents at least 48 hours before the visitor's arrival
- Collect the transit visa the same day (minimum two hours after submission)
- Fax the visa to the visitor and make a copy of the visa

- Deposit the original at the visa counter in the airport (next to the Arrivals hall) at least two hours before the arrival of the visitor and have the copy stamped
- Pay the visa deposit fee at the same counter
- The visitor will exchange his/her copy of the visa for the original upon arrival at the Immigration desk in the airport

Info 96 Hour Transit Visa

Only airlines may issue this type of visa when flight schedules force passengers to spend an extended period of time in Dubai waiting for connecting flights. The airline will apply for the visa and it will be issued at Dubai International Airport. This visa allows transit passengers to stay up to 96 hours in the UAE, under the sponsorship and responsibility of the airline. The Immigration Authority at the airport will stamp the traveller's passport upon arrival and state the permitted period of stay.

Info Visa Change Flight

When your residency application has been approved, you will have to change your visa status from 'visitor' to 'residency'. This can be done in two ways: either leave the UAE, cancelling your previous visa and re-entering on your newly issued residence entry permit, or pay Dhs.500 for the status changeover at the immigration department.

Those nationalities who qualify for a visa on arrival when entering the UAE have a cheap and convenient means to do a visa changeover: as they also qualify for a free entry visa into Oman, they can enter Oman by car at the border post just past Hatta Fort Hotel, and then re-enter the UAE immediately on their residency permit.

However, this road-travel visa change is not an option for those not on the list of nationalities who qualify for a free visa on arrival. These nationalities can either pay for the visa status change at immigration (Dhs.500), or leave and re-enter the country by air. See Visa Run on [p.24].

Visas

Renewing a Visit Visa

1 Overview

If you are on a visit visa and you wish to stay a total of 90 days in Dubai, you will have to renew your visa within 60 days of your arrival. This one-time renewal will allow you another 30 days in Dubai before you must leave the country.

Validity> Additional 30 days

2 Prerequisites

• You have stayed less than 60 days in Dubai

3 What to Bring

☐ Passport (original)

☐ Valid visit visa (original)

Fee> ☐ Dhs.500 (e-Dirhams) – renewal charge

4 Procedure

Location> Immigration Department   Map ref 7-B4

Hours> Sat – Wed 07:30 – 12:00 (submission); 12:00 – 14:30 (collection)

• Up to ten days prior or at least 48 hours before expiration, go to the Visit Visa Renewal Counter

• Submit your passport and the e-Dirham card

• The extension will be stamped into your passport immediately

5 Related Procedures

• Transferring a Visit Visa to an Employment or Residence Visa [p.30]

Tip   Visa Run

For nationalities listed on page 18 there is the option of doing a visa run rather than following the above procedure. You can either fly out (Doha is a popular visa run) or drive through the Omani border at Hatta and then when you re-enter Dubai you will have a new visit visa. If you choose to drive to Oman then you may incur a charge at the border of around Dhs.60, although this is not a steadfast rule. Once you have had your paperwork stamped at the border you can literally u-turn and get your passport stamped for re-entry. For nationalities who don't get a visa on arrival it is possible to leave Dubai, usually to Kish Island, and apply for another visit visa (valid for three months) to re-enter the UAE on. While waiting on Kish Island for the new application to be processed, passengers remain in transit and therefore don't need a visa, however there is nothing much to do, so you should make sure that the agent who is processing your application is efficient and trustworthy.

Obtaining a Residence Permit (Employee)

A Dubai–registered company wants to hire a new employee from abroad

Before employee flies to Dubai ◀·····▶ See *Personal Documents Table* [p.8]

If required, employee attests university degrees in country of issue ◀·····▶ See *Notarising & Attesting Documents* [p.11]

Sponsor applies for Ministry of Labour approval and an entry visa ◀·····▶ See *Applying for a Work Permit & Employment Visa* [p.27]

Employee enters Dubai

Employee takes the health tests ◀·····▶ See *Obtaining a Health Card & Taking the Medical Test* [p.31]

Sponsor applies for the labour card ◀·····▶ See *Applying for a Labour Card* [p.33]

Sponsor applies for the residence visa ◀·····▶ See *Applying for a Residence Permit – Employment* [p.35]

Residence permit is affixed into the employee's passport

Residence Permit

1 Overview

A residence permit allows you to live in the UAE for up to three years, entering and leaving the country freely. Note that if you are out of the country for a period longer than six months, your residence permit will expire.

⚠ Copies of EVERY document, including receipts, must be made.

If in doubt, jump the line to ask if you are in the correct queue.

There are three steps involved in obtaining a residence permit:

- Get a health card, issued by the Ministry of Health and take a medical test
- If sponsored by a company, get a labour card, issued by the Ministry of Labour
- Get a residence permit, issued by the Immigration Department

▢ GCC nationals (Bahrain, Kuwait, Oman, Qatar, Saudi Arabia) do not need a residence permit to live in the UAE.

Validity › General: three years

Student residence permit: one year

Domestic help residence permit: one year

Visa Types

Residence Visa	Sponsor	Maximum Validity
Employment residence visa	Employer (company)	3 years
Family residence visa	Employee (husband, father, wife, son)	3 years
Domestic help residence visa	Employee (head of household)	1 year

Info Public Sector & Free Zone Employment

Application procedures vary depending on whether the sponsor is a private or government–related company. Companies in free zones follow a different set of rules (more closely similar to government organisations), even if they are 'private sector' companies. The Ministry of Labour is involved in the approval of private sector applications. Employees of public and free zone companies do not need approval from the Ministry of Labour. This exemption applies to federal ministries, local departments, the Ruler's offices and representative departments, as well as public firms, companies operating in free zones, and various clubs and societies. Note that in Red-Tape Explorer, procedures relate to the private sector.

Applying for an Employment Visa

1 Overview

This procedure is handled completely by the hiring company prior to the arrival of the employee. More than one employee can be applied for concurrently.

In order for a company to hire an employee, the company must first get permission from the Ministry of Labour. The Visa Committee at the Ministry will assess several criteria such as the profession of the potential employee, the size of the company, the number and nationalities of current employees etc before issuing permission (the work permit) to hire the potential employee.

Once permission has been given, an employment visa must be obtained from the Immigration Department. This visa will allow the employee to enter the country, then apply for a residence visa.

Ministry of Labour Approval

A partner in a company does not need prior approval from the Ministry of Labour to obtain an entry visa. The partner may proceed directly to the Immigration application step in this procedure and apply for a partner visa.

Bank > Certain companies, depending on the type of licence and ownership, arantee must deposit a bank guarantee for each employee they wish to hire. Currently, the guarantee for an employee is set at Dhs.3,000.

Employment Visa – Immigration

ioyment > If a person has a firm job offer, the employment visa will be dealt Visa with by the future employer. This visa allows the employee to enter Dubai and follow the remaining Immigration procedures to become resident.

Partner > In some cases, a partner of a company must pay a guarantee when Visa applying for a visa, depending on the percentage of the partner's ownership in the company and the type of company.

Currently, if the company has a professional trade licence and the partner is working in the field of his degree, no guarantee is required. If it is a commercial company and the partner's share is less than Dhs.70,000, the refundable guarantee to be paid is Dhs.20,000. If the partner's share is more than Dhs.70,000, the refundable guarantee to be paid is Dhs.10,000.

Validity > One entry within two months of date of issue

☐ Application for employment residence permit must occur within 60 days of entry

2 Prerequisites

- Employee is not over 60 or under 19 years of age
- If over 60 years of age, employee must have special qualifications, a highly ranked position, or a specialised job
- Dhs.3,000 guarantee per employee to be paid to the Labour office

Residence Permit (Work)

3 What to Bring

Labour Approval

- ☐ Passport of applicant (copy)
- ☐ One passport photo
- ☐ Valid trade licence (copy)
- ☐ Establishment immigration card (copy) (see Applying for an Establishment Immigration Card [p.253])
- ☐ If the employee is a professional (accountant, consultant, doctor, engineer, lawyer, manager, nurse), all notarised university certificates (see Notarising & Attesting Documents [p.11])

Fees

- ☐ Dhs.200 (e-Dirham) – application fee
- ☐ Dhs.35 – typing fee

Immigration

- ☐ Ministry of Labour work permit approval
- ☐ Valid trade licence (copy)
- ☐ Establishment immigration card (copy) (see Applying for an Establishment Immigration Card [p.253])

Fees

- ☐ Dhs.100 (e-Dirham) – application fee
- ☐ Dhs.100 – urgent receipt from bank
- ☐ Dhs.10 – visa deposit fee

Company

- ☐ Partner's passport (copy)
- ☐ A 'To whom it may concern' certificate from Department of Economic Development listing all partners' names
- ☐ Trade licence (copy)
- ☐ Company memorandum of association attested by a Notary Public
- ☐ Establishment immigration card (copy) (see Applying for an Establishment Immigration Card [p.253])

4 Procedure

Location > Ministry of Labour   Map ref 10-E6

Hours > Sat – Wed 07:30 – 14:30

Approval >
- Go to a typing office near the Ministry of Labour where a typist will fill in the application form for you
- Pay the application and typing fees at the typing office
- Place all required documents into a 'Labour Envelope'
- Submit the envelope at the Ministry of Labour or any post office
- You will be given a submission receipt
- Approval or rejection is sent to your postal address within seven to ten days
- If the work permit is approved, go to the Ministry of Labour or the post office
- Pay Dhs.100 (e-Dirham) and attach the receipt to the approval
- If the work permit has been rejected, return to the Ministry of Labour to verify the reason for the rejection

- There may be a waiting period before a company can re-apply

Bank Guarantee >
- If approval is given, but a bank guarantee is required, go to your bank and deposit the required sum
- The bank will issue a letter addressed to the Labour Office
- Submit the bank letter at the Bank Guarantee Section of the Labour Office
- Two days later, return to collect the original work permit
- Pay Dhs.100 (e-Dirham) at the Ministry of Labour or post office
- Attach the receipt to the approval

Location > Immigration Department   Map ref **7-B4**

Hours > Sat – Wed 07:30 – 12:00 (submission); 12:00 – 14:30 (collection)

Application > • Submit all documents to the Entry Permit office

Only the company owner (sponsor) or PRO may submit the application (see Applying for Immigration & Labour Representative Cards [p.255])

- Immigration will issue an employment visa the same day
- Pick the visa up later that day
- Send a copy of the visa to the employee/partner and make a copy of the visa
- Deposit the original at the visa counter in the airport (next to the Arrivals hall) at least two hours before the arrival of the visitor and have the copy stamped
- Pay the visa deposit fee at the same counter or by e-Dirham
- The visitor will exchange his/her copy of the visa for the original upon arrival at the airport Immigration desk

5 Related Procedures

- Obtaining a Health Card & Taking the Medical Test [p.31]
- Applying for a Residence Permit – Employment [p.35]
- Transferring a Visit Visa to an Employment or Residence Visa [p.30]

Does the job!

If you have just arrived in Dubai, or are thinking about coming to the emirate, and are looking for work there are a vast number of opportunities in various industries from media and hospitality to finance and education. For more information on working in Dubai and recruitment agencies refer to the in the Residents chapter of the **Dubai Explorer** (The Complete Residents Guide) available in all leading bookshops and supermarkets.

Residence Permit (Work)

Transferring a Visit Visa to an Employment or Residence Visa

1 Overview

Family members or certain employees (see below) are entitled to enter the country on a visit visa and change their status to an employment/residence visa without having to leave the UAE. The Immigration Department calls this 'Position Amendment'.

For employees, this procedure is the exception to the rule.

2 Prerequisites

Family > • The sponsor is eligible to sponsor a family member (see Sponsoring Family [p.37])

Employee > • The sponsor has approval from the Ministry of Labour to hire this person (see Applying for a Work Permit & Employment Visa [p.27])

• The employee is in one of the following job categories:

MA/PhD holder, Accountant, Administrator, Consultant, Economist, Legal Expert, Pharmacist, Physician, Bus or Heavy Vehicle Driver, Electronics or IT Specialist, Engineer, Journalist, Laboratory Technician, Medical Technician, Nurse, Petroleum position, Teacher

3 What to Bring

☐ Applicant's passport (original & copy)

☐ Visit visa (original & copy)

Fee > ☐ Dhs.500 – position amendment fee

Employee > ☐ Ministry of Labour work permit approval (see Applying for Work Permit [p.26])

☐ Sponsor's establishment immigration card (original & copy) (see Applying for an Establishment Immigration Card [p.253])

Family > ☐ Birth or marriage certificate

4 Procedure

Location > Immigration Department   Map ref 7-B4

Hours > Sat – Wed 07:30 – 12:00 (submission); 12:00 – (collection)

• Go to a typing office near the Immigration Department, where a typist will fill in the application form for you

• Pay the application and typing fees at the typing office

• Submit documents at the Position Amendment Counter; pay the fee at the same counter

Obtaining a Health Card & Taking the Medical Test

1 Overview

Once you have the correct visa status, i.e. you have entered the country with either an employment (see [p.27]) or family visa (see [p.39]), the next steps to becoming a Dubai resident are to apply for a health card and undergo a medical examination.

The medical examination is an important part of the UAE's immigration requirements, and involves a blood test for communicable diseases, such as HIV and Hepatitis, as well as a chest X-ray. The test has to be taken at one of the Dubai Ministry of Health and Medical Services' clinics. You will be assigned a test location dependent on your sponsor. Common hospitals where you might go for your medical test are Maktoum Hospital, Al Bahara Hospital or the clinic in Jebel Ali (if you work at one of the free zones). Note that the Al Bahara Hospital, in Deira, is commonly known as the Kuwaiti Hospital.

Some employees require further medical tests, depending on their age or profession. You will be informed if you must undergo further examination.

Before your examination, all paperwork is put forward in order to apply for a government health card. This card entitles residents to inexpensive medical treatment at public hospitals and clinics (Dhs.20 per visit, Dhs.50 for a specialist; and urgent/emergency cases are free).

Some employers provide additional private medical insurance to their employees. If yours doesn't, you can sign up with some excellent international medical insurance providers. Such insurance covers most private clinics and hospitals both in the UAE and while travelling overseas. (see Directory [p.274])

Health Card Validity and Fees

Nationality	Validity	Age	Fee (Dhs.)
UAE Nationals	4 Years	0-10 Years	25
		11-18 Years	50
		19 Years and Above	100
GCC Nationals	1 Year	0-10 Years	25
		11-18 Years	50
		19 Years and Above	100
Other Nationalities	1 Year	0-10 Years	100
		11-18 Years	200
		19 Years and Above	300

2 Prerequisites

- Employment visa, residence visa or Dubai residence visa
- Applicant must be at least 18 years of age (those under 18 do not need to take the test to receive a health card)

Residence Permit (Work)

[3 What to Bring

Health Card › ☐ Passport plus entry stamp (original & copy)

☐ Employment or residence visa (copy)

☐ Two passport photos

Fee › ☐ Dhs.25 – 300 cash – health card fee

Medical › ☐ Passport plus entry stamp (original & copy)
Test

☐ Two passport photos

Fees › ☐ Dhs.200 – health test charge

☐ Dhs.7 – Arabic typing charge

[4 Procedure

Location › Rashid Hospital Health Card Section   Map ref 8-F6

Hours › Sat – Wed 07:30 – 14:30

Health Card › • Submit all documents and pay the fee at the same counter

• You will be given a blank test form and health card

Location › Maktoum Hospital Blood Test Section   Map ref 8-H3

Hours › Sat – Wed 07:30 – 20:30

Medical › • Go to any typist next to the hospital and have the blank test form
Test   filled out in Arabic

• Submit all documents in the Blood Test Section

• You will be registered and given a ticket

• Wait for your name to be called

• A blood sample and a chest X-ray are taken

• Return one to two days later to collect your test results

[5 Related Procedure

• Applying for a Residence Permit – Employment [p.35]

• Applying for a Residence Permit – Family [p.39]

• Obtaining a Labour Card when on Family Sponsorship [p.44]

Applying for a Labour Card

1 Overview

To work in the UAE's private sector, you must have a labour card. If your employer is arranging your residency, the employer will arrange for your labour card to be processed directly after the residency visa has been approved.

Regulations in free zones vary. Check with the free zone authority to determine whether labour cards are issued.

Timing › After entering Dubai on an employment visa, application must occur within 30 days.

Validity › Three years

Labour contract › Before a labour card is issued, a labour contract must be signed. This is a standard form issued by the labour authorities detailing your employment information. This contract is printed in both Arabic and English, and as the Arabic version prevails in a court of law, it is advisable to have the Arabic contract reviewed (translated) prior to signing.

2 Prerequisites

- Applicant has an employment visa
- Applicant has signed the employment contract
- Applicant has already taken the medical test

3 What to Bring

Fees ›
- ☐ Dhs.1,000 (e-Dirham) – labour fee
- ☐ Dhs.40 – typing fee (including labour envelope and sticker)
- ☐ Passport (copy)
- ☐ Employment visa with the entry stamp (copy) (see Applying for a Work Permit & Employment Visa [p.27])
- ☐ Official labour contract, signed and stamped
- ☐ Two passport photos
- ☐ Medical test result (copy) (see Obtaining a Health Card & Taking the Medical Test [p.31])
- ☐ If applicable, attested degree(s) (see Notarising & Attesting Documents [p.11])
- ☐ Establishment labour card (copy) (see Applying for an Establishment Labour Card [p.251])
- ☐ Trade licence (copy)

Visas

Residence Permit (Work)

4 Procedure

Location > Ministry of Labour   Map ref 10-E6

Hours > Sat – Wed 07:30 – 14:30

- Take a 'permission to pay' computer printout from the ground floor of the Ministry
- Go to a typing office nearby
- Have the typist fill in the official labour contract; pay with e-Dirhams
- Both the employer (sponsor) and employee must sign and stamp the contract
- To save time, the immigration application form can be completed at this stage
- Place all required documents into the labour envelope
- Submit the envelope at the Ministry of Labour
- You will be given a submission receipt – keep it!
- Return to collect the labour card within two days (in some cases, the card is mailed to the company PO Box)

5 Related Procedure

- Applying for a Work Permit & Employment Visa [p.27]
- Obtaining a Health Card & Taking the Medical Test [p.31]
- Notarising & Attesting Documents [p.11]

Applying for a Residence Permit – Employment

1 Overview

The employment residence permit allows you to live and work in Dubai. In most cases, the employer will take care of this procedure for you.

Validity > Three years

⚠ Once resident, you may not stay outside of the UAE for a period longer than six months, or your residency will lapse. This is particularly relevant to children studying abroad who are on their parent's sponsorship, and wives delivering a child outside of Dubai (see Temporary Entry Permit [p.47]).

Timings > After entering Dubai, completion of this procedure must take place within 60 days.

⚠ If you have not completed the application procedure within 60 days, you will be fined Dhs.200 for the first day overdue, and Dhs.100 each following day until the procedure has been completed.

2 Prerequisites

- Applicant has undergone the medical test (see Obtaining a Health Card & Taking the Medical Test [p.31])
- If applicant is on company sponsorship, the labour card application has been submitted (see Applying for a Labour Card [p.33])

3 What to Bring

- ☐ Passport (original)
- ☐ Employment visa with the entry stamp (original) (see Applying for a Work Permit & Employment Visa [p.27])
- ☐ Three passport photographs
- ☐ Medical test result (original)
- ☐ If applicable, attested degree(s) (see Notarising & Attesting Documents [p.11])
- ☐ Establishment immigration card (copy) (see Applying for an Establishment Immigration Card [p.253])
- ☐ Trade licence (copy)
- ☐ Ministry of Labour envelope submission receipt (copy) (see Applying for a Labour Card [p.251])
- ☐ If you are a partner in the company, a "To whom It may concern" certificate from the Department of Economic Development containing all partners' names

Fees > ☐ Dhs.300 (e-Dirham) – residence permit application fee
- ☐ Dhs.100 – urgent application fee (if required)
- ☐ Dhs.15 – typing fee

4 Procedure

Location > Immigration Department   Map ref **7-B4**

Hours > Sat – Wed 07:30 – 12:00 (submission); 12:00 – 14:30 (collection)

- Go to a typing office near the Immigration Department
- Have the typist fill in the application form; pay the typing fee
- An authorised representative of the company must submit all documents at the Residence Section and pay the fee (e-Dirhams) at the same counter
- Collect a receipt, which will have a date on which to return
- Approximately five days later, return to collect the passport with the residence permit affixed
- For urgent applications, the process can be completed on the same day. Make sure to specify beforehand

5 Related Procedure

- Applying for a Labour Card [p.33]
- Obtaining a Health Card & Taking the Medical Test [p.31]
- Applying for a Work Permit & Employment Visa [p.25]
- Notarising & Attesting Documents [p.11]

Work it out

Working in a new country can be a little bit of a culture shock, especially when you have to get used to having Sunday lunch on a Friday and getting Monday morning blues on a Saturday or Sunday. To find out more about living and working in Dubai, finding a job, employment packages and contracts check out the Residents chapter of the *Dubai Explorer* (The Complete Residents Guide) available in all leading bookshops and supermarkets.

Sponsoring Family and/or a Maid

1 Overview

Family > As an employee of a Dubai-based company, you can sponsor your family so that they can live here – as long as you meet certain requirements. Depending on your company and the conditions of your contract, it may be you who is responsible for taking care of family sponsorship procedures.

Sponsor > The working 'head of the family' will be the sponsor for his/her spouse and children, and will have to apply for residence permits for them (although occasionally your company will do this for you). It is usually the man who will sponsor his family; only those women working in certain categories (teachers, doctors and nurses) are permitted to sponsor their husbands and children.

Work > Spouses and unmarried daughters over 18 years of age, who are on a family residence permit, are allowed to work in Dubai. While no employment visa or permit is required, a labour card must be applied for. An advantage for those working while on family sponsorship is that they can not be 'banned' if they choose to change their employment while in Dubai.

Maid > Those who wish to hire a full-time maid may do so as long as the correct requirements are met. The administrative costs are higher than sponsoring family members, but the actual procedure is more-or-less the same.

Law Sharing Maids?

Unless your domestic helper is sponsored by a specialised maid service you are not allowed to hire a maid who is not on your sponsorship. In other words, 'borrowing' someone else's maid is against the law.

Info How to find a Maid

There are numerous specialised companies in Dubai that offer services ranging from cleaning to babysitting on a regular or one-off basis, to those which offer recruitment of maids from overseas. Those bringing domestic help from abroad will assist you with the entire procedure. Word of mouth may also help you discover women on their husband's sponsorship who are providing cleaning services.

Visas

Residence Permit (Family)

Residence Permit (Family)

Obtaining a Residence Permit for Family

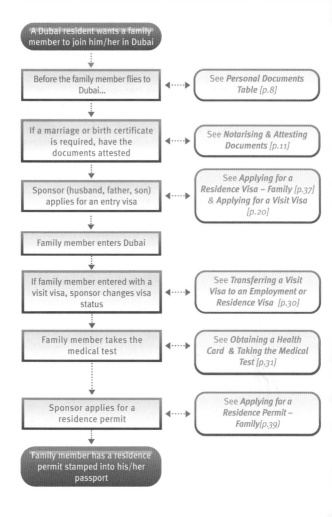

A Dubai resident wants a family member to join him/her in Dubai

Before the family member flies to Dubai... ◀·····▶ See *Personal Documents Table* [p.8]

If a marriage or birth certificate is required, have the documents attested ◀·····▶ See *Notarising & Attesting Documents* [p.11]

Sponsor (husband, father, son) applies for an entry visa ◀·····▶ See *Applying for a Residence Visa – Family* [p.37] & *Applying for a Visit Visa* [p.20]

Family member enters Dubai

If family member entered with a visit visa, sponsor changes visa status ◀·····▶ See *Transferring a Visit Visa to an Employment or Residence Visa* [p.30]

Family member takes the medical test ◀·····▶ See *Obtaining a Health Card & Taking the Medical Test* [p.31]

Sponsor applies for a residence permit ◀·····▶ See *Applying for a Residence Permit – Family* [p.39]

Family member has a residence permit stamped into his/her passport

Applying for a Residence Permit – Family

1 Overview

Family > There are certain conditions which must be met in order to sponsor your family. The most important condition is that you meet the minimum monthly salary requirement (Dhs.4,000, or Dhs.3,500 plus housing). For further conditions, see Prerequisites.

This is a two-step process, beginning with a residence visa application. A residence visa is a one-time entry permit, allowing the family member to enter the country. A residence permit must then be applied for, allowing longer term residency (up to three years) in Dubai.

Maid > The head of the family is permitted to sponsor one maid. The following must be provided to the domestic helper:

- Airfare to home country at least once every two years
- Housing, electricity and air-conditioning
- Generally, salary paid to the maid varies between Dhs.600 plus food to Dhs.1,200 per month

The steps in sponsoring a maid involve applying for a residence visa, then a residence permit, the validity of which is one year. Domestic helpers are not covered by the UAE labour law and thus do not need a labour card.

A family is permitted to sponsor only one maid, unless the sponsor's salary and family size allow for an additional maid.

Fees > In addition, the sponsor must pay a 'maid tax' of Dhs.4,800 yearly. Administration fees, a medical examination, and health card fees are also to be paid to the government, adding up to at least Dhs.6,000 annually.

Validity > • Entry must be made within two months of date of issue
- Valid for 30 days from date of entry
- Application for residence permit must occur within 30 days of entry

⚠ Once resident, you may not stay outside of the UAE for a period longer than six months, or your residency will lapse. This is particularly relevant to children studying abroad who are on their parents' sponsorship, and wives delivering a child outside of Dubai. (See Temporary Entry Permit [p.47])

Tip Family Sponsorship from a Visit Visa

If a family member has already entered the country on a visit visa and then wishes to become resident in Dubai, the sponsor must first apply for a residence visa. Once that has been approved, he/she can make a visa change trip (see Visa Run [p.24]) and re-enter the country with the correct visa; or pay Dhs.500 without having to leave the country.

Visas

Residence Permit (Family)

Residence Permit (Family)

2 Prerequisites

- Sponsor is resident, working in Dubai, and earns a minimum salary according to Ministry regulations

Female > Sponsor
- Women who wish to sponsor a family member need special permission from the Ministry. In general, this privilege is given only to doctors, nurses and teachers.

Family >
- Immediate family members only (including mother and/or father)
- Daughter is unmarried
- Son is under 18 years of age

Maid >
- The sponsor's monthly salary is higher than Dhs.6,000
- The maid is not a relative
- Generally, the maid should not be of the same nationality, although in special circumstances this may be allowed – check with your embassy for additional requirements.
- The maid is under 60 years of age
- The sponsor and his family both live in Dubai
- The sponsor has not sponsored another maid during the past year

If you cannot supply living quarters, you must pay an additional Dhs.500 per month for housing

3 What to Bring

- ☐ Completed application form from a typing office located near the Immigration Department
- ☐ Passport of family member or maid (copy)
- ☐ Passport of sponsor (original & copy)
- ☐ Labour contract of sponsor (original & copy)

Fees >
- ☐ Dhs.100 (e-Dirham) – service charge
- ☐ Dhs.100 – urgent receipt (optional)

Parents >
- ☐ A letter from the consulate/embassy of your home country in the UAE stating that the parent is under your care and responsibility
- ☐ A one–year health insurance policy for the parent

Fees >
- ☐ Dhs.5,000 security bank deposit

Maid >
- ☐ 2 passport photos

Fees >
- ☐ Dhs.4,800 – (cash)

4 Procedure

Location > Immigration Department   Map ref **7-B4**

Hours > Sat-Wed 07:30-12:00 (submission); 12:00-14:30 (collection)

- Submit all relevant documents at the Family Entry Permit Counter (If sponsoring a maid, go to the next counter)
- Make a photocopy of the receipt
- Return to the Family Entry Permit Counter and submit the receipt
- You will be given a ticket
- Return after two days to collect the residence visa; make a copy of the visa – if you requested an urgent application, return either the same or next day
- Send a copy of the visa to the family member or maid
- Deposit the original at the visa counter in the airport (next to the Arrivals hall) at least two hours before the arrival of the visitor and have the copy stamped
- Pay the registration fee by e-Dirham (if online application, e-form) or at the same counter
- The visitor will exchange his/her copy of the visa for the original upon arrival at the Immigration desk in the airport
- The family member must now apply for a residence permit and a health card (see Applying for a Residence Permit – Family [p.39] and Obtaining a Health Card & Taking the Medical Test [p.31])

5 Related Procedures

- Applying for a Residence Permit – Family [p.37]
- Obtaining a Health Card & Taking the Medical Test [p.31]
- Transferring a Visit Visa to an Employment or Residence Visa [p.30]

Info Sole Custody

If you have sole custody of your child and wish to sponsor him/her, you will need some additional documentation.

In addition to the original attested birth certificate, you will need a letter from the non-custodial parent. The letter should include the following:

- Child's name (as per passport & birth certificate)
- Child's nationality
- Child's passport number
- Mention that the non-custodial parent has no objection to the child living with the custodial parent and residing in the UAE

The letter must be endorsed by the legal authority that issued the joint custody, and attested.

Visas

Residence Permit (Family)

Residence Permit (Family)

Applying for a Residence Permit – Family

1 Overview

This is the second step in sponsoring either a family member or maid. The residence permit will allow the person to live in Dubai for a limited period of time (one to three years). The sponsor is responsible for all paperwork and costs related to this procedure.

If you need to register your newborn child, see [p.48] first.

Validity > One to three years, limited to length of time remaining on sponsor's residence permit

2 Prerequisites

- The family member or maid has entered the country with a residence or visit visa (see Applying for a Residence Visa – Family [p.37] or Applying for a Visit Visa [p.15])
- The family member or maid has passed the medical test (see Obtaining a Health Card & Taking the Medical Test [p.31])

3 What to Bring

- ☐ Applicant's passport (original & copy)
- ☐ Residence visa with the entry stamp (original) (see Applying for a Residence Visa – Family [p.39])
- ☐ Sponsor's passport (original & copy)
- ☐ Sponsor's labour contract (original & copy)

Spouse > ☐ Attested marriage certificate (original & copy) (see Notarising & Attesting Documents [p.11])

Child > ☐ Attested birth certificate (original & copy) (see Notarising & Attesting Documents [p.11])

Parent > ☐ A letter from the consulate/embassy of the parent's home country in the UAE stating that the parent is under the sponsor's care and responsibility

Over 18 > ☐ Medical test result (original) (see Obtaining a Health Card & Taking the Medical Test [p.31])

Maid > ☐ Three passport photos of the maid

Fees > ☐ Dhs.300 (e-Dirham) – residence permit application fee
- ☐ Dhs.100 – urgent application fee (optional)
- ☐ Dhs.15 – typing fee

4 Procedure

Location > Immigration Department   Map ref 7-B4

Hours > Sat – Wed 07:30 – 12:00 (submission); 12:00 – 14:30 (collection)

- At any typist's office near the Immigration Department, have the application form (for family or for house maid) completed.
- Pay the residence permit application fee to the typist.
- If the child is on the mother's passport, add the child's name to the mother's application form and pay an additional Dhs.300 per child.

Sponsor > Submit all documents at the Residence Counter

- Collect a receipt with a date, which will be approximately 5 days later
- The process can be completed in the same day if the application is urgent, please mention beforehand
- On the specified date, return to collect the passport with the residence permit stamp affixed

5 Related Procedures

- Transferring From Father to Husband Sponsorship [p.46]
- Obtaining a Labour Card when on Family Sponsorship [p.44]
- Registering a Newborn Child [p.48]
- Applying for a Driving Licence [p.126]

Info Sponsoring a newborn

If you have children whilst residing in Dubai before you can process their residence permit the newborn will need to be registered with both the UAE government and your home country embassy. See page 48 for the procedure.

Family Fun

Moving to a new country is a big step for anyone but when kids are involved it can be a particularly difficult period of adjustment. The best way to make your kids feel at home as soon as possible is to get involved in lots of family and kids' activities. For great ideas on keeping your little angels (and monsters) happy check out the Family Explorer available in all leading bookshops and supermarkets.

Visas

Residence Permit (Family)

Residence Permit (Family)

Obtaining a Labour Card when on Family Sponsorship

1 Overview

If you are on a family residence permit (i.e. on your father's or husband's sponsorship) and find a job in Dubai, your employer (not your sponsor) will need to apply for a labour card for you. The costs for this procedure should be paid by the employer.

Labour > Contract

Before a labour card is issued, a labour contract must be signed. This is a standard form issued by the labour authorities detailing your employment information. This is printed in both Arabic and English, and as the Arabic version prevails in a court of law, it is advisable to have the Arabic contract reviewed (translated) prior to signing.

Validity > One year

2 Prerequisites

- Applicant is on family sponsorship
- Applicant has signed the employment contract

3 What to Bring

Ministry of > Labour Envelope

- ☐ Applicant's passport (copy)
- ☐ Entry stamp in passport (copy)
- ☐ Official labour contract, signed and stamped
- ☐ Two passport photos – one glued (not stapled) and one clipped to the application form
- ☐ Medical test result (copy) (see Obtaining a Health Card & Taking the Medical Test [p.31])
- ☐ If the last medical test was more than three months ago, a second, paid for by the employer, must be undergone
- ☐ If applicable, attested degree(s) (see Notarising & Attesting Documents [p.11])
- ☐ Establishment labour card (copy) (see Applying for an Establishment Labour Card [p.251])
- ☐ Trade licence of employer (copy)
- ☐ Sponsor's passport (copy)

Fees >
- ☐ Dhs.1,200 (e-Dirham) – labour contract and application fee
- ☐ Dhs.40 – typing fee (including labour envelope and sticker)

4 Procedure

Location > Ministry of Labour   Map ref 10-E6

Hours > Sat – Wed 07:30 – 14:30

- Go to a typing office near the Ministry of Labour
- Have the typist fill in the official labour contract; pay with e-Dirhams
- Both the employer and employee must sign and stamp the contract
- Place all required documents into the labour envelope
- Submit the envelope at the Ministry of Labour or any post office
- You will be given a submission receipt – keep it!
- Upon approval, the labour card and contract will be sent to your company's PO Box (up to one month later)

5 Related Procedure

- Transferring from Father to Husband Sponsorship [p.46]

Info Freelance

Dubai Media City's 'Media Business Centre' has made it possible to work as a freelance professional in Dubai by providing the necessary sponsorship and paperwork.

You can get a freelance permit and 'hot desk' space if you fall under one of the various freelance categories, which basically include artists, editors, directors, writers, engineers, producers, photographers/camara operators and technicians in the fields of film, TV, music, radio and print media.

The permit includes a residence visa and access to 10 shared work stations. You will also get to use a shared PO Box address and fax line.

You must spend a minimum of three hours per week at the hot desk, but no more than three hours per day.

Documents required:
- Business plan
- CV
- Bank reference letter
- Portfolio/work samples
- Passport copy

Costs:
- Dhs.5000 security deposit (refundable)
- Dhs.5000 joining fee (one-time payment)
- Dhs.8000 annual permit fee
- Dhs.4000 annual membership fee
- Dhs.1500 annual employee sponsorship fee

For more information on getting a DMC freelance permit, visit their website (www.dubaimediacity.com) or call 391 4555.

Residence Permit (Family)

Transferring from Father's to Husband's Sponsorship

1 Overview

A woman residing in Dubai under her father's sponsorship who marries a man who is also resident in Dubai, must transfer her sponsorship.

2 Prerequisites

- Husband is resident in Dubai
- Husband earns a minimum monthly salary of Dhs.3,500
- At time of marriage, the woman is on her father's sponsorship

3 What to Bring

- ☐ Father's passport (original & copy)
- ☐ Husband's passport (original & copy)
- ☐ Wife's passport (original & copy)
- ☐ Attested marriage certificate (original & copy) (see Notarising & Attesting Documents [p.11])
- ☐ Four passport photos of wife
- ☐ Labour contract (original & copy)
- ☐ If husband is an employee, his employment contract (copy)
- ☐ If husband is a partner in a company, trade licence (copy) and a "To whom it may concern" certificate issued by the DED and listing all partners

Fees ›
- ☐ Dhs.100 – transfer fee
- ☐ Dhs.100 – urgent fee (optional)

4 Procedure

Location › Immigration Department   Map ref 7-B4

Hours › Sat – Wed 07:30 – 12:00 (submission); 12:00 – 14:30 (collection)

- Go to a typing office near the Immigration Department
- Have the typist fill in the sponsorship transfer application form; pay with e-Dirhams
- Submit all relevant documents at the Visa Transfer Counter
- Return within two days to collect the approved application, or on the same day if application is urgent (specify beforehand)
- Once the sponsorship has been transferred, the wife must apply for a health card and undergo a medical examination (see Obtaining a Health Card & Taking the Medical Test [p.31]), and apply for a residence permit (see Applying for a Residence Permit – Family [p.39])

5 Related Procedure

- Obtaining a Health Card & Taking the Medical Test   [p.31]
- Applying for a Residence Permit – Family [p.39]
- Obtaining a Labour Card when on Family Sponsorship [p.44]

Tip | **Temporary Entry Permit**

If a family member has been out of the country for a period longer than 6 months, the residence permit is officially cancelled. The sponsor may, however, apply for a temporary entry permit that will waive the cancellation and allow the 'absconded' person to enter Dubai.

This situation may occur, for example, when a wife delivers a child in her home country. In this case, the husband must go to the Incoming/Outgoing Department on the 1st floor of the Immigration Department. He will submit a 'green card', which is a Dhs.100 receipt from a 'e-Dirham' bank (see [p.274]), his original passport (& copy) and his wife's passport copy. He must fax her a copy of the visa, but there is no need to deposit the visa at the airport. Entry into Dubai must occur within 14 days from the date of issue.

Web Update

While Dubai's government is committed to cutting back on the red-tape involved in setting up in Dubai, both for individuals and businesses, changes in rules and regulations are inevitable. Therefore, if there have been any changes or additions to the procedures included in this book they will appear on the Explorer website. Just log on to **www.Explorer-Publishing.com** and click on the **Red-Tape** link. This page will tell you if there have been any changes to specific procedures – giving you the heads up before you head off to plough through Dubai's administrative maze!

Visas

Residence Permit (Family)

Residence Permit (Family)

Registering a Newborn Child

1 Overview

If you wish to get a residence permit for your child, you must first register the child with the concerned authorities. If the child was born in Dubai, the child must be registered with the embassy/consulate and have a passport (or be entered in the mother's passport). If the child was born outside Dubai, the foreign birth certificate must first be attested by the UAE Ministry of Foreign Affairs.

In general, it is the father who will attend to all the paperwork, as he will be the sponsor and will need to sign all related documents.

If a child born in Dubai has neither a visa nor a residence permit, the child may not leave the country under any circumstances.

Timing › Arrangements for a residence permit for a baby born in the UAE must occur within four months (120 days) of the baby's date of birth.

If you fail to register the baby on time, the legal guardian must pay a fine of Dhs.100 per day until registration is complete.

2 Prerequisites

- Father is resident in Dubai
- Father is eligible to sponsor a child (minimum total monthly salary of Dhs.4,000)
- Child will live in Dubai

3 What to Bring

☐ Attested birth certificate (see Obtaining a Birth Certificate [p.181] and Notarising & Attesting Documents [p.11])

☐ At least three passport pictures of the child with the eyes open

☐ Both parents' passports (original & copy)

☐ If father's name is not indicated in the mother's passport, attested marriage certificate (original & copy)

Fees › ☐ Dhs.10 – Ministry of Health attestation charge (exact change)

☐ Dhs.50 – Ministry of Foreign Affairs attestation charge (exact change)

4 Procedure

Location > Embassy/Consulate (see Directory [p.278])　　　Map ref **Various**

Hours > Normally 08:00-13:00

- Contact your embassy or consulate to determine specific requirements regarding registration of the child and application for a passport
- With all required documents, go to your embassy or consulate to register the birth in your home country and apply for the child's passport

Location > Ministry of Foreign Affairs　　　Map ref **8-H3**

Hours > Sat – Wed 08:30 – 12:00

- Submit all documents at the counter at the end of the hall on the left of the entrance
- Pay the attestation charge at the cashier
- Give the documents (Arabic & English birth certificates) to the guard in the lobby area
- He will take the documents to be signed by an official
- Wait in the lobby
- The guard will return with the documents and call the name written on the birth certificates
- Double check to ensure you have been given the correct documents
- This office is very small. Expect long queues.

Location > Immigration Department　　　Map ref **7-B4**

Hours > Sat – Wed 07:30 – 12:00 (submission); 12:00 – 14:30 (collection)

- Upon receipt of the child's passport and within four months of birth, start immigration procedures for your child (see Applying for a Residence Visa – Family [p.39])

5 Related Procedure

- Applying for a Residence Visa – Family [p.39]

Law Adoption

Sharia law does not permit adoption for Muslims, but expat residents of Dubai have been able to adopt children from abroad and bring them to live here. There is an active Adoption Support Group in Dubai, run by Marion Jalili. The group offers support and advice to those wishing to adopt, as well as organises events for families of adopted children. Call 394 6643.

Overview

How do I get settled into a new home in Dubai?

Web Update

While Dubai's government is committed to cutting back on the red-tape involved in setting up in Dubai, both for individuals and businesses, changes in rules and regulations are inevitable. Therefore, if there have been any changes or additions to the procedures included in this book they will appear on the Explorer website. Just log on to **www.Explorer-Publishing.com** and click on the **Red Tape** link. This page will tell you if there have been any changes to specific procedures – giving you the heads up before you head off to plough through Dubai's administrative maze!

Overview

Housing

The buzz surrounding the property market in Dubai is difficult to ignore. In the three years that freehold property has been available for purchase by expats, the industry has experienced a boom of staggering proportions. Property prices have climbed dramatically, and new freehold developments are announced on what seems like a daily basis!

In this chapter, you'll find some basic guidelines to reaping the benefits and avoiding the pitfalls associated with purchasing freehold property in Dubai. Apart from providing details on the freehold phenomenon and the attached residence visa, it also gives a detailed comparison of costs and services offered by property developers and mortgage providers.

Should you decide that buying property is not right for you, this chapter also has a section on renting a home in Dubai, from finding a suitable property to signing the lease.

Water & Electricity

Once the lease has been signed, utilities need to be hooked up. All procedures related to water and electricity are listed, from connecting service to reconnecting service if you forget to pay your bills and have your service cut off, to disconnecting water and electricity prior to moving on from Dubai.

DEWA

The Dubai Electricity & Water Authority, commonly known as DEWA, provides all of Dubai with electricity and water supply, as well as sewerage. This government department provides excellent service, with extremely rare electricity or water shortages or stoppages. The head office is modern and service is both swift and efficient. DEWA has been awarded numerous prizes for customer service and its drive for greater efficiency. Following the e-government initiative, DEWA has a Website (www.dewa.gov.ae) offering various services to consumers, provided you have the correct encryption software.

Gas

As there is no real procedure involved with obtaining gas for your stove, we have a quick overview of the subject, including costs and a list of the main gas suppliers in Dubai. Make the call and you'll have gas hooked up in your home within an hour - no headaches at all!

Home Sweet Home

There are number of popular residential areas in Dubai, all with their own set of pros and cons, be it price, space or amenities. If you are trying to decide where to lay your hat then check out the Residential Areas section within the Residents chapter of the **Dubai Explorer** (The Complete Residents' Guide) available in all leading bookshops and supermarkets.

Moving

Shipping Your Personal Belongings

1 Overview

The two main options when moving your belongings to or from Dubai are air freight and sea freight. Air freight is best for moving small amounts, whereas sea freight is better (and cheaper) for larger consignments. Booking an entire container reduces the amount your goods are handled, but obviously some destinations are not easily accessible by sea.

2 Prerequisites

- You are moving to Dubai from overseas, or leaving Dubai for another country, and wish to ship your belongings.

3 What to Bring

If collecting goods shipped to Dubai:

    Airway Bill/Tracking number

    Passport (copy)

If you are picking goods up for someone else:

    An authorisation letter written and signed by owner

    Copy of their passport as well as your own

4 Procedure

If collecting goods shipped by air:

Location > Dubai Cargo Village (04 211 1111)   Map ref 9-B7

Hours > 24hrs

- Call ahead, quoting the Airway Bill/Tracking number, to confirm your shipment has arrived
- Take the Airway Bill/Tracking number to the desk to locate shipment
- Pay fees:

    Delivery Cost   Dhs.35

    Handling Cost   Dhs.12 (for 200kg and less); Dhs.0.6 per kg (for over 200kg)

- From here move to the customs desk (04 282 8888) with your invoice and your airway bill number or tracking number
- Your shipment will be searched by customs officers
- Depending on the agreement you have with the removal company, either their representative in Dubai will help you transport the boxes, or you can make the arrangements locally.

Tip Moving Tips

- Book moving dates well in advance
- Don't forget insurance – purchase additional insurance for irreplaceable items
- Make an inventory of the items you want moved (keep your own copy!)
- Ensure everything is packed extremely well and in a way that can be checked by customs and repacked with the least possible damage; check and sign the packing list
- Keep a camera handy to take pictures at each stage of the move (valuable in case of a dispute)
- Do not pack restricted goods of any kind
- Ensure videos, DVDs and books are not offensive to Muslim sensibilities

Info Expert Help

Removal Companies

Unless you send your personal belongings with the airline you are flying on, you will need a removal company. A company with a wide international network is usually the best and safest option. Most offer free consultations, advice, and samples of packing materials.

Relocation Experts

Relocation experts help you settle into your new life overseas as quickly and painlessly as possible. Assistance includes finding accommodation and a school for your children. They may also offer advice on the way of life in the city, and put you in touch with social networks.

Info Customs

It is normal for customs to search your shipment. You will be asked to remain present while the authorities open your boxes to ensure nothing illegal or inappropriate is brought into the country.

Renting

Renting a Home

1 Overview

Renting a property is still a popular option for expat residents in Dubai. Rent is paid on an annual or biannual basis with postdated cheques. For new residents, this advance payment can create difficulties, but some companies pay the landlord directly and deduct the rent from your salary on a monthly basis; alternatively, banks are quick to offer loans. As cheques must be local, a bank account is a prerequisite to renting a home. 'Bouncing' cheques is a criminal offence here, and can result in a jail term, so make sure you have enough money in your account when your cheques are due!

Additional Rental Costs
- Refundable water and electricity deposit (see p.75])
- Real estate commission (5% of annual rent in a one-off payment)
- Maintenance charge (5% of annual rent)
- Municipality tax (5% of annual rent)
- Refundable rental security deposit (Dhs.2,000 - 5,000)
- In some cases, a damage deposit is also required (usually a fully refundable, one-off payment)

2 Prerequisites

☐ Dubai bank account
☐ Valid Dubai residence permit
☐ Passport (copy)

3 What to Bring

Individual>
☐ Residence permit (copy)
☐ No objection letter (NOC) from employer
☐ Salary certificate (copy)
☐ Rent cheque (or agreed-upon number of post-dated cheques covering the remaining period of the lease)
☐ Deposit
☐ Real estate commission

Company>
☐ Valid trade licence (copy)
☐ Passport of the person signing the rent cheque (copy)

4 Procedure

- Find a home you like
- Try to negotiate the rent and terms
- Sign the lease
- Read the lease agreement thoroughly to be aware of termination, damage, subletting, liability clauses, etc, which may affect you

- Hand over the rent cheque(s), deposit and commission
- Connect water and electricity [p.68]

5 Related Procedure

- Purchasing Gas [p.77]
- Applying for a Telephone Line [p.82]

Info Lease Termination

Security Deposit

Before returning your security deposit, the landlord may ask you to submit final utilities bills and/or clearance certificates (see Obtaining a Clearance Certificate (Utilities) [p.76] and Obtaining a Clearance Certificate (Telecom Bills) [p.76])

Damage Deposit

When vacating the premises, return the apartment in the same condition (or better) as you received it.

Note that the apartment should be both clean and usually freshly painted before taking over the lease.

Home Improvements

If you have made 'improvements' to your home, do not expect the landlord to compensate you for your investments; on the contrary, you may be asked to compensate the landlord to return the home to its original condition.

Tip Search Tips

Negotiation

There may be some room for negotiation when renting a home. Payment of the lease in one cheque may reduce the rent, as may signing a long-term lease.

Waiting Lists

Certain buildings with unique amenities, a prime location, or particularly good value often have a waiting list. It costs nothing to place your name on the list.

Older Buildings

If you are interested in an older building or villa, determine whether there are any plans for demolition before signing the lease!

Info Government Subsidised Housing

The Dubai government owns and manages thousands of residential and commercial properties all around Dubai, with varying rents suitable for all levels of income. As the rents tend to be very good value for money, some of the properties are highly sought after, and there are long waiting lists. For homes, married couples and families with children are given preference. To find out more or to put your name on a waiting list, contact the Dubai Real Estate Department (398 6666), or check their Website on www.realestate-dubai.gov.ae.

Housing

Renting

Buying a Home

1 Overview

Currently, non-GCC Nationals are permitted to own land only in various property developments. New developments are being announced all the time. Some developments (such as the Springs, the Meadows and Arabian Ranches) feature villa-style living For further information contact Dubai Palm Developers (399 1400), Emaar Properties (399 3366) or Jumeirah Beach Residence (391 1114).

Research and register with the property development you would like to purchase in.

Decide whether you need to apply for a mortgage. Speak to the mortgage company to determine the amount you can borrow.

If you are not applying for a mortgage, arrange payment plans and cheques with your bank.

• Passport (original)
• Deposit as down-payment
• Mortgage agreement (if there is one)

For new property (still not built):

• Register your interest by contacting the real estate agents
• Visit the real estate office, pay deposit and claim contract

For property already built:

• Arrange for a contract to be drawn up
• Visit real estate office with passport (original) and 100% payment
  – unless a mortgage is being arranged

What is Freehold?

As the owner of a freehold property, you are the absolute owner of the buildings and the land they are on for the duration of your life. You have the right to sell the property to another owner, or to pass it on to somebody in your will, after your death.

In Dubai, many developers include a clause in the agreement that requires a property owner to get the developer's consent before selling the property to a third party.

Even though the owner of a freehold property is the absolute owner of the buildings and the land, he or she must still follow any laws and regulations controlling the property. For example, there may be regulations preventing you from painting the exterior of your house a different colour, and you may have to use approved service companies (to install your satellite dish or carry out any maintenance).

Other Costs Involved in Buying a Home

Apart from the actual purchase price of the house, there are several other costs involved in buying.

Processing fee: This is payable to the bank and is usually around 1% of the loan amount.

Registration fee: usually around Dhs.3000 or 0.5% of the loan amount.

Valuation fee: Before the bank will grant you a mortgage, they will send someone round to make sure the value of the property is not under-rated or inflated. This is usually done for a fee of around Dhs.3000, but some banks may bear this cost on your behalf.

Remember that there will be other costs as well once you get ownership of the property and move in. Many developers charge an annual maintenance fee, of which payment is compulsory. This amount may be a flat rate, or it may be charged per square metre. To avoid any nasty surprises, always ask about these costs before you sign anything, and clarify what they cover.

Homeowner's Residence Visa

One of the attractions of buying freehold property in Dubai is the chance to get a residency visa. Some developers offer to get residency visas for homeowners, if they are unable to get one in any other way (through work, for example).

There are no work rights attached to this visa however, so if you want to work here then you have to get your employer to provide you with a residency visa. The homeowner's visa is more suited towards people who do not wish to work in Dubai, yet who want to stay longer than a visit visa would allow.

Developers charge for this service (as an example, a three-year visa to live on the Palm Jumeirah will cost Dhs.5000 per person). The visa can only be given to the principal owner, his spouse and immediate children below the age of 18. In the case of joint ownership, only one visa will be given (to the primary owner).

Housing

Buying

Info | **Secondary Market**

It is advisable to use a well-known agency if you are buying a resale property. As the seller, you are (usually) required to get permission from the developers to sell your house. The developer will charge a transfer fee, so check who is responsible for paying this fee – is it the buyer or the seller? The current transfer fee is anything from 1% to 8% of the value of the property, but plans are underway to introduce a standard transfer fee.

In the Market for a New Home

If you are on the look out for a new property, be it for investment purposes or for a new home - or both then you'll be spoilt for choice. For more information about the types of properties available and their amenities check out the Property section in the **Dubai Explorer** (The Complete Residents' Guide) available in all leading bookshops and supermarkets.

Property Developers

Company	Telephone	Website
Emaar Propertries	367 3333	www.emaar.com
Estithmaar Realty	391 1114	www.jbr.ae
Nakheel	390 3333	www.nakheel.ae
Damac Properties	390 8804, 399 9500	www.damacproperties.com
Saba Real Estate	330 0086	www.saba-re.com
RMJM	332 2171	www.arshiamarina.com
ARY	226 3535	www.arymarinaveiw.com
Vakson Real Estate	393 9977	www.vakson.com
B&M FZ CO	299 6968	www.larivieratower.com
Mega Properties	222 5586	www.magaprodubai.com
Tident International Holdings	299 7333	www.thewaterfrontdubai.com
Ahmed Hashim Khoory & Brothers	331 6789	www.fortunetower.com
Dubai Properties	391 1114	www.dubai-properties.ae

Info Legal Advice

The new law to open up the real estate arena to non-Nationals is still in its infancy and there are a number of ambiguous issues surrounding the status of ownership. If a property is referred to as 'freehold' do not assume it means the same as in your country of origin. Not only because of the issues involved with legal ownership but also with restrictions on the property. For example, it may not be as straightforward as you think to sell the property on to a third party or to make structural changes to it. Additionally, most developments require payments of annual service charges and significant transfer fees when you sell. Problems may also arise in the event of the owner's death, since under Sharia law (which applies in the UAE from a family law perspective) it may not necessarily be transferred to the spouse. With this ambiguity existing in current legislation it is important that you seek legal advice from a firm specialising in real estate law. Hadef Al Dhahiri & Associates (www.hadalaw.com) has a dedicated Real Estate department.

Payment Terms	
Nakheel	
The Palm, Jebel Ali	
Purchasing Process	
On booking property	10%
On start of construction	20%
180 days thereafter	20%
180 days thereafter	20%
180 days thereafter	20%
On completion of construction	10%
Jumeirah Islands	
Purchasing Process	
On booking of property	10%
30 days thereafter	10%
30 days thereafter	15%
120 days thereafter	20%
On completion of construction	45%
Garden View Villas	
Purchasing Process	
On booking property	10%
On moving in	90%
Estithmaar	
Jumeirah Beach Residence	
Studio, 1, 2, 3 and 4 bedroom Apartments	
Purchasing Process	
On selection of the apartment	25% current cheque
Second installment	25% post dated cheque
Third installment	25% post dated cheque
At the time of possession	25%
Sign the sale and purchase Agreement	
Exclusive Appartments	
Purchasing Process	
On selection of the apartment	20% current cheque
Second installment	20% post dated cheque
Third installment	20% post dated cheque
Forth installment	20% post dated cheque
At the time of possession	20%
Sign the sale and purchase Agreement	
Emaar	
Purchasing Process	
On signing purchasing agreement	10% deposit
Within 120 days of signing purchase agreement	10%
Within 240 days of signing purchase agreement	10%
On closing of unit	Balance of 70% due

Housing

Buying

Obtaining a Mortgage

1 Overview

The maximum mortgage granted is Dhs.5 million. Financing companies are offering up to 90% of the purchase price to UAE Nationals and residents, and up to 70% for non-residents. Mortgages are paid back in monthly installments within a maximum of 25 years. The mortgage amount depends on the chosen plan and is limited to an amount no greater than 60 times the monthly household income.

🗌 Monthly payments should not exceed 55% of your monthly salary.

🗌 Mortgage rates fluctuate according to the market rate; financing charges are adjusted on an annual basis.

2 Prerequisites

- Applicant is between the ages of 21 and 65 years
- Applicant has been employed full-time for at least three years
- Applicant's sponsoring company has been in operation at least three years
- Insurance policy covering the property and the life of the person responsible for mortgage payment
- Your property reservation has been confirmed by the developers/management company

3 What to Bring

☐ Passport (original & copy)

☐ Labour card (original & copy)

☐ Salary certificate

☐ Bank statements for the last six months

☐ Letter from your bank confirming you have no outstanding loans

☐ Registration form with the reserved plot

4 Procedure

- Contact the financing office linked with the property
- Agree on the financing details for your new home
- Submit all documents and sign the relevant paperwork
- Once a holding deposit of 5% has been paid, your mortgage will be processed

Nearly all developers ask for a 10% deposit to reserve a property. The balance of the purchase price should then be paid in installments during the construction of the property (unless it is not a new property). The final installment is due when you take possession of the property. If you change your mind and wish to withdraw from the purchase, you may stand to lose most or all of the money that you have already paid during the construction phase. At the very least, you will have to pay a penalty of 1% of the purchase price.

Info   Long Term Visas

The Immigration authorities are currently working on a system that will grant property owners a residence permit. These long-term visas will be valid for the duration of your property contract but must be renewed every three years. A fee is paid to the real estate agents (in addition to any fees payable to the Department of Immigration & Naturalisation) for the arrangement and renewal of your residency permit.

Tip   Keep up to date

Being relatively new, the area of property ownership for non-Nationals is constantly changing and evolving. Watch the Explorer website for any new information and updates (www.Explorer-Publishing.com).

Web Update

While Dubai's government is committed to cutting back on the red-tape involved in setting up in Dubai, both for individuals and businesses, changes in rules and regulations are inevitable. Therefore, if there have been any changes or additions to the procedures included in this book they will appear on the Explorer website. Just log on to **www.Explorer-Publishing.com** and click on the **Red-Tape** link. This page will tell you if there have been any changes to specific procedures – giving you the heads up before you head off to plough through Dubai's administrative maze!

Bank/Mortgage Provider	Bank Account*	Age	Employment	Self Employment	Loan Amount	Loan Tenor	Do I have to take insurance with bank?
Amlak	Yes (Dubai bank)	21-60	Min 3 years	Min 3 years	60 times monthly salary, max 5 million	15 years	Yes-property No-building
Dubai Islamic Bank	Yes	21-50	Min 3 years	Min 3 years	60 times monthly salary, max 5 million	12 years	Yes
HSBC	Yes	25-60	Min 1 year	Min 1 year	Up to 70% of market value villas/townhouses- 20 years	Apartments-15 years	No
RAK	No	21-65	Last 6 months statements, min salary DHS 8,000 pm	Min 2 years	Depends on individuals financial status,	15 years	Yes- life insurance No- building
Mashreq Bank	No	21-65	3 months same employer	Min 3 years	DHS 100,000 to 3 million	15 years	Yes

Bank	Processing	Registration	Valuation	Lump Sum Payments	Paying of Mortgage early	Interest Rate
Amlak	1%	Dhs.3,000	Dhs.3,000	No Fee	No Fee	Down payment 10%-7.25%, 20%- 6.95%, 30%-6.75%
Dubai Islamic Bank	1.25%	0.05% of Loan amount	Dhs.3,000	2% of the amount	2% of the outstanding balance	8% fixed installments with reducing profits
HSBC	1%	0.25% amount of home loan	Completed property Dhs.2,500-3,000 uncompleted property Dhs. 3,500-4,000	2% of amount left	if under 10% is left to pay on mortgage, then there is no fee	6.25%
RAK	1.25%	1.25%	Dhs. 3,000	Dhs.1,500	1% within 5 years, 0.5% within 5-10 years, above 10 years no charge	6.5% on deposit, 6.95% on property
Mashreq Bank	1%	No Fee	No Fee	5% of amount if from another bank, 1% of amount if paid in cash	5% of outstanding balance if paid from another bank, 1% if balance is paid in cash	6.95%

Housing

Buying

Bank/Mortgage Provider	Bank Account*	Age	Employment	Self Employment	Loan Amount	Loan Tenor	Do I have to take insurance with bank?
Tamweel	Yes	21-60	Min1 year, Min salary Dhs. 10,000 pm	Min 2 years Min salary Dhs. 10,000 pm	180,000 - 5million	25 years	Yes
Lloyds TSB	Yes	21-65	Must be in permanant employment, Min Salary Dhs. 12,000 pm	Min 3 years, Min Salary Dhs. 12,000 pm	Upto 70% of the market evaluation	15 years	Yes
Abudhabi Commercial Bank	No	21-60	2 years	Last 6 months bank statements	Up to 80% of the market evaluation	20 years	Yes
National Bank of Dubai	No	21-60	3 years	3 years	Up to 4 million	15 years	Yes

Bank	Processing	Registration	Valuation	Lump Sum Payments	Paying of Mortgage early	Interest Rate
Tamweel	1.25%	0.5% of Loan amount	Dhs. 3,000	2% of the amount	2% of the outstanding balance	6.90%
Lloyds TSB	0.5% of Loan amount	Dhs. 3,000	Dhs. 2,500	No fee	No fee	7%
Abu Dhabi Commercial Bank	0.75%	No Fee	No Fee	5% of amount if paid from another bank, 3% if paid in cash	5% of amount if paid from another bank 3% if paid in cash	6.5% for one year. After one year goes to market value
National Bank of Dubai	1%	1%	Go through Cluttons	1% of the amount	1% of the remaining amount	1st 6 months-5.99% after 6 months-ebor + 3.5%

Housing

Buying

Water & Electricity

Connecting Water & Electricity

1 Overview

DEWA (Dubai Electricity & Water Authority) is the only supplier of water and electricity in Dubai.

Before moving into a property, you will have to connect the water and electricity supply. Most premises are registered and connected by the landlord upon completion of construction, and then disconnected until the tenant moves in. Therefore, DEWA considers the procedure outlined below a 'reconnection' of the service.

- The name on the tenancy agreement will be the DEWA consumer name.
- Accounts can no longer be transferred from one tenant to another without prior settlement of the final bill.
- Accounts can no longer be transferred between premises.

2 Prerequisites

- Premises have been connected before and there is a consumer account number (see below)

3 What to Bring

- ☐ Consumer account number
- ☐ Tenancy agreement (copy)

Security Deposit >
- ☐ Apartment – Dhs.1,000
- ☐ Villa – Dhs.2,000

Reconnection Fees >
- ☐ Small meter – Dhs.30
- ☐ Large meter – Dhs.100

4 Procedure

Location > DEWA Head Office   Map ref 7-D8

Hours > Sat-Wed 07:30-20:30

- Pick up the Security Deposit/Change of Address application form from the Security Deposit Counter at the DEWA head office
- Complete the form in English or Arabic (hand-written)
- Submit all documents at the Security Deposit Counter to determine the required security deposit
- Submit the application form and pay both the determined security deposit and reconnection charge at the Cashier

Ensure the name on the security deposit receipt is that of the person authorised to collect the security deposit refund. Keep this receipt for future reference and to claim the security deposit when you move out of the premises.

5 Related Procedures

- Paying for Water & Electricity [p.70]
- Reconnecting Service (When Service Cut Off) [p.72]
- Disconnecting Service & Settling Accounts [p.74]

Info Consumer Account Number

The consumer account number is a unique 9-digit reference number that is assigned permanently to each premises. You will need this number for every transaction made with DEWA. The account number can be found:

- With the landlord or the real estate agent
- On the tenancy agreement
- On the DEWA number plate next to the front door or near the meter

E Online Utilities Connection

Connection ('reconnection') can be arranged online at www.dewa.gov.ae. You will need access to a high-speed connection (ADSL) as well as a fax machine or scanner.

Follow the prompts, pay with your credit card, and you will receive a security deposit receipt number. Write this number on your tenancy agreement, then either fax it to 324 9345 or scan and upload it on the same site. Your utilities will be connected the same day.

Info Contact DEWA

You can call the 24 hour DEWA Customer Care Centre on (04) 304 1444, or email dewa@dewa.gov.ae. In an emergency call 991.

Housing

Water & Electricity

Paying for Water & Electricity

1 Overview

To avoid being disconnected, DEWA bills must be paid within 14 days of the due date. Bills are sent monthly to the premises or to a postal address, depending on the location you have specified.

DEWA also offers an email and SMS service notifying you of unpaid bills. Apply for this at any DEWA office.

2 Prerequisites

• Existing DEWA account

3 What to Bring

☐ Bill or consumer account number (see DEWA Overview [p.68])

☐ Depending on chosen method of payment (see below): cash, cheque or credit card (online)

4 Procedure

See table below

Payment	Location	Comments
In Person		
Cashier	Any DEWA office	• Cash and cheque accepted
Deposit Box	Any DEWA office	• Insert bill and crossed cheque in an envelope
By Post		
Mail to:	DEWA PO Box 564, Dubai	• Enclose bill and crossed cheque
Online		
Log on to:	www.dewa.gov.ae	• View and pay bills online (credit card or bank account) • Both current and the last 13 months' bills, adjustments and payments can be viewed
At a Bank		
Various banks offer payment services to DEWA customers	Check the back of the DEWA bill to determine which banks offer these services	• Note: some banks offer payment services to their own customers, while others offer services to all DEWA customers

5 Related Procedure

- Consolidating Bill Statements [p.73]

Info Change of Mailing Address

Either collect and complete a 'Security Deposit/Change of Address' application form at the Consumer Billing Department at any DEWA office, or make a change of address request by letter, fax or email. The Dhs.10 service charge for each change of address will be debited from your account. Remember to include your consumer account number and the name of the account holder.

E Online Registration

To use DEWA's online services, you must first register. Log on to www.dewa.gov.ae and follow the prompts. You will be asked to enter at least one consumer account number or the statement account number (consolidated bills), your telephone number, email address, plus a username and password. The service will usually be activated within 24 hours. A DEWA employee may contact you to validate your information.

Once the registration has been approved, you can view and pay your DEWA bills online. Whenever a new bill has been issued, you will be informed via email. For further information about online services or for registration enquiries, contact DEWA by phone (307 2563) or by email (ebpp.support@dewa.gov.ae).

Info Utilities Charges

- Electricity: 20 fils per kW/h
- Water: 3 fils per gallon
- Sewerage: 0.05 fils per gallon

Reconnecting Service (When Service Cut Off)

1 Overview

If you fail to pay the bill within 14 days of the due date, you w
receive a reminder, then your water and electricity service will be c
off by DEWA. Once your services have been cut, you will have to g
to DEWA in person to request reconnection, and pay all outstandir
amounts plus a penalty charge.

2 Prerequisites

- Services have been cut off

3 What to Bring

☐ Bill or consumer account number

☐ Outstanding amount to be paid (cash or cheque)

Fee> ☐ Dhs.30 – reconnection charge (small meter)

☐ Dhs.100 – reconnection charge (large meter)

4 Procedure

Location> DEWA Head Office   Map ref 7-D

Hours> Sat-Wed 07:30-20:30

- Pay the amount outstanding plus the reconnection charge at t
  Cashier at any DEWA office
- Retain your receipt
- A technician will come to the premises and reconnect services
  the same day

5 Related Procedure

- Disconnecting Service & Settling Accounts [p.74]

Tip 24 Hour Reconnection Service

If you need to be reconnected urgently, the following DEWA
Complaint Centres offer a 24 hour reconnection service :

Satwa: 398 5560

Burj Nahhar: 271 4777

Rashidiya: 285 0622

You can pay the bill and reconnection charge any time of day o
night. A technician will go to your premises and reconnect supply
the same day/night.

Consolidating Bill Statements

1 Overview

As an additional service, DEWA allows individual or commercial consumers with more than 10 DEWA consumer account numbers to consolidate all accounts into one bill statement with an independent statement code number.

If any deletions or changes in the statement account are required, follow the same procedure as detailed below.

2 Prerequisites

- The company or individual has more than 10 consumer account numbers in the same name

3 What to Bring

☐ All consumer account numbers

☐ A written request addressed to the Head of the Consumer Billing Department indicating the consumer account numbers and asking that they be grouped together ('consolidated')

4 Procedure

Location > DEWA Head Office Consumer Billing Dept.   Map ref 7-D8

Hours > Sat-Wed 07:30-20:30

- Submit the request to the Consumer Billing Department in person or
  - Mail to: PO Box 564, Dubai
  - Fax to: 324 9345
  - Email to: cbd@dewa.gov.ae
- You will receive an independent statement code with your next bill
- Paying for Water & Electricity [p.70]

5 Related Procedure

- Disconecting Service & Settling Accounts [p.74]

Disconnecting Service & Settling Accounts

1 Overview

Disconnecting DEWA service consists of two steps: paying the final bill and having the security deposit refunded. DEWA will need at least two days' warning for disconnection of services, so this is not a procedure that can be done on the same day that you leave the country.

You must disconnect DEWA services and settle all accounts first before your rental security deposit will be returned.

2 Prerequisites

- The premises will be vacated in a minimum of two days

3 What to Bring

Account Closure >
- ☐ Consumer account number
- ☐ Date you will be vacating the premises
- ☐ A contact telephone number

Security Deposit >
- ☐ Original security deposit receipt (see Connecting Water & Electricity [p.68])
- ☐ If you have lost the original receipt, a completed indemnity form from the Security Deposit Counter.
- ☐ If the security deposit is in a company name, a stamped letter from the company requesting that the deposit be refunded. The name of the person who will receive the money or cheque should be mentioned in the letter.
- ☐ Recipient's passport (copy) or labour card (copy) to verify identity
- ☐ Final bill payment receipt

4 Procedure

Location > DEWA Head Office Consumer Billing Dept.   Map ref 7-D8

Hours > Sat-Wed 07:30-20:30

Disconnection >
- At least two days before vacating the premises, go to the Consumer Billing Department
- Present your consumer account number
- Indicate when the premises will be vacated
- Leave a contact telephone number
- A technician will visit your premises and record the final meter reading
- The supply will be disconnected immediately afterwards

ification > • You will be notified when the final bill is ready (if you have a mobile phone, you will receive notification by SMS)

• You will receive the final bill by post, or you can collect it personally from the Consumer Billing Department

Bill > Two options exist for settling final bills:
Payment

Option 1 > **Pay Final Bill**

• Pay the final bill at the Cashier at any DEWA office

• Collect the final receipt

• Ensure the bill is stamped 'final bill' by the Cashier

Refund Security Deposit

• Submit the relevant documents and the final bill receipt at the Security Deposit Counter at the DEWA head office and request a refund

• Sign the refund voucher and submit it to the Cashier

• Collect the security deposit from the Cashier (if you are closing a commercial account, you will receive a cheque)

Option 2 > **Settle Final Bill with Security Deposit**

• Submit the relevant documents and the final bill at the Security Deposit Counter at the DEWA head office and request a refund

• Go to the main Cashier where the final bill is adjusted through the security deposit

• If there is a credit, you will receive the remaining amount in the form of cash or a cheque

• If there is a debit, pay the remaining amount (cash only)

5 Related Procedure

• Obtaining a Clearance Certificate [p.76]

Tip Urgent Disconnection

In the case of an emergency, you may request an immediate disconnection of the water and electricity supply. With your consumer account number, request urgent disconnection from the Disconnection/Reconnection Department at the DEWA head office. A technician will accompany you to the premises to record the final meter reading and disconnect the service. You can collect the final bill immediately after the technician has read the meter.

Water & Electricity

Obtaining a Clearance Certificate

1 Overview

In general, the final bill payment receipt is considered a final settlement when you move out of the premises. However, some landlords request a clearance certificate as additional proof that all outstanding amounts have been paid to DEWA, before they will return your rental security deposit.

2 Prerequisites

- The water and electricity supply has been disconnected
- The final bill has been paid

3 What to Bring

☐ Final bill/receipt (paid)

☐ Passport copy (if consumer not registered with DEWA)

Fee ❯ ☐ Dhs.10 service charge

4 Procedure

Location ❯ DEWA Head Office   Map ref 7-D8

Hours ❯ Sat-Wed 07:30-20:30

- Submit the final bill/receipt (paid)
- If consumer is not registered with DEWA (living in other emirate and working in Dubai), submit copy of passport
- Collect Service Charge Slip for payment
- Pay the service charge
- Present the service charge receipt and collect the clearance certificate

Overview

There is no mains gas supply in Dubai. Individual gas cylinders can be purchased from numerous gas companies around town. The supplier will deliver and connect the cylinders for you. Customers are no longer required to pay a security deposit for gas cylinders.

Charges > **New Connection:** (includes price of regulator, pipe, clips & cylinder)

- Large cylinder (44kgs/100lbs) – Dhs.380
- Medium cylinder (22kgs/50lbs) – Dhs.280
- Small cylinder (11kgs/25lbs) – Dhs.230

Gas Refill:

- Large cylinder (44kgs/100lbs) – Dhs.98
- Medium cylinder (22kgs/50lbs) – Dhs.53
- Small cylinder (11kgs/25lbs) – Dhs.31

Info Gas Suppliers

• New City Gas Distributors	351 8282
• Oasis Gas Suppliers	396 1812
• Salam Gas	344 8823
• Union Gas Company	266 1479

Check the commercial telephone directories for other suppliers in Dubai.

Setting up Home

From getting your phone connected to working out how your sewerage works there is a whole host of things to get your head round when moving into your new abode. For more information on setting up home in Dubai check out the Residents section of the *Dubai Explorer* (The Complete Residents' Guide) available in all leading bookshops and supermarkets.

Housing

Gas

A square book but not for squares!

Explore Dubai's decadent range of restaurants, bars, cafes and clubs in this beautiful book with stunning images and informative reviews. More than just a guidebook, it's at home on a coffee table while you're out on the town.

Communications

Telecommunications

The bulk of this chapter is about getting connected, be it by telephone, mobile phone or Internet. Thanks to the well-established telecommunications sector in Dubai, you won't feel isolated; staying in touch with friends, family and colleagues around the world is never a problem. Dubai's main service provider, Etisalat and its sister company, Emirates Internet & Multimedia, control the majority of telecommunication services in Dubai, although Dubai Internet and Media City control the landline telephone systems and internet for Emaar properties, which should be automatically processed for you by the maintenance office of your property.

Etisalat and e-Company (Previously known as Emirates Internet and Multimedia – EIM)

Etisalat's head offices can be easily recognised by the massive golf ball on the top of their building in Deira. Inside, all counters are clearly marked and well-organised. Etisalat also has a website: www.e4me.ae that allows customers to follow many procedures online. Etisalat and e-Company are generally extremely efficient and innovative, continuously introducing new services and even cutting bills to the consumer! You should face few problems in processing paperwork, receiving services or rectifying problems with Etisalat.

Post

In Dubai, you will not find a postman knocking at your door unless you subscribe to a special service. Here, all mail is sent to post boxes rather than to the address of your home or office. In Red-Tape, we cover how to rent a PO Box, which is a must for most people, and certainly for all companies setting up in Dubai.

Emirates Post (Empost)

Emirates Post, formerly known as "General Post Authority", is the government authority responsible for all postal service in Dubai. They offer a variety of services to individuals and companies. View their Website: www.emiratespostuae.com. Emirates Post has recently undergone a face-lift with a new name and logo, and is attempting to become a more service-oriented organisation.

Web Update

While Dubai's government is committed to cutting back on the red-tape involved in setting up in Dubai, both for individuals and businesses, changes in rules and regulations are inevitable. Therefore, if there have been any changes or additions to the procedures included in this book they will appear on the Explorer website. Just log on to **www.Explorer-Publishing.com** and click on the **Red-Tape** link. This page will tell you if there have been any changes to specific procedures - giving you the heads up before you head off to plough through Dubai's administrative maze!

Telephone

Applying for a Telephone Line

1 Overview

Etisalat will install up to five telephone lines at a residence. A business may install more lines, depending on its size. If you live in an Emaar property your landline will be controlled by DIMC and will be connected for you by the property maintenance company

Telephone Costs

Charges > Calls made within an emirate and to a landline are free.

For international dialling charges, see the tariff guide in the customer care section of www.etisalat.ae

Dhs.45 – current quarterly rental charges for a telephone line

Telephone Sets

Dhs.80 – one standard telephone

Dhs.135 – one additional CLIP (caller identification) enabled telephone

2 Prerequisites

Private > Line • Subscriber must be resident in Dubai

Commercial > Line • Company must be registered in Dubai

3 What to Bring

☐ Tenancy agreement or proof of premises ownership (copy)

☐ Telephone number of any working telephone at the same premises (or the nearest one)

If neither you nor the Etisalat salesperson can supply a number, a surveyor number (the Etisalat identification for your building location) must be obtained (see Obtaining a Surveyor Number [p.88])

Private > Line ☐ Passport (copy)

☐ Residence permit (copy)

☐ No objection letter from sponsor in either English or Arabic

Commercial > Line ☐ Completed application form in English or Arabic (typed) signed by the National partner, sponsor or authorised nominee, with the company stamp

☐ Passport of National partner, sponsor or authorised nominee (copy)

☐ Passport of non GCC owner/partner (copy)

☐ Residence permit of non GCC owner/partner (copy)

☐ Valid trade licence (copy)

☐ If the trade licence does not mention the location: a no objection letter from the Economic Department (original)

☐ If the premises is a site: an office site plan (copy)

☐ If the premises are a warehouse: a tenancy contract (copy) mentioning whether it is a warehouse, shed or store

☐ If the above details are not mentioned in the tenancy contract: a letter (original typed and stamped) from the company confirming that the premises will be used either as a warehouse, shed or store

Fee › ☐ Dhs.245 – registration fee including first quarter rental

☐ Additional cash for supplementary services, additional sockets or a CLIP (caller identification) enabled telephone set (for further services, see [p.96])

4 Procedure

Location › Etisalat, Various (see [p.294])   Map ref Various

Hours › Sat-Wed 07:00-15:00; 17:00-19:00

- Collect the application form from any Etisalat office
- Complete the form in English or Arabic (typed or hand-written) and select any supplementary services needed (call waiting, call barring, etc)
- Take a ticket and wait for your number to be displayed
- Submit all documents
- Pay the fees (cash or credit card) at the same counter
- The salesperson will assign you a telephone number
- Ensure you are able to provide access to your residence or business so that the Etisalat technician can install the connection

Activation › • One to four working days
- International dialling activation: one day after the local line is connected

5 Related Procedures

- Paying Bills [p.85]
- Transferring a Line to Another Subscriber [p.91]
- Applying for Supplementary Services [p.96]

Communications

Telephone

Tip Subscription Through 182,101 or www.e4me.ae

There is no subscription fee if supplementary services are applied for on 182,182,101 & e-shop (online). For a list of subscription fees when applying in person, see [p.84].

Additional Sockets

If you want more than one socket in your home or office, request extra sockets when applying for the line to avoid having the technician return at a later date. The first additional socket is Dhs.50, and sockets thereafter are Dhs.15, with no rental charge.

Communications

Telephone

Charges (in Dhs.)

Service	Subscription Through e-shop, 182 or 101	Subscription at Etisalat Offices	Rental Charges per Quarter
Call waiting	Free	50	15
Call forwarding -			
• Unconditional	Free	50	15
• On busy	Free	50	15
• On no reply	Free	50	15
• On switched off	Free	50	15
Conference calling	Free	50	15
STAR package	Free	50	30
CLIP service	Free	50	15
Code control barring -STD	Free	50	25
Code control barring -ISD	Free	50	25
Do not Disturb	Free	50	15
Follow Me	Free	50	5
Hot Line with Time Out	Not possible	50	45
Hot Line without Time out	Not possible	50	120
Automatic Alarm Service	Not possible	30fils per usage	0
Al Mersal Messaging Service	Not possible	Free	15
GSM Ishaar Package	Free	50	25

Activation and Deactivation Codes

Service	Activation Codes	Deactivation Codes
Call Waiting	*43#	#43#
Call Forwarding -		
• Unconditional	*21* (desired no.) #	#21#
• On Busy	*67* (desired no.) #	#67#
• On No reply	*61* (desired no.) #	#61#
• On switched off	*62* (desired no.) #	#62#
Add on Conference (3 party conference)	* *	Not applicable
STAR Package	Not applicable-	Not applicable
CLIP Service	Not applicable	Not applicable
Code Control barring -ISD &STD	*33* (personal code) #	#33(personal code) #
Do not Disturb	*26#	#26#
Follow Me	Not applicable	Not applicable
Hot Line with or without Time out	*53* (desired no.) #	#53#
Automatic Alarm Service	*55*(00hrs &00 min) #	#55*(00hrs &00 min) #
Al Mersal Messaging Service	Dial 125 for subscription then dial 123 for set up	

Paying Bills

1 Overview

Etisalat bills are itemised for international and mobile telephone calls and must be paid within 30 days. All service charges are clearly noted, with descriptions on the back of the bill. Bills are mailed monthly, and computer generated recorded reminders are sent to both GSM phones and landlines. An SMS reminder is also sent to mobile users who have missed their payment due date, noting the amount that must be paid and the due date.

Internet > charges

See Residential Service Overview [p.108]

See Commercial Service Overview [p.110]

phone > charges

Local Calls

Calls made within an emirate on and to a landline are free.

Calls made between mobile phones or from a mobile phone to a landline and vice versa are charged at a rate of:

- 24 fils/minute peak (07:00-14:00; 16:00-24:00)
- 18 fils/minute off–peak (00:00-07:00; 14:00-16:00)

International Calls

For a listing of international telephone call charges, visit Etisalat's www.etisalat.ae site, call 101, or look in the front of Etisalat's annual telephone book (available free of charge at any Etisalat office).

SMS

Short Message Service charges do not change according to peak or off peak timing and are charged at a rate of:

- 30 fils/local SMS
- 90 fils/international SMS

Tip Bill Inquiry

Call 142, go to any of Etisalat's public payment machines or check online at www.e4me.ae.

Communications

Telephone

Payment Options	Location	Comments
In Person		
Counter	Any Etisalat office	• Present bill, telephone number, or user name • Cash and credit card accepted
Payment Machine	Any Etisalat office and most shopping malls	• 24-hour payment using a touch-screen machine
Cheque Deposit Box	Any Etisalat office	• Insert bill counterfoil and crossed cheque in an envelope • Receipt will be mailed to you
By Post		
Mail to:	The Chief Cashier Etisalat Accounts Department PO Box 400, Dubai	• Mail bill counterfoil and crossed cheque • Receipt will be mailed to you
Online		
Log on to:	www.e4me.ae	• View and pay bills online • Both current and past bills, adjustments and payments can be viewed • See **Applying for Online Services** [p.94] to learn how to access this service
At a Bank		
Bank Counters, Telebanking & ATMs	Banks listed on [p.271]	If your bank is not listed in this table, check with your bank to determine if it has started offering this service

Communications

Telephone

Info Maysour

This is a prepaid telephone service for landlines. It is ideal for residential or business telephone lines as it gives you the convenience of receiving incoming calls for a full year, while making outgoing calls on a prepaid basis to match your budget needs.

The package is available for Dhs.190, which includes an annual subscription and rental. A standard telephone set is provided along with an initial credit of Dhs.10 worth of outgoing calls. Subsequent annual renewal is available for Dhs.120 only.

For further information, assistance or subscription to Etisalat's Maysour Prepaid Telephone Service please contact your nearest Etisalat Office/Business Center.

Reactivating a Disconnected Line

1 Overview

If the telephone bill is not paid within a specified period, the line will be disconnected in two stages. The first stage allows only receipt of calls; the second stage involves complete deactivation of the line.

nection > **Landline Telephone**

- Outgoing calls will be cut 10 days after bill payment due date
- Incoming calls can still be received (non-payment penalty already applies)
- The line will be disconnected 5 days later
- The number will be cancelled 3 months later

GSM Telephone

- Outgoing calls will be cut 45 days after bill payment due date
- Incoming calls can still be received (non-payment penalty does not yet apply)
- The line will be disconnected 15 days later
- The number will be cancelled 6 months later

2 Prerequisites

- Existing telephone or GSM line – unpaid, bill overdue

3 What to Bring

- ☐ Bill or subscriber name or telephone number
- ☐ Amount due

Fee >
- ☐ Dhs.50 – landline penalty charge
- ☐ Dhs.25 – GSM penalty charge

4 Procedure

cation > Etisalat, Various (see [p.294])   Map ref Various

Hours > Sat-Wed 07:00-15:00; 17:00-19:00

oming >
s Only
- Pay the outstanding amount (plus penalty in case of a landline) at the Cashier at any Etisalat office
- Outgoing call service will be reconnected within 1 day

nected >
Line
- Pay the outstanding amount plus the penalty at the Cashier at any Etisalat office
- Collect and complete the application form in English or Arabic (typed or hand-written)

Communications

Telephone

- Take a ticket and wait for your number to be displayed
- Submit the form and receipt
- The telephone line will be reactivated the same day

After Cancellation Deadline • Once the line has been cancelled, arrears must be settled at any Etisalat office before a new line can be applied for

> It is not always possible to obtain the same telephone number again

Reactivation > Same day

5 Related Procedures

- Paying Bills [p.85]
- Closing Accounts & Settling Final Bills [p.92]

Tip Total Disconnection!

Beware, if you have two lines in your name and one number remains unpaid, the second number may be disconnected as well.

Info Obtaining a Surveyor Number

When applying for a new telephone line, or when transferring a line to new premises, a working telephone number near the new premises must be supplied. If neither you nor the Etisalat salesperson can supply a number, a surveyor number (the Etisalat identification for your building location) must be obtained. To get the surveyor number you need to know the exact location of the new premises (use the Street Map Explorer) and if possible go to the Etisalat office in the district of your new premises (if there is one). You will need to take a copy of the tenancy agreement or proof of premises ownership, a passport copy and residence permit copy. At the Etisalat office you need to complete the required form and take it to the Surveyor Counter and show the tenancy agreement with the land plot number on it.

Transferring a Line (Account) to a New Location

1 Overview

When moving to new premises, the telephone line(s) (accounts) may be transferred. If the new location is in the same exchange area, it may be possible that the telephone number is transferred along with the line.

2 Prerequisites

- Existing telephone line

3 What to Bring

- ☐ Tenancy agreement or proof of premises ownership of the new location (copy)
- ☐ Telephone number of any working telephone at the new premises, or the nearest premises, or the surveyor number (see Obtaining a Surveyor Number [p.88])
- ☐ Last paid bill (copy)

Private > Line
- ☐ Passport (copy)
- ☐ Residence permit (copy)
- ☐ No objection letter from sponsor in either English or Arabic

mercial > Line
- ☐ Completed application form in English or Arabic (typed) signed by the National partner, sponsor or authorised nominee, with the company stamp, or
- ☐ A written request signed by the National partner, sponsor or authorised nominee
- ☐ Passport of National partner, sponsor or authorised nominee (copy)
- ☐ Valid trade licence with the location where the service is required (copy)
- ☐ If the trade licence is not updated with the new location: a no objection letter from the Economic Department (original)
- ☐ If the new premises are a site: an office site plan (copy)
- ☐ If the new premises are a warehouse: a tenancy contract (copy) mentioning whether it is a warehouse, shed or store
- ☐ If the above details are not mentioned in the tenancy contract: a letter (original typed and stamped) from the company confirming that the premises will be used either as a warehouse, shed or store

Fee >
- ☐ Dhs.100 service charge

Communications

Telephone

4 Procedure

Location > Etisalat, Various (see [p.294])   Map ref Various

Hours > Sat - Wed 07:00 - 15:00; 17:00-19:00

- Collect the application form from any Etisalat office
- Complete the form in English or Arabic (typed or hand-written)
- Pay the final bill (cash or credit card) at the Cashier by providing either the bill or the telephone number; collect the receipt
- Take a ticket and wait for your number to be displayed
- Submit all documents (including receipt)
- You will be given a new telephone number (if the previous number is not being transferred)

The service charge will be included in your next bill

Activation > 3 working days.

5 Related Procedures

- Obtaining a Surveyor Number [p.88]

Tip   Recorded Message

A recording can be installed on the old number to inform callers of your new telephone number.

Simply fill in the application form and request interactive voice recording (IVR) service. Subscription costs Dhs.150 per month, and Dhs.100 for the next two months, and will be included in your next bill.

Note that this service can only be ordered once and cannot be re-ordered. Hence, order the recording for a longer than shorter period just in case.

Setting Up Home

From getting your phone connected to working out how your sewerage works there is a whole host of things to get your head round when moving into your new abode. For more information on setting up home in Dubai check out the Residents section of the *Dubai Explorer* (The Complete Residents Guide) available in all leading bookshops and supermarkets.

Transferring a Line to Another Subscriber

1 Overview

It is possible to transfer a telephone line to another person or company ('subscriber') rather than cancel the current line and activate a new one.

GSM, Wasel and landlines can be transferred.

2 Prerequisites

- Existing telephone, GSM or Wasel line
- New subscriber must be resident in Dubai

3 What to Bring

☐ Tenancy agreement or proof of premises ownership (copy)

☐ Last paid bill (copy)

Private > Line

☐ Passport of the party releasing the line (copy)

☐ Residence permit of the party releasing the line (copy)

☐ Passport of the new subscriber (copy)

☐ Residence permit of the new subscriber (copy)

Commercial > Line

☐ Completed application form in English or Arabic (typed) signed by the National partner, sponsor or authorised nominee, with the company stamp

☐ Passport of National partner, sponsor or authorised nominee (for both parties) (copy)

☐ Valid trade licence (copy)

Fee >

☐ Dhs.50 – service charge

4 Procedure

Location > Etisalat, Various (see [p.292])   Map ref Various

Hours > Sat-Wed 07:00-15:00; 17:00-19:00

- The final bill must first be paid by the original telephone line subscriber
- Collect and complete the application form in English or Arabic (typed or hand-written)

Both parties must sign the 'Transfer' section on the back of the form

- Take a ticket and wait for your number to be displayed
- Submit all documents (including final receipt)
- Pay the fee (cash or credit card) at the same counter

Activation > Same day.

Communications

Telephone

Telephone

Closing Accounts & Settling Final Bills

1 Overview

A telephone line may be cancelled at any time, but it must be done in person at any Etisalat office.

2 Prerequisites

• Existing Etisalat telephone line

3 What to Bring

☐ Passport (copy)

☐ The last telephone bill or telephone number or subscriber name

4 Procedure

Location > Etisalat, Various (see [p.294])   Map ref Various

Hours > Sat – Wed 07:00 – 15:00; 17:00 – 19:00

• Collect the application form from any Etisalat office
• Complete the form in English or Arabic (typed or hand-written)
• Tick 'Disconnect the Line (Permanent) From:' (enter date)
• Attach your passport copy to the form
• Proceed to the Cashier and request a final bill
• Pay the bill and obtain a receipt

Disconnection > Immediate.
Timings

5 Related Procedures

• Transferring a line to a new location [p.89]

Info Getting a Clearance Certificate

In general, the final bill is considered proof of final settlement when you move out of your premises. However, some landlords may request a clearance certificate as additional proof before returning the rental security deposit to the tenant. In order to get a clearance certificate you will first have to pay the final bill and have the telephone line disconnected. You need to submit the final bill receipt to the cashier at any Etisalat office and request a clearance certificate. The certificate will be issued immediately and there is a service charge of Dhs.20.

Applying for an Etisalat Calling Card (ECC)

1 Overview

An Etisalat Calling Card (ECC) is available free of charge to every telephone line subscriber. This PIN–protected card is not pre-paid and all calls made using this card are charged to your monthly bill. With this card, both local and international calls can be made from any telephone in the UAE. Calls from international destinations can also be made to the UAE.

Rates are the same as dialling from a regular telephone when calling within and from the UAE. When dialling from overseas, standard international rates apply.

2 Prerequisites

• An existing Etisalat telephone or GSM account

3 What to Bring

☐ Telephone or GSM application form, depending on which account you wish to use

☐ One form of valid ID

4 Procedure

Location ❯ Etisalat, Various (see [p.294])   Map ref Various

Hours ❯ Sat-Wed 07:00-15:00; 17:00-19:00

• Collect the application form from any Etisalat office
• Complete the form in English or Arabic (typed or hand-written)
• Tick "Etisalat Calling Card Service" on the form
• Take a ticket and wait for your number to be displayed
• Submit all documents to the salesperson
• The salesperson will give you an Etisalat Calling Card

🗋 You may request a personalised card, though this will take up to three days to process

Within the UAE ❯ • Dial 800 8080 (toll-free) and follow the voice prompts

Abroad ❯ • Dial the HCD (Home Country Direct Telephone Service) telephone number of the country you are visiting

🗋 To find this number, see the instructions on the reverse of your Etisalat Calling Card

• HCD numbers are also listed on www.etisalat.ae on the Business Solutions page

Activation ❯ Up to four working days.

General Telecom Services

Applying for Online Services

1 Overview

Emirates Telecommunications Corporation, generally known as Etisalat, provides telephone, fax and mobile lines as well as Internet connection and email. Etisalat customers may access personal billing information and make payments or changes to the current services they subscribe to by logging on to www.e4me.ae.

The first step in being able to access this information is to register online at the above website.

2 Prerequisites

- Any Etisalat account in your name

3 What to Bring

Depending on how you wish to contact and be contacted by Etisalat:

Option 1 ›   ☐ By SMS: a mobile phone registered in your name

Option 2 ›   ☐ By telephone: Internet address or landline number and your personal details as per the Etisalat database

4 Procedure

Location ›   Etisalat, Various (see [p.294])   Map ref Various

Hours ›   Sat – Wed 07:00 – 15:00; 17:00 – 19:00

Log on ›   • Log on to www.e4me.ae
- Fill in the registration form following the prompts

Registration › Number

Option 1
- Enter your GSM number
- You will instantly receive an SMS message with a number
- Enter this number onto the site within 15 minutes
- If registration is successful, you will instantly receive a registration number, customer number and username on the screen

Option 2
- Enter your Internet address or landline number
- Call 800 888 3463
- The customer service agent will verify your identity by asking for some personal details
- If you answer the questions correctly, the agent will give you a registration number, customer number and username

With the above steps, you may access general billing information online. If you wish to have access to specific call details, you will have to obtain a password from Etisalat first. Go to the E4Me Counter at any Etisalat Business Centre and present your registration number and username (see facing page). The salesperson will give you a password to access your personal information online.

Immediate.

:tivation > • Paying Bills [p.85]

5 Related Procedures

Tip Application Assistance

If you do not feel comfortable with the online application procedure, go to any Etisalat Business Centre and a salesperson will gladly guide you through this procedure on a computer provided by Etisalat for this purpose.

Tip Helpful Numbers

Directory Enquiries	181
(landline – 30 fils per enquiry; mobile – 30 fils per minute)	
Fault Reporting	171
(free of cost)	
Customer Service Helpline	101
(landline – 30 fils per enquiry; mobile – 30 fils per minute	

Communications

General Telecom Services

Eastenders, Desperate Housewives, 24 and ER

Just because you've left your home country it doesn't mean you have to say goodbye to all your home comforts, especially not your favourite TV shows. There are a number of satellite television providers in Dubai showcasing popular shows and movies from around the world. For more information see the Residents section of the *Dubai Explorer* (The Complete Residents Guide) available in all leading bookshops and supermarkets.

10th Edition EXPLORER
The Complete Residents' Guide

Dubai

Applying for Supplementary Services

1 Overview

Etisalat offers its clients a variety of additional services from call forwarding to call waiting to code controlled barring and these services can be applied for in person at the Etisalat office for a charge. For a comprehensive list of services and the corresponding charges, see [p.84]. If you activate supplementary services through 182, 101 or e-shop (online) there are no charges, see the table on p.95 for further details.

2 Prerequisites

• Existing telephone or GSM line

3 What to Bring

Private Line ›
☐ Passport (copy)
☐ Residence permit (copy)

Commercial Line ›
☐ Completed application form in English or Arabic (typed) signed by the National partner, sponsor or authorised nominee, with the company stamp, or

☐ A written request signed by the National partner, sponsor or authorised nominee

☐ Passport of National partner, sponsor or authorised nominee (copy)

☐ Valid trade licence (copy)

4 Procedure

Location › Etisalat, Various (see [p.294])   Map ref Various

Hours › Sat-Wed 07:00-15:00; 17:00-19:00

• Collect the application form from any Etisalat office
• Complete the form in English or Arabic (typed or hand-written)
• Take a ticket and wait for your number to be called
• Submit all documents at the counter
• In order to activate the services requested, specific codes must be entered into the phone (for a listing of these codes, see [p.84])
• Service charges will be included in the next bill

Activation › Immediate.

5 Related Procedures

•   Paying Bills [p.85]

Communications

General Telecom Services

Supplementary Service Definitions & Availability

Service	Description	Tel.	GSM	Al Wasel
Call waiting	Allows receipt of a second call while you are on another call	Yes	Yes	Yes
Call forwarding -	Diverts all incoming calls to any telephone, GSM or voice mail	Yes	Yes	Yes
• Unconditional	All calls			
• On busy	When your line is busy			
• On no reply	When you don't answer			
• On switched off	When your phone is switched off	No	Yes	Yes
Conference calling	Allows a 5-party conference call	Yes	Yes	No
STAR package	Combination of 3 services: call forwarding (unconditional), call waiting and add-on conference	Yes	Yes	Yes
CLIP service	Enables you to see the number of the person calling you.	Yes	No	No
Code control barring -STD	Bars UAE and international calls (0+00)	Yes	Yes	No
Code control barring -ISD	Bars international calls (00)	Yes	Yes	No
Do not disturb	Diverts all calls to a pre-recorded announcement	Yes	No	No
Follow me	Allows you to forward calls remotely from any telephone to any other telephone within the UAE by dialling 146	Yes	No	No
Hot line with time out	Calls a frequently dialled number automatically each time you lift the handset (within 5 seconds)	Yes	No	No
Hot line without time out	Immediately calls a frequently dialled number each time you lift the handset	Yes	No	No
Automatic alarm service	Allows you to set an alarm	Yes	No	No
Messaging service (Al Mersal)	Automatic answering service greets callers with your personal greetings, inviting them to leave a message and which you can listen to from any phone in the UAE	Yes	Yes	Yes
EW@p	Access of Internet on Mobile	No	Yes	Yes

Tip Free!

To avoid paying application charges for supplementary services, either call 182, 101 or use the Web. Register your details with Etisalat's 'e-shop' to access a number of services, including adding supplementary services to your telephone line.   Log on to www.e4me.ae to register. For a listing of available services and their charges (for walk-in customers), see [p 84].

Mobile Phone

Overview

Etisalat, the only mobile service provider in the UAE, puts the number of GSM subscribers in the UAE at almost 3.7 million. Mobile phones (also known as 'cell phones', GSM or 'handy phones') are prevalent in the UAE and can be purchased from Etisalat, specialised telecommunications shops, electronics shops, as well as large supermarkets.

In order to use a mobile phone with a Dubai telephone number, you will first have to obtain a SIM card from Etisalat, which is inserted into the back of the phone. There are two GSM service options available, and each depends on your needs/requirements.

Standard GSM allows you to make an unlimited number of calls, as long as the monthly bills are paid. Wasel GSM works on a pre-paid credit basis, which must be recharged in order to continue making calls. This is a popular choice for new arrivals to Dubai, as no residence permit is required for registration. For a detailed comparison of the services, see the table on the facing page.

Unlike in many other countries, there are no free calling times or mobile package options offering unlimited evening and weekend calls etc. In the UAE, you must simply pay for each call you make from your mobile.

Info WAP & GPRS

Etisalat offers EWAP Service to customers with WAP (Wireless Application Protocol) enabled handsets.

GPRS (General Packet Radio Service) is also available and provides customers access to information with their GPRS enabled mobile phones.

Tip GSM Help

For Etisalat GSM assistance service, dial 101 (free of charge from a landline; 24fils/minute from a mobile).

Supplementary Services

To avoid paying application charges for supplementary services, either call 182, 101 or register your details with Etisalat's 'e-shop' to access a number of services. Log on to www.e4me.ae to register. For a listing of available services and their charges (for walk-in customers), see the tables on [p.84].

Info Najm

Najm is perfect for people who spend a lot of time on their mobile phone. You can pay a set amount for 500, 1000 or 2,000 minute packages (with free text) a month which works out cheaper than your normal call rate. A variety of other services are included, but international calls are not part of the package and will be billed separately.

Mobile Phone Services – Options		
	GSM	**Wasel**
Product	Standard mobile service	Prepaid mobile service
Residence permit required	Yes	No
Subscription duration	Unlimited	1 year of incoming calls
Target group	Residents without limitations on calls	Residents with control of call expenses & frequent visitors
Minimum salary	Dhs.5,000	No
Payment	Monthly bill	Prepaid credit
SMS (Short Message Service)	Yes	Yes
Roaming	Yes (Dhs.2,000 deposit) (see [p.101])	Yes (limited)
Cost: peak/min	24 fils	24 fils
Cost: off-peak/min	18 fils	18 fils
Subscription charge (1 time only)	Dhs.185	Dhs.165
Renewal ('Rental')	Dhs.60 every 3 months after first 3 months	Dhs.100 per year after first year
SMS Message Centre Number	+971 50 606 0000	+971 50 606 0000
Help	101	101 (120 and the prepaid card number to recharge)

Info Need Two SIM Cards?

A new service, 'Taw'am' has recently been introduced by Etisalat, allowing you to have two SIM cards with the same number (GSM and Wasel).

There is a one-time charge of Dhs.100, with no additional rental charges. Call 101 or log on to www.etisalat.ae for further details or to sign up.

Note: In case a card is lost, blocked or damaged, replacement of both SIM cards will take place. A new dual SIM card will be issued at a price of Dhs. 100

Tip Subscription in Stores

It is possible to subscribe to Wasel service at several electronics stores around Dubai. Bring a passport copy with a valid residence permit, or entry permit, pay, and you will be given a telephone number on the spot. Keep an eye open for special offers including free Wasel subscription with mobile purchase. You may also order Wasel4me by logging on www.e4me.ae or call 7000 11 111 and your card will be delivered to you anywhere in the UAE within 24 hrs through a new partnership deal between Etisalat, the Corporation's Contact Centre, and Empost.

Mobile Phone

Applying for a Standard GSM Line

1 Overview

Standard mobile phone service allows both local and international dialling and call receipt. Unless roaming as a supplementary service is added to the GSM line (see the Info box [p.103]), it cannot be used outside the UAE. For an overview of the two mobile line options offered Etisalat, see the Mobile Phone Services – Options table on [p.99]. Standard GSM lines are billed monthly and have a quarterly rental charge included in the bill.

Validity › Unlimited

Charges › • Dhs.185 – subscription fee (one time only)
  • Dhs.60 – quarterly rental fee
  • 24fils – cost: peak/min (07:00 – 14:00; 16:00 – 24:00)
  • 18fils – cost: off-peak/min (14:00 – 16:00; 00:00 – 07:00)

2 Prerequisites

  • Subscriber must be resident in Dubai and over 21 years of age
  • Minimum monthly salary of approximately Dhs.5,000

3 What to Bring

  ☐ Passport (copy)
  ☐ Residence permit (copy)
  ☐ Salary certificate from employer demonstrating that monthly salary is at least Dhs.5,000 (original)

Fee › ☐ Dhs.185 – subscription fee including first quarter rental

4 Procedure

Location › Etisalat, Various (see [p.292])   Map ref Various

Hours › Sat-Wed 07:00-15:00; 17:00-19:00

  • Collect the application form from any Etisalat office
  • Complete the form in English or Arabic (typed or hand-written) and select any supplementary services needed
  • Take a ticket and wait for your number to be displayed
  • Submit all documents
  • Pay the fee (cash or credit card) at the same counter

  ☐ Supplementary service charges are included in your next bill

  • The salesperson will give you a SIM card

Procedure › Within one hour.
Time

5 Related Procedures

- Paying Bills [p.85]
- Replacing a SIM Card [p.104]

Tip SMS ('Risala')

SMS (Short Message Service) messages can be sent and received from a GSM telephone. The Service Centre Number for GSM SMS is +971(0)50 606 0000. Enter this number into the message menu of the GSM handset (once only) in order to activate message sending.

Info Reporting a Lost or Stolen Mobile

If your mobile is either lost or stolen, report the loss immediately to Etisalat by calling 101. You will be asked for your name, telephone number and your passport number. The operator will then deactivate the SIM card.

Note: You are liable for all calls made from your phone until it is reported lost or stolen to Etisalat. To avoid abuse, ensure your phone is always locked with a code, and report losses immediately.

Info Mobile Service Info Box

GSM Roaming

If you wish to receive and/or make calls while outside the UAE, roaming must be applied for at Etisalat, and a refundable deposit of Dhs.2, 000 paid in advance.

This deposit is not applicable to UAE Nationals and locally-owned companies.

When overseas, calls received from the UAE are billed at Etisalat's international rate to that country plus 15%. The caller in the UAE will only pay the local call to the mobile.

GSM roaming customers can also use GPRS internationally with networks that offer the service.

3G Service

For a subscription fee of Dhs.200 and a fixed monthly fee of Dhs.25, mobile phone users can use Etisalat's third generation ('Mubashir') service. It includes multi media messaging, video calling, and high speed mobile Internet access. Video calls are charged at a rate of 75 fils a minute and data services one fil per kb of information.

GSM customers call 125 and Wasel customers 122 to sign up.

Communications

Mobile Phone

Applying for a Wasel4me Prepaid GSM Line

1 Overview

Wasel service unlimited incoming calls and pre-paid (pay-as-you-go) outgoing calls via purchased phone cards (Dhs.30 each, available from shops, petrol stations, supermarkets, etc.) This service includes connection, one year's rental, SIM card charges and Dhs.10 free credit. You can receive calls while outside the UAE, provided you have enough credit in your card, but international rates apply. As this is a prepaid service, there are no monthly telephone bills.

▢ You do not have to be a resident of Dubai to apply for this service; visitors to Dubai may also use Wasel.

Validity › One year, renewable

Charges › • Dhs.165 – one year's subscription
• Dhs.100 – annual renewal including call waiting service
• 24fils – cost: peak/min (07:00-14:00; 16:00-24:00)
• 18fils – cost: off-peak/min (14:00 - 16:00; 00:00 - 07:00)

2 Prerequisites

• Subscriber must be over 21 years of age

3 What to Bring

☐ Passport (copy)
☐ Residence permit (copy), or
☐ Entry stamp in passport (copy)

Fee › ☐ Dhs.165 – subscription fee

4 Procedure

Location › Etisalat, Various (see [p.294])   Map ref Various

Hours › Sat-Wed 07:00-15:00; 17:00-19:00

• Collect the application form from any Etisalat office or authorised reseller
• Complete the form in English or Arabic (typed or hand-written)
• Take a ticket and wait for your number to be displayed
• Submit all documents
• Pay the fee (cash or credit card) at the same counter
• The salesperson will give you a SIM card

Acticvation › Immediate

5 Related Procedures

• Replacing a SIM Card [p.104]

ven if you have no credit on your phone, SMS messages can be received while in the UAE. In order to send messages, there must be credit on the phone. Enter +971 (0)50 606 0000 into the message menu of the phone (once only) in order to activate message sending.

Call Waiting

Call waiting is not available to Wasel customers in the first year of subscription. When renewing your registration after one year, this service is automatically included in the package. If you want call waiting in the first year, just pay one year in advance.

Recharging/Adding Credit

Options to recharge the card for outgoing calls:

- Pay at any Etisalat cashier
- Use a prepaid Etisalat phone card (Dhs.30 per card)
- Log on to www.e4me.ae and pay by credit card (minimum Dhs.50)
- Use an Etisalat payment machine (for locations see [p.294]) but note that credit is payable in Dhs.50 units only
- Some banks allow the use of their ATM to credit a Wasel connection.
- Emirates Post outlets in the UAE have machines that accept cash to credit a Wasel connection

Subscription Renewal

- You will need four Dhs.30 Etisalat phone cards as annual renewal costs Dhs.100
- Enter 122 followed immediately by the numbers on the four cards, each separated by the # key
- Press "call" or "OK"
- Dhs.20 is automatically added to the SIM card as credit
- Log on to www.e4me.ae and pay by credit card

Balance Inquiry

To determine the balance amount, dial 121 (free call) or press *121# then press the 'send' key

Kallemni

The Kallemni service allows a prepaid Wasel user outside the UAE to send a call request to any fixed line or mobile number in the UAE. The request will be delivered as a text message to a mobile phone and as a voice message to a fixed line. This service is available only when the Wasel user is outside the UAE, and these requests can only be sent to numbers within the UAE. A complete list of countries in which Kallemni can be used is available on www.etisalat.ae.

Wasel Roaming

Wasel customers can receive calls and messages when overseas. While roaming charges apply for incoming calls, incoming messages are free. Around 70 countries support Wasel customers to make outgoing calls and send messages too, as long as they have enough credit.

Free of Charge Roaming: Dial as follows: *111*destination number#send.

Mobile Services

Replacing a SIM Card

1 Overview

If the SIM card is lost or damaged, Etisalat will replace it with a new SIM card and the same telephone number for a Dhs.50 fee.

You are liable for all calls made from your phone, even if it has been stolen, until the loss has been reported to Etisalat. To avoid abuse, report losses immediately. See [p.101] for more information.

2 Prerequisites

• Existing GSM line

3 What to Bring

☐ Passport (copy)

Fee ⟩ ☐ Dhs.50 – replacement fee

4 Procedure

Location ⟩ Etisalat, Various (see [p.294])   Map ref Various

Hours ⟩ Sat-Wed 07:00-15:00; 17:00-19:00

• Collect the application form from any Etisalat office
• Complete the form in English or Arabic (typed or hand-written)
• Take a ticket and wait for your number to be called
• Submit all documents
• Pay the replacement fee (cash or credit card) at the same counter
• The salesperson will give you a replacement SIM card with the same telephone number

Activation ⟩ Within 15 minutes

Info Tarjim

The service offers mobile users the ability to translate Arabic text into English and vice versa.

• Send a text message that contains words/sentence to be translated to 1001.
• Arabic messages should be 70 Characters.
• English messages should be 160 Characters.
• Pricing – Each SMS would cost 60 fils. For assistance please call 101

Internet Overview

1 Overview

Emirates Internet & Multimedia

Etisalat is the sole provider of Internet services in the UAE through its proxy server. Due to the popularity of the Internet in the UAE, Emirates Internet & Multimedia has developed into a separate, well-organised business unit within Etisalat. It provides individuals and companies with Internet access and all related services such as email addresses, domain names and Websites.

For a detailed comparison of services, commercial and residential, offered, see the tables on [p.106].

With the proxy server in place, certain sites are restricted. If you find a blocked site that you believe should be unblocked, report it to Etisalat on help@emirates.net.ae.

Useful > Websites **www.ecompany.ae** – homepage of Emirates Internet & Multimedia, offering products and services, billing inquiries, online change of passwords, change of ISDN access speed

Internet Help   800 6100

Related > cedures
- Residential Service Overview [p.108]
- Commercial Service Overview [p.110]
- Internet Roaming [p.113]
- Applying for a UAE Domain Name [p.112]
- Paying Bills [p.85]

Tip   Dial 'n' Surf

This facility allows you to surf the Internet without subscribing to Emirates Internet services. You will need a computer with a modem and a regular phone line; no account number or password is required. The Dial 'N' Surf service is nominally priced and you have to pay 12 fils/minute which is charged directly to the telephone you are connecting from. Simply dial 500 5555 to gain access.

Tip   Installation Assistance

If you are not comfortable with computers, request paid installation service (Dhs.100) when applying for residential Internet service. A technician will come to your residence to install the package for you.

Communications

Internet Services

Residential Internet Services

Technology Description	PSTN (telephone line)	ISDN (digital line)	ADSL line	PSTN or ISDN
Maximum Speed	Up to speed of modem	64 or 128 kb/s	Up to 256 kb/s (upstream) Up to 2Mb/s (downstream)	As per PSTN or ISDN speeds
Connection Type	Dial-up	Dial-up	Continuous connection	Dial-up
Services Included	Email address	Email address	Basic dial-up: email address	–
Registration Fee	Dhs.100	Dhs.200	Dhs.200 (ADSL) +Dhs.0 (Basic dial-up)	Not applicable
Monthly Charges	Dhs.20	Dhs.20 (Dhs.100/quarter)	Dhs.190 (ADSL) 256K Dhs.250 (ADSL) 512K Dhs.450 (ADSL) 1M Dhs.650 (ADSL) 2M	Directly billed to the telephone you are connection from
Cost – Peak (06:00–01:00)	Dhs.1.80/hour	64 kbps: Dhs.1.80/hour 128 kbps: Dhs.3.60/hour	Not applicable	12 fils/minute Dhs.7.2 per hour
Cost – Off Peak	Dhs.1/hour 128 kbps: Dhs.2/hour	64 kbps: Dhs.1/hour	Not applicable	12 fils/minute Dhs.7.2 per hour
Dial-Up Number	400 4444	400 4444	Not applicable	500 5555

Commercial Internet Services

	Dial-Plus	ISDN LAN (local area network)	'Business One'	Dedicated Access
Technology Description	PSTN & ISDN	ISDN	ADSL	Leased line (ISDN or ADSL)
Target Company	Small to medium	Medium to large	Medium to large	Very large and/or publishers information on the Web
Maximum Speed	PSTN: up to modem speed ISDN: 64kb/s to 128kb/s	64 kb/s	Up to 1 Mb/s (upstream) Up to 8 Mb/s (downstream)	128 kb/s to 2 Mb/s
Connection Type	Dial-up	Unlimited: continuous Limited: click connected	Continuous connection	Continuous connection
Services Included	• Domain name registration • 10MB Web hosting space	• Domain name registration • 10MB Web hosting space • Static IP address	• Domain name registration • 20 MB Web hosting space • 30 GB/month data transfer • upto 40 email accounts	• Domain name registration • 10 MB web hosting space • Static IP address • No download limitation
Subscription/Installation Fee	Dhs.200	Dhs.1,000	Dhs.200	Dhs.2,000-4,000 (depending on speed)
Monthly Charges	Dhs.50	Unlimited Connection:Dhs.3,000 Limited Access: Dhs.500	Dhs.350-1,995 (depending on the package you take	Dhs.2,900 - Dhs.23,550 (depending on speed)
Cost – Peak (06:00-01:00)	64kb/s: Dhs.1.80/hour 128kb/s: Dhs.3.60/hour	Unlimited connection: Not applicable Limited Access: Dhs.6/hour	Not applicable	Not applicable
Cost – Off Peak (01:00-06:00)	64kb/s: Dhs.1/hour 128kb/s: Dhs.2/hour	Limited Access: Dhs.6/ hour	Not applicable	Not applicable
Dial-Up Number	400 4444	Not applicable	Not applicable	Not applicable

Applying for Residential Service

1 Overview

Emirates Internet offers various internet access options for residential users, from basic dial-up connection, to high-speed ADSL connection. See Residential Service Table [p.106] for a listing of speeds, charges and services. Note that this service can not be used for commercial/business purposes. For a listing of commercial Internet services, see [p.107].

Charges > • See Residential Service Table [p.106]

2 Prerequisites

- Subscriber must be resident in Dubai
- Standard telephone line
- Modem with a minimum speed of 56K

ISDN > • Digital line

ADSL > • An appropriate telephone line (call 800 6100 or log on to
(Al Shamil) www.alshamil.net.ae to determine whether your area has telephone lines which can provide this service)

☐ An Etisalat technician may also need to check the capacity of the line and location before accepting the application

- An Etisalat-approved modem (recommended)

☐ If you purchase a modem on the market, check for the Etisalat approval stamp to ensure system compatibility

3 What to Bring

☐ Passport (copy)

☐ Residence permit (copy)

Fee > ☐ Subscription fee (see Residential Service Overview [p.106])

ADSL > ☐ Dhs.600-775 external; Dhs.600 internal (ADSL modem purchase)

4 Procedure

Location > Etisalat, Various (see [p.294])   Map ref Various

Hours > Sat – Wed 07:00 – 15:00; 17:00 – 19:00

- Collect the internet services application form from any Etisalat office
- Complete the form in English or Arabic (typed or hand-written)
- Take a ticket and wait for your number to be called
- Submit all documents
- Pay the subscription fee (cash or credit card) at the same counter
- The salesperson will give you your Internet package and email address

Communications

Internet

- Billing commences with the first log-in or 21 days from the date of application, whichever is first

cedure> Same day if there is no technician visit.

Info   Prepaid Internet

Prepaid Internet cards are available for use which allow you to access the internet without having an account. From the computer's modem you can dial 128 plus the 14 digit number on the card and you will be given immediate access to the internet. This means you can access the internet from any phone line in the UAE. Credit on prepaid scratch cards is 12 fils per minute. Etisalat prepaid scratchcards are available in denominations of Dhs.30.

Info   ADSL Service

Emirates Internet's ADSL service (also known as 'Al Shamil') does not provide you with an email address. If you wish to have an emirates email address, you will have to register for the basic dial-up connection as well. This will provide you with a username and password, which allows you to check your mail from any computer, both in the UAE and when you are overseas. Note that if you subscribe to ADSL and basic dial-up at the same time, the basic dial-up subscription fee will be waived, though you will have to pay both monthly charges. For more information about ADSL service, log on to www.alshamil.net.ae.

Internet Software

Etisalat can provide you with a basic internet software package, which includes Netscape, Microsoft Explorer and Eudora, for free.

Communications

Internet

Surfing UAE

The internet is a fantastic resource for extensive research on all things Dubai (at least that's a good excuse for a bit of surfing) - whether you want to find out services, events, shopping or just expat activities. For a list of some of the best websites check out the General Information chapter of the *Dubai Explorer* (The Complete Residents' Guide) available in all leading bookshops and supermarkets.

Applying for Commercial Service

1 Overview

Etisalat/Emirates Internet offers various Internet access options for business users, from basic dial-up connection, to dedicated access, depending on the size and needs of the company. See Commercial Service Table [p.107] for a listing of speeds, charges and services.

Charges ❯ See Commercial Service Table [p.107]

2 Prerequisites

• Company is registered in Dubai or in one of Dubai's free zones

3 What to Bring

☐ Completed application for Internet services form in English or Arabic (typed) signed by the National partner, sponsor or authorised nominee, with the company stamp

☐ Passport of National partner, sponsor or authorised nominee (copy)

☐ Passport of non GCC owner/partner (copy)

☐ Residence permit of non GCC owner/partner (copy)

☐ Valid trade licence (copy)

☐ Power of attorney to sign on behalf of the company

☐ If a free zone company: a letter from the free zone authority verifying registration with the free zone

Fee ❯ ☐ See Commercial Service Overview [p.107]

Business ❯ ☐ Modem purchase – Dhs.775 external; Dhs.600 internal
One

4 Procedure

Location ❯ Etisalat, Various (see [p.294])   Map ref Various

Hours ❯ Sat – Wed 07:00 – 15:00; 17:00 – 19:00

• Go to any Etisalat office, take a ticket and wait for your number to be called

• Submit all documents

• Pay the subscription fee (cash or credit card) at the same counter

• The salesperson will give you your Internet package and email address

• Billing commences after installation

Activation ❯ Depends upon service applied for.

5 Related Procedures

• Applying for a UAE Domain Name [p.112]

Tip | Installation Assistance

Companies receive automatic installation assistance on sign-up for business service. A technician will install the commercial Internet package and hardware (if applicable) on your computer for you. Contact Etisalat/Emirates Internet for installation fees, which depend on the services applied for.

Info | Obtaining an Email Address

In order to obtain an email address in the UAE, you must subscribe to any Emirates Internet service. A commercial user name is limited to eight characters and the address depends on the nature and status of the company (co.ae = company, org.ae = non-profit organisation, sch.ae = school, mil.ae = military, gov.ae = government, ac.ae = academy or university). A typical commercial email address will be: user@company.co.ae.

Communications

Internet

Internet

Applying for a UAE Domain Name

1 Overview

UAE domain names for the internet may be registered and reserved for future use without signing up for Internet services. Domain names are now available to all customers. As predominantly commercial customers will use this service, Red-Tape focuses on commercial application. For more information, visit www.uaenic.ae.

2 Prerequisites

• Residential or commercial internet customer

3 What to Bring

☐ Completed & signed Web Hosting Service application form in English or Arabic

☐ Passport copy with valid residency page of sponsor

☐ Valid trade licence copy

☐ Power of attorney to sign on behalf of the company

☐ If a free zone company: a letter from the free zone authority verifying registration with the free zone

4 Procedure

Location › Etisalat, Various (see [p.294])   Map ref Various

Hours › Sat – Wed 07:00 – 15:00; 17:00 – 19:00

• Visit www.uaenic.ae to determine availability of the domain name you would like to reserve

• Go to any Etisalat sales office, take a ticket and wait for your number to be called

• Submit all documents and pay the subscription fee (cash or credit card) at the same counter

• The salesperson will give you confirmation of the registered domain name

Activation › Immediate

Internet Roaming

1 Overview

Internet Roaming allows Emirates Internet customers to go online from almost anywhere in the world, at the price of a local call. Emirates Internet is member of the GRIC (Global Roaming Internet Centre) Alliance, allowing access from over 500 internet service providers (ISPs) world-wide. For a list of the 150 countries in which this service can be used, log on to www.gric.com.

Charges > • 30 fils per minute (Dhs.18 per hour)

• A one-time service charge of Dhs.10 per month, during the month in which the roaming service is used

2 Prerequisites

• An Emirates Internet account
• Computer with a modem and access to a telephone line

3 What to Bring

☐ Your Emirates Internet username and password

4 Procedure

• Log on to www.gric.com and go to the ISP locator page to determine whether there is a GRIC Internet Service Provider in the country to which you are travelling

• If yes, download (onto the computer you will use while travelling) a free user-friendly software package called 'GRICdial'

▢ GRICdial has an updateable phonebook containing dialup numbers of every ISP in the GRIC world-wide network

▢ GRICdial also frees you from having to configure network settings while travelling

• When travelling, to locate the nearest ISP in the GRIC network, check in the GRIC phonebook on your computer

• Dial that ISP number

• Log on with your Emirates Internet username (e.g. username@emirates.net.ae)

• All international access will be billed to your Emirates Internet account

Help! > 800-5244 or help@emirates.net.ae

▢ International users dial 500 3535 to access the Internet while in the UAE

Communications

Internet

Tip Help!

For assistance or further information on any of the listed Internet services, call 800 6100 or log on to www.emirates.net.ae.

DIC Telecom

Applying for Telecommunications

1 Overview

Dubai Internet City operates the telephone, internet and television services for all Emaar properties, both business and residential (Dubai marina, Arabian ranches, Emirates Hills, the Greens/Springs/Lakes). All villas and apartments are equipped with multiple sockets, through which the telephone, internet, and TV signals are routed, eliminating the need for further cables and dishes.This also means that residents get just one bill for all services and they can use various connecters in their home for TV and Internet interchangeably.

2 Prerequisites

Customers must own or reside in an Emaar property – residential or business

3 What to Bring

☐ Application form (obtained from the Telecom office, Dubai Marina Centre or downloaded from www.telecom.dic.ae)

☐ Required documents:

Individuals

☐ Owners: passport and proof of ownership copies

☐ Tenants: passport and tenancy agreement copies

Companies

☐ Company pays: Copy of valid trade license, tenancy agreement, proof of ownership and a stamped Dubai application form

☐ Company employee pays: Copy of passport, tenancy agreement, proof of ownership and a authorization letter from the company stating employee's name.

Activation > ☐ A one off installation payment, DHS 200 for each service required e.g., telephone, Internet and TV will cost you DHS600.

4 Procedure

Location > Telecom office, Dubai Marina Centre, 3905555

Hours > 8.00-4.00pm Sat-Thurs.

Complete the application form having chosen the services you would like (telephone, internet, broadband, choice of satellite company etc).

Submit the form along with the correct documents to the office above (only one visit to the office is required)

Pay the installation fee (cost depending on your chosen services)

Fees > A basic telephone line rental will cost an additional DHS 15 a month, one months payment is also required in advance depending on your overall chosen package (this is usually added to your 1st bill)

Activation > 4-5 days to get connected

There are no minimum contracts for telephone and Internet, but satellite companies will charge for a broken subscription (usually a minimum of one year)

Paying your Bills

If you wish to pay for your bill by credit card, you can by filling out a credit card standing order form available from the tecom office or download from www.telecom.dic.ae and returning it to the office or faxing it back on 04395554.

If you would prefer to pay by cash, you will need to pay DHS 200 deposit and pay your bill in person at the end of each month.

Wi Fi (wireless Internet Broadband Connection)

Wi Fi allows you to connect to the Internet from you laptop or any other wireless device. Wi Fi enabled computers send and receive data indoors and out within the range of the DIC telecom base.

There are pre paid cards made available in 3 denominations.

1 hour which can be used to try out the service

4+1 free hours to catch up on work or send emails.

Unlimited for one month

You can use your hours anywhere the service is required. To use Wi Fi you need one of two things, a Centimo enabled laptop or a laptop with a network card.

DIC Internet Service Options

	Email address	Do I need a modem	Cost	Installation charge
64 Kbps	1x 5Mb	No	Dhs 75/m	Free
512 Kbps	2x5 Mb	No	Dhs 225/m	200
1 Mbps	10x5 Mb	No	Dhs 500/m	200
2 Mbps	20x5 Mb	No	Dhs 1000/m	200

TV Package Options

	Basic Package	ORBIT	SHOWTIME	ADD
Subscription	Dhs. 10 per month	From Dhs. 129 per month	From Dhs.129 per month	From Dhs.83 per month
Additional Subscription		From Dhs. 40 per month	From Dhs. 32.25 per month	Same as subscription
Installation Dhs. per decoder	199	1st decoder free, Dhs.199 2nd decoder onwards	1st decoder free, Dhs.199 2nd decoder onwards	199

TV Package Options

Requires	TV1	TV2
Decorder	1. Orbit and Showtime(free decoder) 2. ADD decoder purchase DHS 799 or DHS 799 or Dhs49 rental/ monthly after 3 years you own Decoder is Dhs 1500 if subscribing to the basic package only. 3. Decoder is DHS 1500 if subscribing to the basic package only.	Free, if you subscribe for DIC Telecom Services
Activation	Free activation for the 1st decoder with Orbit and Showtime DHS 199 one time payment for ADD.	DHS 199 one time Payment
Monthly Charges	Depends on what package you chose	Same

Different satellite companies offer a different selection of channels and programs from each other, before deciding on which company you would like to subscribe to it is worth having a look at what each one is offering before making your decision.

Web Update

While Dubai's government is committed to cutting back on the red-tape involved in setting up in Dubai, both for individuals and businesses, changes in rules and regulations are inevitable. Therefore, if there have been any changes or additions to the procedures included in this book they will appear on the Explorer website. Just log on to **www.Explorer-Publishing.com** and click on the **Red-Tape** link. This page will tell you if there have been any changes to specific procedures - giving you the heads up before you head off to plough through Dubai's administrative maze!

Tip   Freedom and choice

One of the distinct advantages (or disadvantages, depending on which way you look at it!) of having DIC as your internet service provider is that they use a different proxy to Etisilat and therefore you don't get sites being banned. Other benefits include the ability to watch more than one pay TV package on the same receiver thanks to the fact that all the services are pre-wired and routed through one cable. You do, of course, have to pay for the second subscription.

Home Sweet Home

While Emaar have an choice of dwellings there are number of additional residential areas in Dubai, all with their own set of pros and cons, be it price, space or amenities. If you are trying to decide where to lay your hat then check out the Residential Areas section within the Residents chapter of the *Dubai Explorer* (The Complete Residents' Guide) available in all leading bookshops and supermarkets.

Postal Services

Applying for a PO Box

1 Overview

There is no home address-based mail system in the UAE; all mail is delivered to the Central Post Office and subsequently distributed to post boxes in one of 22 centrally located post offices. For post office locations, see [p.292].

While many residents direct mail to a company mailbox, it is also possible to rent a personal post office box.

Validity › The rental period runs from January 1st - December 31st. You can rent it for one year or a portion of a year and it can be renewed for up to 3 years.

2 Prerequisites

• Applicant must be resident in Dubai

3 What to Bring

Private › Box
☐ Passport (two copies)

☐ Valid residence permit (two copies)

☐ Two passport photographs

Fees ›
☐ Dhs.230 – private rental key charge (3 keys) & registration fee

☐ Dhs.150 – Annual Renewal

Company › Box
☐ Completed and signed application form with a company stamp

☐ Valid trade licence (copy)

☐ If trade licence is not ready yet, a letter from the Dubai Department of Economic confirming that the company has applied for a trade licence and that the Department has no objection to the applicant opening a post box

Fee ›
☐ Dhs.330 – commercial rental & key charge (3 keys)

☐ Dhs.250 – Annual Renewal

4 Procedure

Location › Post Office, Various (see [p.292])   Map ref Various

Hours › Sat-Thu 08:00-20:00, Public Holidays 08:00-12:00

• Select a post office where you would like to rent a post box, for convenience, near your office or home

• Go to that post office, submit all documents and pay the rental fee

• You will be assigned a PO Box number

• Renew rental yearly by paying the annual rental fee

Validity › Rental is for one calendar year.

Additional Services

Info You've Got Mail!

Rather than popping by your PO box to check whether you have mail, you can track your deliveries online at www.emiratespost.co.ae (you can also apply for or renew a PO box online). Customers can also pay an annual fee of Dhs.50 and they will be informed by email when postal items that require a signature or company stamp have been delivered. In addition, EziMail offers the personal collection of customers' mail from their PO box, delivered in a sealed satchel to an office or residence at a convenient time.

Info EMPOST Service

To save time and effort, Emirates Commercial Services Corporation, Empost, has introduced a brand new service to Emirates Post's customers who wish to rent private post boxes. Empost facilitates the renting process by delivering the post box key to the subscriber as well as collecting forms required for only Dhs 9.

Info Business Mail

If an individual or company receives mail in such large volumes that their post box is simply not big enough to accommodate it all, they can rent a bag to hold the mail. The Private Mail Bag Service is not available to commercial building post box subscribers. Service features meet the needs of subscribers who receive large quantities of mail. Pricing: Dhs.400 per annum (over and above the annual post box rental fee). Other business services from Empost include Mandoub, a PRO service, Direct Mail and tailormade logistical services for mailroom management.

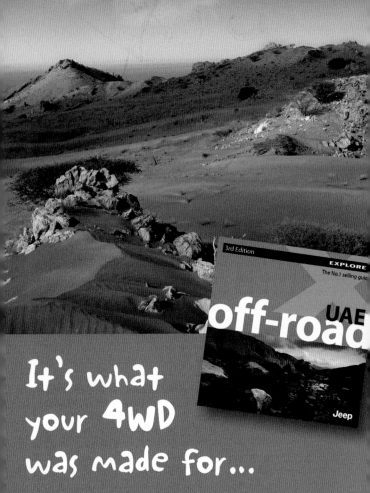

Overview

Overview

Driving

Overview

This chapter deals with everything to do with getting around Dubai in a vehicle. For ease of reference, the chapter has been divided into three sections: Driving Licence, Vehicle, and Traffic Accidents & Fines.

Driving Licence

It is essential that you have the correct documents when driving in Dubai. If not, the insurance on the vehicle may become invalid, and you will find yourself in trouble with the Police. If you currently have a foreign licence, you may be permitted to transfer it to a Dubai licence. With several steps involved in obtaining a licence, the flowchart on [p.125] will guide you.

Vehicle

Once permitted to drive a private vehicle in Dubai, the next step for many is to purchase a car. To obtain Dubai licence plates, you will have to register the car with the Dubai Traffic Police. If you have purchased an older car, it must be tested first, [p.149].

Traffic Accidents & Fines

Sadly, serious traffic accidents have become a daily occurrence on Dubai's busy roads. Repair shops are forbidden to repair any car (even with minor damage) without a police report, hence the procedure outlining police reports is detailed.

Dubai Traffic Police

For most procedures described here, you will need to visit the Dubai Traffic Police. Unlike the traffic police of other emirates, Dubai's are usually very friendly, relaxed and calm. For a list of police stations including external police desks, see [p.283].

EPPCO Tasjeel and Emarat Shamil Centres

EPPCO Tasjeel and Emarat Shamil Centres will test your vehicle prior to registration. Several testing stations exist around Dubai and both centres have done an impressive job in creating a pleasant atmosphere and in streamlining the procedure. For a list of the various locations, see [p153].

Overview

Driving

Web Update

While Dubai's government is committed to cutting back on the red-tape involved in setting up in Dubai, both for individuals and businesses, changes in rules and regulations are inevitable. Therefore, if there have been any changes or additions to the procedures included in this book they will appear on the Explorer website. Just log on to **www.Explorer-Publishing.com** and click on the *Red-Tape* link. This page will tell you if there have been any changes to specific procedures – giving you the heads up before you head off to plough through Dubai's administrative maze!

Driving Licence Overview

1 Overview

This section covers procedures for both new and experienced drivers. Everything from applying for a temporary Dubai driving licence when visiting the UAE, to transferring your current driving licence, to registering with a driving school and taking all tests is listed in full detail.

To drive a private vehicle (non-rental/leased vehicles) in Dubai you must have a temporary or permanent Dubai driving licence. Your insurance will be invalid if a private vehicle is driven with just an international or foreign driving licence.

Info Road Control Committee

Plainclothes policemen in unmarked cars regularly patrol the streets for traffic offenders. Be warned that if a driver disregards the law, a full report will be made and a fine imposed, but the driver will not necessarily be stopped at the time.

If you see a dangerous driver on the road, call 800 4353 to lodge a complaint.

Info Eye Tests

To apply for a Dubai driving licence, you must first take an eye test. You can do so at any authorised optician around Dubai, and at most hospitals & clinics. Let them know it's for a driving licence. You will need two passport photos, and will be charged a small fee. You'll receive a certificate to present when applying for your licence.

Tip Ladies' Section

Vehicle registration and all driving licence procedures can be done in the ladies' section of the Dubai Traffic Police Driving Licence Section. This is a dedicated area in which all documents are processed, photos taken, and where you can wait in peace for your licence or registration to be prepared.

Obtaining a Dubai Driving Licence

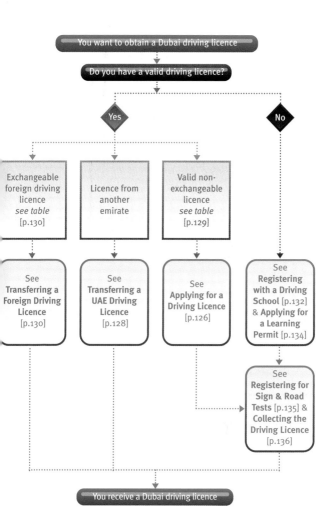

You want to obtain a Dubai driving licence

Do you have a valid driving licence?

Yes

No

Exchangeable foreign driving licence
see table
[p.130]

Licence from another emirate

Valid non-exchangeable licence
see table
[p.129]

See **Transferring a Foreign Driving Licence** [p.130]

See **Transferring a UAE Driving Licence** [p.128]

See **Applying for a Driving Licence** [p.126]

See **Registering with a Driving School** [p.132] & **Applying for a Learning Permit** [p.134]

See **Registering for Sign & Road Tests** [p.135] & **Collecting the Driving Licence** [p.136]

You receive a Dubai driving licence

Driving Licence

Driving

Driving Licence

Applying for a Driving Licence

1 Overview

Once you have obtained a Dubai residence permit and you wish to drive private vehicles (non-rental/leased) in the UAE, you must apply for a Dubai driving licence. The aim of this procedure is to 'open' a file in order to proceed further.

If you have a valid exchangeable licence from another country, see Transferring a Foreign Driving Licence [p.130], you may transfer it to a Dubai licence the same day and you do not need to follow this procedure.

International and foreign driving licences are valid for use only up to the date on which the residence permit is issued. Whilst on a visit visa, a temporary licence may be applied for (see Applying for a Temporary Driving Licence [p.142]).

Validity > 10 years

2 Prerequisites

- Applicant must be resident in Dubai
- Applicant must be at least 18 years of age

3 What to Bring

- ☐ Passport (original & copy)
- ☐ Residence permit (copy)
- ☐ 1 passport photograph (6cm x 4cm)
- ☐ Eye test certificate (see [p.124])

Fee > ☐ Dhs.100 – application fee

4 Procedure

Location > Dubai Traffic Police, Driving Licence Section   Map ref 10-E9

Hours > Sat – Wed 07:30 – 14:30

Registration >
- Collect the driving licence application form from any Traffic Police office.
- Complete the form in Arabic (typed or hand-written)
- Submit all documents at the Control Counter
- The officer will process the paperwork and return the documents to you
- Take the documents to the Cashier and pay the required application fee
- The officer will inform you which step you will need to take next

Next >
Steps • If you have an invalid or non-exchangeable driving licence, you will either have to take a road test or attend a driving school (see Registering for Sign & Road Tests [p.135] or Registering with a Driving School [p.132])

• If you do not have a driving licence, you will have to attend driving school (see Registering with a Driving School [p.132])

Tip Driving School Assistance

If you are learning to drive with an approved driving school, then the school should be able to help with your licence application.

Law Probationary Driving Licence

Drivers between the ages of 18 and 21 years receive annual renewable probationary driving licences. Strict regulations apply with probationary licences. If the driver is found guilty of a dangerous offence or of causing a serious accident, running a red light, or accumulates more than 12 black points (see [p.166]) in one year, the licence is withdrawn and the application procedure must be started again from the beginning (this includes sitting all tests).

Be Prepared

Before you get behind the wheel make sure you have your wits about you. The driving in Dubai leaves rather a lot to be desired and the number of traffic accidents are quite shocking. For more information on driving habits refer to the Driving section of the Residents chapter in the *Dubai Explorer* (The Complete Residents' Guide) available in all leading bookshops and supermarkets.

Driving Licence

Driving

Driving Licence

Transferring a UAE Driving Licence to Dubai

1 Overview

If you are changing your residency to Dubai from another emirate, and already have a driving licence issued in that emirate, you may want to transfer it to a Dubai licence. However, this isn't strictly necessary, as you could continue driving with your existing licence, and even renew it in your original emirate once it expires.

Validity > 10 years

2 Prerequisites

- Applicant must be resident in Dubai
- Driving licence from other emirate

3 What to Bring

☐ Passport (original & copy)
☐ Residence permit (copy)
☐ Driving licence (original & copy)
☐ NOC from Dubai Traffic Police (see below)
☐ Traffic Police file from current emirate (see below)
☐ Driving licence application form typed/hand-written in Arabic (see below)
☐ 1 passport photograph (6cm x 4cm)
☐ Eye test certificate (see [p.124])

Fee > Dhs.100 – application fee

4 Procedure

Location > Dubai Traffic Police, Driving Licence Section   Map ref 10-E9

Hours > Sat – Wed 07:30 – 14:30
- Go to the Transfer Licence Counter
- Request a no objection certificate from the Dubai Traffic Police addressed to the Traffic Police of the emirate which issued your current driving licence

Other Emirate > • Present the letter to the Traffic Police of the emirate which issued your current licence
- They will give you a stamped and sealed copy of your Traffic Police file

Location > Dubai Traffic Police, Driving Licence Section   Map ref 10-E9

Hours > Sat – Wed 07:30 – 14:30
- Collect the driving licence application form from any Traffic Police office.

- Complete the form in Arabic (typed or hand-written)
- Submit all documents at the Control Counter
- The officer will process the paperwork and return the documents to you
- Take the documents to the Cashier and pay the required application fee

Women may go to the Ladies' Section to submit all documents (see opposite)

- Submit all documents and the receipt at the Data Entry Counter
- Wait for your name to be called and your document will be given back to you
- Queue for your photograph to be taken
- Your licence will be ready within 5-10 minutes

5 Related Procedure

- Renewing a Driving Licence [p.138]
- Importing a Vehicle (UAE) [p.157]

Info Car Rental

Until you acquire full residency you may drive a rental car with an international licence, or with a valid exchangeable foreign licence (see Exchangeable Foreign Driving Licences table [p.130]). If you have neither, apply for a temporary Dubai driving licence from the Traffic Police (see[p.142]). A temporary licence is valid until you become a resident, or until your visit visa expires.

Passport? Deposit?

Note that car rental firms are not permitted to retain customer passports; give them a photocopy of your passport and if they insist on having the original, speak to the police! The same applies if they request a deposit from you – it's also illegal.

Driving Licence

Driving

Driving Licence

Transferring a Foreign Driving Licence to Dubai

1 Overview

The Dubai Traffic Police allows licence holders of certain countries to transfer (or exchange) their valid licence to a Dubai licence without having to take a driving test.

Validity › 10 years

Exchangeable Driving Licences

Australia	Germany	Netherlands	South Africa
Austria	Greece	New Zealand	Spain
Bahrain	Holland	Norway	Sweden
Belgium	Iceland	Oman	Switzerland
Canada	Ireland	Poland	Turkey
Cyprus	Italy	Portugal	United Kingdom
Czech Republic	Japan	Qatar	United States
Denmark	Korea	Saudi Arabia	
Finland	Kuwait	Singapore	
France	Luxembourg	Slovakia	

Iranian › Nationals
Some Iranian government employees may exchange their licence for a Dubai driving licence. Others must take the sign and road tests with the Dubai Traffic Police (see Registering for Sign & Road Tests [p.135]).

Canadian › Nationals
Holders of Canadian driving licences must obtain an affidavit (in English) from the Canadian Consulate in Dubai verifying that the licence is genuine, before applying for a licence transfer.

Other › Nationals
Licences from Greece, Portugal, the Czech Republic, Slovakia, Cyprus, Canada, Turkey, Japan and Korea must be translated at the respective consulate before a licence transfer can be applied for. If in doubt, check with your consulate first.

2 Prerequisites

- Applicant must be resident in Dubai
- Driving licence from one of the countries listed above must be valid, or within one year of the date of expiry.

3 What to Bring

☐ Passport (original & copy)

☐ Residence permit (copy)

☐ Current driving licence (original & copy)

☐ 1 passport photograph (6cm x 4cm)

☐ Eye test certificate (see [p.124])

☐ Driving Licence Applicaton form in Arabic (typed or hand-written)

☐ Letter from your consulate verifying the driving licence (if applicable, eg Canada)

☐ Translation of Driving Licence (if applicable – see list opposite)

Fee > ☐ Dhs.100 – application fee

4 Procedure

Location > Dubai Traffic Police, Driving Licence Section   Map ref 10-E9

Hours > Sat – Wed 07:30 – 14:30

- Collect the driving licence application form from any Traffic Police office.
- Complete the form in Arabic (typed or hand-written)
- Submit all documents at the Control Counter
- The officer will process the paperwork and return the documents to you
- Take the documents to the Cashier and pay the required application fee

  Women may go to the Ladies' Section to submit all documents (see [p.128])

- Submit all documents and the receipt at the Data Entry Counter
- Wait for your name to be called for your photograph to be taken
- Your licence will be ready within 5-10 minutes

5 Related Procedure

- Renewing a Driving Licence [p.138]
- Replacing a Driving Licence [p.140]
- Buying a Vehicle [p.146]

Tip Expired Licence?

If your licence expired more than one year ago, you will have to take all driving tests prior to receiving your Dubai driving licence.

Driving Licence

Driving

Driving Licence

Registering with a Driving School

1 Overview

If you have never owned a driving licence, or if you cannot transfer your licence issued in your previous country of residence, you will have to attend a driving school and take the Dubai Traffic Police driving tests.

Many driving schools will take care of the application process for their students. Students then only need to go to the Traffic Police to sit the tests and pick up the driving licence.

Depending on the competency of the driver, the process of learning to drive and passing the tests could take between two and five months.

Testing > The testing process consists of three components:

- Internal test: parking test, overseen by the driving school
- Sign (highway code) test, overseen by the Traffic Police
- Road test, overseen by the Traffic Police (see Registering for Sign & Road Tests [p.135])

2 Prerequisites

- Applicant must be at least 18 years of age
- Motorbike: applicant must be at least 17 years of age

3 What to Bring

☐ Passport (original & copy)
☐ Residence permit (copy)
☐ 8 photgraphs
☐ Eye Test certificate [p.124]

Fee > ☐ Dhs.1,500 (approx.) – driving school fee (cost varies according to school and number of lessons)

4 Procedure

Driving > School
- Choose a reputable driving school
- Sign up and submit all documents
- The school will process the paperwork with the Traffic Police
- You will receive a learning permit after approximately two days
- Attend classes

- When your instructor feels you are prepared, you will take the first test (internal test) with the driving school
- Once you have passed that test, your instructor will apply for a test date with the Traffic Police for the second and third tests (sign and road tests)

5 Related Procedure

- Applying for a Driving Licence [p.126]
- Registering for Sign & Road Tests [p.135]

Info Manual or Automatic?

Learners have the option to apply for a licence for either manual or automatic vehicles.

Female or Male Instructor?

Women are required to take lessons with a female instructor, at a higher cost than those with a male instructor. If a woman wishes to take lessons with a male instructor, she must first obtain a no objection letter from her sponsor and the Traffic Police. This letter must indicate the name of the instructor and the driving school. Submit the letter at the 'Certificates for Women' Counter at the Traffic Police; pay Dhs.10. The Traffic Police will attest this letter, which you then give to the driving school.

Tip Pre-Booked Driving Lessons

Some driving schools insist that you pay for a set of pre-booked lessons. In some cases the package extends to 35 lessons and can cost up to Dhs.1,500 (approx.). These lessons must be taken on consecutive days and usually last 45 minutes.

On the other hand, some companies offer lessons on an hourly basis, as and when you like, at a cost of Dhs.35 per hour. Choose according to your needs and word of mouth regarding reputation of the school.

Driving Licence

Driving

Driving Licence

Applying for a Learning Permit

1 Overview

A learning permit allows a new driver to practise in the company of a driving instructor. Normally the driving school applies for the permit for the student, but it is possible that you will have to apply on your own.

2 Prerequisites

- Applicant must be resident in Dubai
- Applicant has applied for a permanent driving licence (see Applying for a Driving Licence [p.126])

3 What to Bring

- ☐ Passport (original & copy)
- ☐ Residence permit (copy)
- ☐ 2 passport photographs (6cm x 4cm)
- ☐ Eye test certificate (see [p.124])
- ☐ Driving licence application form
- Fee > ☐ Dhs.40 – application fee

4 Procedure

Location > Dubai Traffic Police, Driving Licence Section   Map ref 10-E9

Hours > Sat – Wed 07:30 – 14:30

- Collect the driving licence application form from any Traffic Police office
- Complete the form in Arabic (typed or hand-written)
- Submit all documents at the Control Counter
- The officer will process the paperwork and return the documents to you
- Take the documents to the Cashier and pay the application fee
- The application will be approved the same day
- Give the approval to the driving school

5 Related Procedure

- Registering with a Driving School [p.132]
- Registering for Sign & Road Tests [p.135]

Driving Licence

Registering for Sign & Road Tests

1 Overview

After passing the internal test with the driving school, you must register for the subsequent sign and road tests with the Traffic Police. You will sit two different tests, each on a different date.

2 Prerequisites

- Applicant has already applied for a Dubai driving licence (see Applying for a Driving Licence [p.126])
- If attending a driving school, applicant has passed the internal test

3 What to Bring

☐ Passport (original & copy) & Residence permit (copy)

☐ 2 passport photographs (6cm x 4cm)

☐ Eye test certificate (see [p.124])

☐ Application form

Fee > ☐ Dhs.35 – sign test fee + Dhs.35 – road test fee

4 Procedure

Location > Dubai Traffic Police, Driving Licence Section   Map ref 10-E9

Hours > Sat – Wed 07:30 – 14:30

- Collect the driving licence application form from any Traffic Police office and complete the form in Arabic
- Submit all documents at the Control Counter
- The officer will process the paperwork and return your documents to you; the remaining documents will be placed in your file
- Take the documents to the Cashier and pay the test fee
- You will be given a time and date for the sign test
- Once you have passed the sign test, return to the same counter with the passing certificate
- You will be given a time and date for the road test

There is a long waiting period for the road test (average three months for men and 20 days for women)

- If you fail the test, return to the same counter, pay the test fee and you will be given a new test time and date
- After passing all tests, collect your driving licence (see Collecting the Driving Licence [p.136])

5 Related Procedure

- Applying for a Driving Licence [p.126]
- Collecting the Driving Licence [p.136]

Driving Licence

Collecting the Driving Licence

1 Overview

This is the final step in obtaining your Dubai driving licence after you have passed all driving tests.

2 Prerequisites

- Applicant has passed the internal, road and sign tests (See Registering for Sign & Road Tests [p.135])

3 What to Bring

☐ Passing receipt

☐ One form of ID (passport or labour card)

Fee > ☐ Dhs.100 – service charge

4 Procedure

Location > Dubai Traffic Police, Driving Licence Section   Map ref 10-E9

Hours > Sat – Wed 07:30 – 14:30

- After having passed all the tests, submit the passing receipt at the 'Passing Transactions' Counter
- You will be handed your test file
- Submit the file at the Control Counter
- The officer will process the paperwork and return the documents to you
- Pay the required fee at the Cashier
- Submit all documents and the receipt at the Entry Counter
- Wait for your name to be called for your photograph to be taken
- Your licence will be ready within 5-10 minutes

5 Related Procedure

- Renewing a Driving Licence [p.138]
- Replacing a Driving Licence [p.140]

Law Carry your Driving Licence

If you fail to produce your driving licence during a police spot check, you will be fined, and risk having the car impounded and having to appear in court. If you bring your licence to the police within 24 hours, your fine will be reduced.

Applying for an International Driving Licence

1 Overview

Residents of Dubai who are travelling overseas and who wish to drive in another country can apply for an international driving licence at one of three locations in Dubai. Note that the Dubai Traffic Police do not handle this procedure.

⚠ If you wish to use your Dubai Driving Licence as a form of identification while travelling, note that your date of birth is not shown on it.

Validity > One year

2 Prerequisites

• Applicant has a valid Dubai driving licence

3 What to Bring

☐ Dubai driving licence (original & copy)

☐ Passport (copy)

☐ Two passport photos

Fee > ☐ Dhs.100 – Dhs.200 licence fee (varies depending on company)

4 Procedure

• Go to one of the companies listed below
• Submit all documents
• Pay the licence fee
• The licence will be prepared for you while you wait

🗋 Before purchasing an international licence, check the requirements of the country you are visiting; some countries allow visitors to drive with a UAE-issued driving licence

5 Related Procedure

• Applying for a Tourism Certificate [p.154]

Law Zero Tolerance

The Dubai Police exercise a strict zero tolerance policy when it comes to drinking and driving. If you are involved in an accident, regardless of whose fault it is, and you have consumed any alcohol, your insurance is automatically void and you are likely to end up in jail. Be smart – don't drink and drive.

Driving Licence

Driving

Driving Licence

Renewing a Driving Licence

1 Overview

Driving licences must be renewed every ten years, and probationary licences yearly. The procedure for renewal is similar to licence registration. Before the licence is renewed, all outstanding traffic fines must be cleared (see Paying Fines [p.164]).

2 Prerequisites

- Dubai driving licence (valid or expired)

3 What to Bring

- ☐ Passport (original & copy)
- ☐ Driving licence (original)
- ☐ Eye test certificate (see [p.124])

Fee ›
- ☐ Dhs.100 – renewal charge
- ☐ Dhs.100 – probationary/temporary driving licence renewal charge
- ☐ Money for outstanding traffic fines (if applicable)

4 Procedure

Location › Dubai Traffic Police, Driving Licence Section   Map ref 10-E9

Hours › Sat – Wed 07:30 – 14:30

- Submit all documents at the Control Counter
- The officer will process the paperwork and return the documents to you
- Take the documents to the Cashier and pay the required fee and any outstanding fines
- Submit all documents and the receipt at Entry Counter
- Wait for your name to be called for your new photograph to be taken
- Your licence will be ready within 5-10 minutes

Driving Licence Offices		
Al Safa Union Coop.	394 5007 Jumeira Sat – Wed 09:00 – 14:00	Map ref 4-G3
Al Tawar Union Coop.	263 4857 Al Qusais Sat – Wed 09:00 – 14:00	Map ref 6-G5
Jumeira Plaza	342 0737 Jumeira Sat – Wed 09:00 – 14:00	Map ref 5-B2

Tip Time Saver

To save time and avoid the crowds, renew your driving licence at any Driving Licence Office (see above table for a list of these outlets). Each has only one counter and your new photo is taken instantly.

Tip Licence Renewal Outside Dubai

No matter where you are, you can renew your Dubai driving licence by logging on to www.dxbtraffic.gov.ae. While you will be charged a credit card commission and courier service charge, you will not have to undergo the prerequisite eye test.

Provide the personal details requested; the police will validate the information and send you a username and password by email. Log on with your username and password and follow the prompts. The Traffic Police will courier your new driving licence to you. Note that when renewing this way, your previous photo will be used for your new licence.

Driving Licence

Driving

Driving Licence

Replacing a Driving Licence

1 Overview

If you lose or damage your driving licence, you can have it replaced by the Traffic Police for a fee.

In the case of a lost licence, you will first be issued with a temporary (two month) licence. If your licence has not been recovered within two months, you must then apply for a new Dubai licence and you will follow the procedure for replacing a damaged licence.

2 Prerequisites

• Current driving licence has been lost or damaged

3 What to Bring

☐ Passport (original & copy)

☐ Damaged driving licence (if applicable)

☐ 2 passport photographs (6cm x 4cm)

☐ Application form for temporary licence (if original is lost)

☐ Application form for replacing damaged licence (if applicable)

Fee > ☐ Dhs.100 – replacement fee (lost or damaged)

4 Procedure

Location > Dubai Traffic Police, Driving Licence Section   Map ref 10-E9

Hours > Sat – Wed 07:30 – 14:30

Lost > Licence
• Fill in the application for a temporary licence (typed or hand-written)

• Report the loss at the Control Counter; give the driving licence number or passport copy

• The officer will check whether the licence has been found

• Submit all documents at the Temporary Licence Counter

• Pay the temporary licence application fee at the Cashier

• Return to Temporary Licence Counter to collect your temporary licence (validity: two months)

After two months, follow the damaged licence procedure below

Damaged > Licence
• Collect the driving licence application form from any Traffic Police office

• Complete the form in Arabic (typed or hand-written) and write "issue against loss"

• Go to the Driving Licence Section

- Submit all documents at the Control Counter
- The officer will process the paperwork and return the documents to you
- Take the documents to the Cashier and pay the replacement fee
- Submit all documents and the receipt at the Data Entry Counter
- Wait for your name to be called for your photograph to be taken
- Your licence will be ready within 5-10 minutes

5 Related Procedure

Applying for a temporary licence [p.142]

Info Obnoxious Driver Hassling You?

Dubai Police would like motorists to assist with keeping errant drivers under tabs. Call 800 4353 or log on to www.dubaipolice.gov.ae to report lawbreakers and maniacs on the road.

Web Update

While Dubai's government is committed to cutting back on the red-tape involved in setting up in Dubai, both for individuals and businesses, changes in rules and regulations are inevitable. Therefore, if there have been any changes or additions to the procedures included in this book they will appear on the Explorer website. Just log on to **www.Explorer-Publishing.com** and click on the **Red-Tape** link. This page will tell you if there have been any changes to specific procedures – giving you the heads up before you head off to plough through Dubai's administrative maze!

Driving Licence

Driving

Driving Licence

Applying for a Temporary Driving Licence

1 Overview

Visitors to Dubai or those on an employment visa who are waiting for residence permit processing may drive private or rental vehicles if they first register and apply with the Dubai Traffic Police. A valid foreign driving licence (any) is needed to apply for a temporary licence.

Dubai residents who have lost their Dubai driving licence, or who have passed all driving tests but the permanent licence processing is being held up, may in the meantime apply for a temporary driving licence with the Traffic Police.

☐ Nationalities listed in the Exchangeable Driving Licences table [p.130] may drive rental vehicles in Dubai without a temporary licence; the valid foreign licence is sufficient. But in order to drive private vehicles, a temporary licence is necessary.

Validity > Corresponds with the length of visa (tourist: 30 days; visit: 60 days); two months if replacing a lost licence.

2 Prerequisites

- Valid driving licence
- Valid tourist, visit or residence visa

3 What to Bring

☐ Passport (original & copy)

☐ Tourist, employment, residence or visit visa (copy)

☐ Foreign driving licence (original & copy)

☐ 2 passport photographs (6cm x 4cm)

☐ Driving Licence Application Form

Fee > ☐ Dhs.100

4 Procedure

Location > Dubai Traffic Police, Driving Licence Section   Map ref 10-E9

Hours > Sat – Wed 07:30 – 14:30

- Collect the driving licence application form from any Traffic Police office
- Complete the form in Arabic (typed or hand-written)

If Sponsored >
- Go to the Driving Licence Section
- Submit all documents at the Temporary Licence Counter

☐ The application form must be stamped by the company sponsoring you

- The officer will process the paperwork and return the documents to you
- Take the documents to the Cashier and pay the application fee
- Return to the Temporary Licence Counter to collect your temporary licence
- Leave your foreign licence with the Traffic Police

Non > angeable • Before leaving the country, return to collect the licence

5 Related Procedure

- Transferring a Foreign Driving Licence [p.130]

Acceptable Licences	
Visitor to Dubai	
Rental vehicle	Foreign exchangeable licence
	Temporary driving licence
Private vehicle	Temporary driving licence
Residency under Process	
Rental vehicle	Temporary driving licence
Private vehicle	Temporary driving licence
Dubai Resident	
Rental vehicle	Dubai driving licence
	Temporary driving licence
Private vehicle	Dubai driving licence
	Temporary driving licence

Driving Licence

Driving

Be Prepared

Before you get behind the wheel make sure you have your wits about you. The driving in Dubai leaves rather a lot to be desired and the number of traffic accidents are quite shocking. For more information on driving habits refer to the Driving section of the Residents chapter in the *Dubai Explorer* (The Complete Residents Guide) available in all leading bookshops and supermarkets.

Vehicle Overview

1 Overview

☐ Remember that car dealers, shipping companies and various other service companies will assist you with many of the following procedures, for a fee.

☐ All application forms listed can be filled out in either English or Arabic and can be either hand-written or typed.

Law Blood Money

If you cause someone's death while driving, even accidentally, you are liable to pay a sum of money known as 'blood money' to the family of the deceased. The limit is set at Dhs.200,000 per victim. Make sure that your insurance policy covers this cost, and check the terms and conditions very carefully. Insurance companies will only pay if they cannot find a way of claiming that the insurance was invalid (eg the driver was speeding, driving without a licence, under the influence of alcohol etc). You will be locked up until you or the insurance company comes up with the amount, or the family of the deceased waives the right to blood money.

Info Oman Insurance & Tolls

It is wise to check whether your insurance covers you for the Sultanate of Oman, as within the Emirates you may find yourself driving through small Omani enclaves, especially if you are driving off-road near Hatta, through Wadi Bih, or on the East Coast. Short-term insurance for Oman can be easily arranged.

If you cross a formal border post, such as the one at Hatta, you will be charged a Dhs.20 – 30 'border toll' as well. Have cash on hand.

Buying a Vehicle

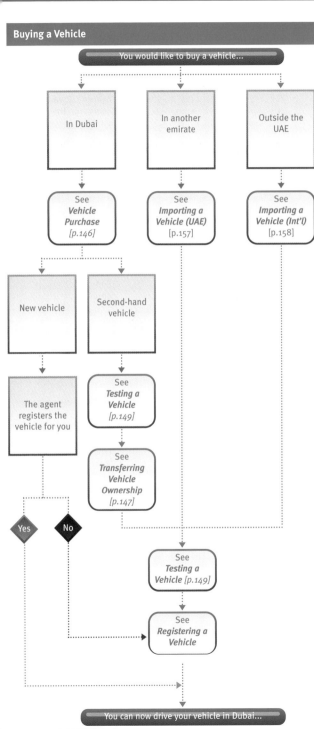

You would like to buy a vehicle...

In Dubai

In another emirate

Outside the UAE

See *Vehicle Purchase* [p.146]

See *Importing a Vehicle (UAE)* [p.157]

See *Importing a Vehicle (Int'l)* [p.158]

New vehicle

Second-hand vehicle

The agent registers the vehicle for you

See *Testing a Vehicle* [p.149]

See *Transferring Vehicle Ownership* [p.147]

Yes **No**

See *Testing a Vehicle* [p.149]

See *Registering a Vehicle*

You can now drive your vehicle in Dubai...

Vehicle

Driving

Buying a Vehicle

1 Overview

The actual process of buying a vehicle in Dubai is fairly straightforward. A new vehicle is obviously more expensive than one that is second-hand, but you will not have to deal with vehicle testing for two years, nor will you have to worry about whether the vehicle sale is legitimate.

2 Prerequisites

- Unless you are a cash buyer, you need to meet the requirements for auto finance through one of the UAE banks (see below). If you are buying the car through a dealer, they will assist you with this procedure.

3 What to Bring

☐ Cash for purchase, or if financing:

If Sponsored ❯ ☐ Passport (copy)

☐ Residence permit (copy)

☐ Driving licence (original & copy)

☐ Bank statements for the past three months

☐ Salary certificate from employer

☐ If financing is for a company car: valid trade licence (copy)

4 Procedure

Location ❯ New or used car dealer, or private sale   Map ref na

Hours ❯ na

- Find a vehicle you would like to purchase
- If the vehicle is second-hand, have it checked (tested)
- Ensure the vehicle is neither stolen nor has any liens or fines attached to it
- Obtain financing if necessary (at a bank or with the dealer)
- After you have purchased the vehicle, you will need to insure it and register it with the Dubai Traffic Police

The above procedures will probably be done for you if you purchase the vehicle from a dealer.

5 Related Procedure

- Transferring Vehicle Ownership [p.147]
- Testing a Vehicle [p.149]
- Registering a Vehicle [p.151]
- Buying a Vehicle (Flowchart) [p.145]

Transferring Vehicle Ownership

1 Overview

To register a second-hand car or motorcycle in your name, you must first officially transfer vehicle ownership.

⚠ Before purchasing a second-hand vehicle, check with the Traffic Police to ensure there are no outstanding fines or defaulted loan payments, and the car is not wanted or stolen.

⚠ A Dhs.3,000 fine is imposed on both the buyer and seller if a vehicle is sold unofficially (i.e. ownership is not transferred through the Dubai Traffic Police).

2 Prerequisites

- Buyer is resident in Dubai
- All outstanding fines have been paid
- Insurance is valid a minimum of 13 months

3 What to Bring

Buyer ›
- ☐ Passport or Dubai driving licence (original)
- ☐ Vehicle registration card (original)
- ☐ Original licence plates
- ☐ Vehicle permit application form
- ☐ No objection letter from the finance company (if applicable)
- ☐ Insurance certificate (original)
- ☐ Transfer of loan by the finance company or bank (if applicable)

Seller ›
- ☐ Seller must be present to sign documents or bring a sale deed letter from a car showroom or dealer
- ☐ Passport (original & copy)
- ☐ Residence permit (copy)

Fee ›
- ☐ Dhs.20 – transfer fee for light vehicle or motorcycle

4 Procedure

Insurance ›
- Take a copy of the vehicle registration card to the seller's insurance provider
- The seller terminates the insurance policy and either requests a refund or transfers the policy to the buyer

5 Related Procedure

- Testing a Vehicle [p.149]
- Registering a Vehicle [p.151]
- Buying a Vehicle (Flowchart) [p.145]

Vehicle

Driving

> Insurance should be refundable if it is valid for more than six months.

- If the insurance policy is not transferable, the buyer must obtain his/her own insurance cover from any insurance provider

Location > Dubai Traffic Police   Map ref 10-E9

Hours > Sat – Wed 07:00 – 14:30

Registration >
- Both parties go to any vehicle licensing centre or the Traffic Police Headquarters
- At the typing booth, the clerk will fill out the vehicle permit application form for you
- Submit all documents at the Registration Counter where a check for outstanding fines will be run
- Seller must pay all outstanding fines before proceeding

Buyer >
- Pay the transfer fee at the Cashier
- Submit all documents and receipt at the Control Counter
- Wait for your name to be called
- The new registration card will be issued within 5-10 minutes
- Send a copy of the new registration card to your finance company

Seller >
- It is advisable that you photocopy the new registration card and send it to your insurance company as proof that the car has been sold and ownership officially transferred

5 Related Procedure

- Registering a Vehicle [p.151]
- Paying Fines [p.164]

Tip Quick Vehicle Ownership Transfer

For convenience, there are now 10 centres around Dubai offering ownership transfer service at no extra cost. All transfer procedures will be performed, including checking for outstanding fines. Licence plates and the vehicle registration card will be issued on the spot. See the table on [p.291] for a list of external police desks around Dubai.

Vehicle

Driving

Testing a Vehicle

1 Overview

This is an annual procedure for all vehicles older than two years. As well as being carried out by the Dubai Traffic Police, vehicle testing has been outsourced to EPPCO Tasjeel and Emarat Shamil. There are four Tasjeel testing stations and three Shamil testing stations in Dubai where you can have the vehicle tested & registered. The following procedure refers to Eppco Tasjeel, but the Shamil service is virtually the same. See [p.153] for testing station locations.

Normal Test > The technical inspection involves the following:

- Brake test
- Exhaust test
- Visual inspection (body & frame)

Used Car/ Auction Test >
- Light test
- Side slip test
- Shock absorber test
- Brake test and brake quality test
- Exhaust test
- Visual inspection (body & frame)
- Road test (engine performance & gears)

2 Prerequisites

- Any vehicle needing to be tested

3 What to Bring

- ☐ Vehicle registration card or
- ☐ Export/import documents

Normal Test >
- ☐ Dhs.50 – light vehicle or motorcycle testing fee
- ☐ Dhs.75 – heavy vehicle testing fee
- ☐ Dhs.25 – second vehicle retest within 31 days
- ☐ Dhs.50 – vehicle retest after 31 days

Auction Test Fee >
- ☐ Dhs.250 – testing fee

Vehicle

Driving

4 Procedure

Location> EPPCO Tasjeel or Shamil, Various (see [p.153])   Map ref Various

Hours> Various

Check-in>
- Drive to the registration/Tasjeel lane
- Submit your registration card or export/import documents at the check-in booth
- The registration card will be punched and returned to you

Testing Bay>
- Pull forward to any available testing bay and park your vehicle
- Remove all valuables
- Leave the key and registration card with the inspector
- Go to the Tasjeel building and wait for your name to be called

Tasjeel Building>
- When your name is called, pay the test fee at the Counter
- You will receive a Test Result Certificate
- Return to your vehicle and remove the licence plates, if they are not the new licence plates
- Proceed with vehicle registration (see Registering a Vehicle [p.151] or Renewing Vehicle Registration [p.155])

Failed Test>
- If your vehicle fails the inspection, have it repaired and re-tested within 31 days for no additional fee
- If the vehicle fails a second time, the second re-test within (first) 31 days costs Dhs.25
- If the vehicle is re-tested after (first) 31 days, the original testing fee (Dhs.50) will be charged

Vehicle

Driving

Tip **Pre-inspected Second-Hand Vehicles**

All vehicles for sale at the Dubai Municipality's Used Car Complex at Al Awir/Ras Al Khor have been pre-inspected by EPPCO Tasjeel.

Out Drive Your Neighbours

If you were smart enough to get yourself a 4WD then don't hesitate to get hold of a copy of the *UAE Off-Road Explorer* With 18 awesome routes, satellite maps, tips on driving, ideas for diversions and a whole host of other activities such as off-road biking and hiking it is a must own for anyone with a licence.

Registering a Vehicle

1 Overview

In order to obtain licence plates for the vehicle, the car must first be registered with the Dubai Traffic Police. There are no longer any restrictions on the number of cars anyone may register.

Dealer > Purchase

If you have purchased a new vehicle from a dealer, the dealer will register the car for you. You do not need to test new vehicles for the first two years, though you must re-register it after one year. In some cases, second-hand dealers will register the car for you.

⚠ If you purchase a second-hand vehicle, the registration date is not necessarily the anniversary of the date of purchase.

2 Prerequisites

- Buyer is resident in Dubai
- Insurance is valid a minimum of 13 months
- Vehicle has been tested (see Testing a Vehicle [p.149])

Imported > Vehicle

- Vehicle has Gulf specifications (see Importing a Vehicle (International) [p.159])
- Vehicle has been cleared through customs, or
- If transferred / imported from another emirate, vehicle registration has been cancelled in that emirate

3 What to Bring

☐ Vehicle insurance certificate (original, valid 13 months)

🗎 If you do not have an insurance policy, insurance providers have booths at the testing/registration centres

☐ Vehicle transfer or customs certificate (if applicable)

☐ Proof of purchase agreement (original)

☐ If second-hand or imported, current registration card

☐ If imported, blue temporary licence plates

Private > Vehicle

☐ Valid Dubai driving licence (original & copy), or

☐ Home country driving licence (original & copy)

☐ Passport (original & copy)

🗎 The above items are only necessary if you do not already have a Traffic Police file

Commercial > Car

☐ Valid trade licence (copy)

Imported > Vehicle

☐ Application form from Traffice office department

☐ Blue temporary export licence plates

☐ Vehicle clearance certificate or customs papers

☐ GCC specification letter (if applicable)

□ Proof of residence in Dubai – tenancy contract, DEWA or Etisalat bill (original)

Failed ❭
Test

□ Dhs.10 – typing fee

□ Dhs.70 – long number plates, or

□ Dhs.50 – short number plates

□ Dhs.420 – annual vehicle registration fee or

□ Dhs.165 – annual motorcycle registration fee

□ Dhs.20 – import registration fee (if applicable)

4 Procedure

Location ❭ EPPCO Tasjeel or Shamil, Various (see opposite)   Map ref Various

Hours ❭ Various

Registration ❭
- Take the passed test certificate (see Testing a Vehicle [p.149]), the old licence plates (if not new Dubai plates) and the insurance papers to the typing counter

- Your application form will be typed for you; pay Dhs.10 at the same counter

- At the Traffic Police Counter, submit all documents and the licence plates

- Your application will be validated and entered into the system

- Go to the Cashier and pay the registration fee, the licence plate fee and any outstanding fines (cash or credit card)

- Wait for your name to be called

- You will receive your vehicle registration card and insurance papers

Licence ❭
Plates
- Go to the last police counter

- Submit the receipt and vehicle registration card

- You will be given new plates and a date sticker for the rear licence plate; your registration card will be returned to you

- Affix the sticker to the licence plate

- Mount the plates on your vehicle

- Keep the vehicle registration card and the insurance documents in the car at all times

5 Related Procedure

- Paying Fines [p.164]

Vehicle

Driving

EPPCO Tasjeel Centres — www.eppcouae.com

Light Vehicles, 4x4's & Motorbikes

Al Qusais	267 3940	Map ref 6-H5
	New Sharjah Rd	
	Sat – Wed 07:00 – 21:00; Thu 07:00 – 14:00	
Sheikh Zayed Rd	347 6620	Map ref 2-D4
	Jct 4, next to Dubai Traffic Police HQ	
	Sat – Wed 07:00 – 21:00; Thu 07:00 – 14:00	

Used Car Complex & Pre-Auction Testing

Al Awir	333 1510	Map ref 5-C8
	Ras Al Khor Rd	
	Sat – Wed 07:00 – 21:00; Thu 07:00 – 14:00	

Heavy Vehicles (2.5+ tons)

Warsan	333 6470	Map ref Off Map
	Dubai Hatta Rd	
	Sat – Wed 07:00 -15:00; Thu 07:00 -14:00	

Emarat Shamil Centres — www.shamil.ae

Light Vehicles, 4x4's & Motorbikes

Al Adhed	398 6006	Map ref 5-C2
	Opp.Port Rashid, Bur Dubai	
	Sat – Wed 09:00 – 13:00; 16:00 – 20:00; Thu 09:00 – 13:00	
Nad Al Hamar	289 4440	Map ref 5-D7
	Nr.Coca Cola bld., Rashidiya	
	Sat – Wed 09:00 – 13:00; 16:00 – 20:00; Thu 09:00 – 13:00	
Al Muhaisna	267 1117	Map ref 6-H5
	Nr Cattle Market, Al Qusais	
	Sat – Wed 09:00 – 13:00; 16:00 – 20:00; Thu 09:00 – 13:00	

Vehicle

Driving

Tip Registration Service Companies

For those who do not wish to register the vehicle themselves, some companies offer full registration service for a fee (in addition to the normal registration costs). They will need the vehicle's registration card, the insurance papers (with 13 months' validity) and cash for the fees and fines.

- EPPCO Tasjeel: 800 4258
- AAA: 285 8989
- Midland Cars: 396 7521/2
- Protectol: 285 7182
- Shamil: 800 4559

Info Special Licence Plate Number?

The Traffic Police set aside licence plates with unique or short number combinations, and sell them for anywhere between Dhs.1000 and Dhs.35,000. If you are interested in purchasing one of these plates, visit the Administration Department in the Traffic Police HQ or log on to www.dxbtraffic.gov.ae.

Applying for a Tourism Certificate

1 Overview

If you wish to leave the UAE by car, you may need to apply for a tourism certificate. Those countries which require a tourism certificate include Saudi Arabia, Lebanon, Syria and Jordan. The Sultanate of Oman does not require this certificate. If the driver is the owner, then a certificate is not required for visiting GCC countries, but if the vehicle is driven by someone else, a tourism certificate will be necessary.

Note that the Border Control may wish to see the tourism certificate when leaving and re-entering the UAE. The countries you intend to drive to may also request to see the tourism certificate when you apply for a visa. As the vehicle licence number may be entered into your passport together with the visa, you will then only be able to enter that country with that specific vehicle.

Contact the relevant embassy or the UAE Automobile & Touring Club (228 4019) to enquire whether this certificate is required.

2 Prerequisites

- Valid registration card
- Private vehicle, registered in the name of the driver
- Driving Licence number of the driver, if the vehicle is not registered in his/her name

3 What to Bring

- ☐ Vehicle registration card
- Fee › ☐ Dhs.20 – service charge

4 Procedure

Location › Dubai Traffic Police, Various   Map ref Various

Hours › Sat – Wed 07:30 – 14:30

- Submit documents at the Vehicle Permits Section
- Pay the service charge to the Cashier
- A tourism certificate will be issued immediately
- Upon return to the UAE, cancel the tourism certificate

Tip   **Additional Insurance**

As your vehicle insurance is most likely valid only for the UAE, it is advisable to take out third party insurance for the country to which you'll be travelling.

Vehicle

Driving

Renewing Vehicle Registration

1 Overview

Car registration must be renewed on an annual basis with the Traffic Police. Re-registration involves a vehicle test, performed by EPPCO Tasjeel or Emarat Shamil while you begin the paperwork process.

There is a 40 day grace period after your registration has expired in which to have your car re-registered.

2 Prerequisites

• Vehicle has been tested (See Testing a Vehicle [p.149])

3 What to Bring

☐ Vehicle registration card

☐ Vehicle insurance certificate (valid at least 13 months)

Private > ☐ Passport copy
Car

mpany > ☐ Valid trade licence (copy)
Car

Fees > ☐ Dhs.10 – typing fee

☐ Dhs.360 – vehicle registration fee (light vehicle)

☐ Dhs.735 – vehicle registration fee (heavy vehicle)

☐ Dhs.130 – motorcycle registration fee

☐ Dhs.73 – overdue registration penalty charge per quarter (if applicable)

4 Procedure

cation > EPPCO Tasjeel or Shamil, Various (see [p.153]) Map ref Various

Hours > Various

• Take the passed test certificate (see Testing a Vehicle [p.145]), the old licence plates (if old style) and the insurance papers to the typing counter

• Your application form will be typed for you; pay Dhs.10 at the same counter

• At the Traffic Police Counter, submit all documents and the licence plates (if not new plates)

• Your application will be validated and entered into the system

• Go to the Cashier and pay the registration fee, the licence plate fee and any outstanding fines (cash only)

• Wait for your name to be called

Vehicle

Driving

- You will receive your vehicle registration card and insurance papers

Licence >
Plates
- Submit the receipt and vehicle registration card
- You will be given new plates and a date sticker for the rear licence plate; your registration card will be returned to you
- Affix the sticker to the plate
- Mount the plates on your vehicle
- Keep the vehicle registration card and insurance documents in the car at all times

5 Related Procedure

- Paying Fines [p.164]

Info Vehicle Insurance

The insurance provider will need to know the make, model, year of manufacture and chassis number of the vehicle. Annual insurance policies are 13 months in length, covering the one month grace period the Traffic Police allows you after your registration expires.

Rates depend on the age and model of the car as well as your previous insurance history, and normally range from 4 – 7% of the listed value of the vehicle. Cars older than five years are insured at a rate of 5% of the listed value. Fully comprehensive and personal accident insurance are strongly advised.

Rates also depend on whether agency repairs are specifically requested. Normally, agency repairs are only offered on vehicles less than three years old.

Insurance Discount?

That depends on the insurer, but it's worth asking. Some give a discount to 'good drivers' (accident free), others to women over 21 and men over 25, then a further discount to those over 50. Safety features in your vehicle such as airbags and ABS might also get you a discount.

Tip Temporary Insurance

While driving with blue temporary export licence plates, regular insurance may not be valid. Special temporary insurance may be purchased for a period of three days for export within the UAE and 14 days for international export.

Importing a Vehicle (UAE)

1 Overview

Dubai residents may not own vehicles registered in another emirate. Vehicles may be purchased in other emirates, but must be imported into Dubai and registered with the Dubai Traffic Police. Note that the Traffic Police refers to this procedure as 'vehicle export'.

If you purchase a new vehicle in another emirate, the dealer may obtain blue temporary export plates from the police for you before you register the car with the Dubai Traffic Police.

2 Prerequisites

- Owner is resident in Dubai
- Vehicle is registered in another emirate

3 What to Bring

- ☐ Passport (original & copy)
- ☐ Residence permit (copy)
- ☐ Blue temporary export licence plates (provided by the police of the other emirate)
- ☐ No objection letter from the financing agency or bank (if applicable)

Fees >
- ☐ Dhs.60 – temporary licence plate fee (if applicable)
- ☐ Dhs.50 – testing fee
- ☐ Dhs.420 – vehicle registration fee

4 Procedure

Location > Traffic Police of other emirate   Map ref Various

Hours > na

- Obtain blue temporary export licence plates from the police of the emirate in which the vehicle was purchased
- Affix the licence plates and take the vehicle to any EPPCO Tasjeel centre (see [p.149])

These plates have a validity of three days, and allow you to drive in Dubai until your vehicle is officially registered with the Dubai Traffic Police

- Have the vehicle tested and registered (see Testing a Vehicle [p.149] and Registering a Vehicle [p.151])

5 Related Procedure

- Registering a Vehicle [p.151]
- Testing a Vehicle [p.149]

Vehicle

Driving

Importing a Vehicle (International)

1 Overview

Any vehicle may be imported to Dubai from another country with relative ease. Once the initial step of obtaining a vehicle clearance certificate has been obtained from the Customs Authority of any UAE port, the vehicle must be registered with the Dubai Traffic Police (see Registering a Vehicle [p.151]).

You will be given blue temporary export licence plates, then must obtain an NOC from the Ministry of Finance & Industry. Individuals may only import one vehicle for personal use.

Charges › Note that customs duty will be charged at a rate of 5% of the Dubai market value of the vehicle. The customs authorities will determine the value of the vehicle upon arrival.

2 Prerequisites

- Owner is resident in Dubai
- Vehicle complies with GCC specifications and is left-hand drive

3 What to Bring

- ☐ Passport (original & copy)
- ☐ Residence permit (copy)
- ☐ Vehicle papers
- ☐ Bill of entry

Fees › ☐ 5% customs duty (cash or cheque)

- ☐ Dhs.60 – blue temporary export licence plates
- ☐ Dhs.10 – registration fee
- ☐ Ports Authority vehicle handling & storage fee is as follows:

    RORO(Roll on Roll Off) handling fee depends on the weight of the vehicle. For vehicles up to 1.5 tonnes the fee is Dhs.138. For vehicles up to 5 tons the fee is Dhs.193.

    Storage is free for the first 15 days, after which vehicles weighing up to 1.5 tonnes are charged Dhs.10 per day and vehicles up to 5 tonnes Dhs.12 per day.

4 Procedure

- Ship the vehicle to Dubai
- When the vehicle arrives at the port, collect the delivery order from the shipping agent

  If possible, have the delivery order issued in the name of the person who will register the car

Vehicle

Driving

Location > Ports & Customs Vehicle Department, Port Rashid & Jebel Ali

Hours > Sat – Wed 07:30 – 14:30; Thu 08:00 – 12:00   Map ref 7-D1

Clearance > • Submit the delivery order, vehicle papers and passport copy to the Customs Authority

• Except for new cars brought in by car dealers, all cars are inspected by customs and an inspection report is produced.

• The customs duty will be calculated

• Pay the customs duty and fee (cash or cheque) at the Customs clearance counter. Get a receipt.

• A vehicle clearance certificate will be issued

Location > Dubai Customs Inspection Office, Port Rashid   Map ref 7-D1

Hours > Sat – Wed 07:30 – 19:00; Thu 08:00 – 17:00

Temporary > • Submit all documents at the Customs Office

• Next to the Traffic Police desk, obtain temporary insurance for your vehicle

• The Traffic Police will provide you with blue temporary export licence plates valid for three days

• Take the vehicle to be registered with the Dubai Traffic Police (see Registering a Vehicle [p.151])

Location > Industry Department, Ministry of Finance & Industry   Map ref 8-F1

Hours > Sat – Wed 08:00 – 14:00

NOC > • Take all paperwork provided by the Customs Authority and e-Dhs.200 (see e-Dirham [p.6]) to the counter on the ground floor

• The no objection certificate will be issued within five minutes

5   Related Procedure

• Registering a Vehicle [p.151]

Tip   Import Assistance

It is advisable to have the clearing & forwarding company handle the import procedures for you, if possible.

Info   GCC Specifications

Vehicles manufactured between 1987 and 2000, imported by individuals or private car showrooms will need a no objection certificate from the Ministry of Finance and Industry. This procedure ensures that the vehicle complies with GCC specifications.

Vehicle

Driving

Exporting a Vehicle

[1] Overview

Before exporting a vehicle to another country or emirate, vehicle registration must first be cancelled with the Dubai Traffic Police.

Testing > If the vehicle has never been tested by the Dubai Traffic Police, or if the registration has expired, the vehicle must be inspected prior to export to ensure that the chassis (body) number corresponds with the engine number.

[2] Prerequisites

• Vehicle has no outstanding liens, fines or loans

[3] What to Bring

Testing > If a test is required, bring the vehicle to be exported

☐ Vehicle registration card

Fee > ☐ Dhs.25 – testing fee

Cancellation > ☐ Vehicle registration card

☐ Licence plates (no car necessary)

☐ Passport copy of person who will receive the car in other country/emirate (if applicable)

☐ Settlement of loan certificate (if applicable)

☐ If temporary plates are needed, temporary insurance papers valid for three days if exporting to another emirate, and 14 days if exporting overseas

Fees > ☐ Dhs.10 – export fee

☐ Dhs.10 – transfer to another individual fee

☐ Dhs.10 – typing fee

☐ Dhs.60 – blue temporary licence plate fee (if applicable)

[4] Procedure

Location > EPPCO Tasjeel, Various (see [p.153])   Map ref Various

Hours > Sat – Wed 07:00 – 21:00; Thu 07:00 – 14:00

Testing > • Take the vehicle to any EPPCO Tasjeel centre

• Tell the registration officer that you wish to have the export test done

• Submit your vehicle registration card and export documents

• The registration card will be cancelled

• Pull forward to any available testing bay and park the car

• Remove all valuables

Vehicle

Driving

- Leave the key and registration card with the Tasjeel inspector
- Remove the licence plates
- Go to the Tasjeel building and wait for your name to be called
- A visual test of the vehicle and all paperwork will be performed
- Pay the testing fee at the Tasjeel Counter
- You will be issued a 'Test Result Certificate'

stration >
ellation

- Go to the typing counter
- A vehicle permit application form will be prepared for you
- Pay the typing fee
- Submit the vehicle registration card, insurance certificate, licence plates and receipt at the Traffic Police Counter
- Pay fees and fines (if applicable) at the Cashier
- You will receive blue temporary export licence plates, which you must mount on your vehicle

  These plates are valid for a maximum of three days if you are exporting to another emirate, and 14 days for overseas export

- The police will give you a transfer document (export form) in the buyer's name
- Vehicle registration is cancelled automatically
- If you are exporting the vehicle to an international destination, take the vehicle to the shipping agency

Tip **Export to Another Emirate**

If you are exporting the vehicle to another emirate, contact the Traffic Police in the other emirate to determine import requirements first.

Export to the UK

If you are planning to export your vehicle to the UK and want to make your life a lot easier when you arrive, keep the Dubai export plates on the vehicle. This will allow you to avoid having to register the car and pay taxes on it for six months.

Vehicle

Driving

Traffic Accidents & Fines

Traffic Accidents

[1 Overview

If you are involved in a traffic accident in which no one is injured and vehicle damage is minor, move your vehicle to the side of the road in order to avoid blocking traffic.

[2 Prerequisites

- Any damage whatsoever to the vehicle

[3 What to Bring

- ☐ Valid driving licence
- ☐ Vehicle registration card

[4 Procedure

- Determine whether anyone has sustained injuries
- Call the Traffic Police (999)
- If necessary, call Ambulance Services (998)
- Wait for the police to arrive
- Provide your driving licence, vehicle registration card and insurance papers
- Do not argue over responsibility; the police will hear both sides and determine liability
- The police will document all details and give each party a copy of the accident report
- If you receive a pink form, you are at fault
- If you receive a green form, you are not at fault
- If necessary, contact a recovery company to tow away your vehicle (see facing page)

Insurance ▸
- Submit the accident report to your insurance provider in order to repair the vehicle

🗋 The police may retain your driving licence until you obtain the necessary documentation from the insurance company demonstrating that the claim is being processed. If this is the case, the insurance provider will give you a letter entitling you to retrieve your licence from the police

- Take the car to the designated garage for repair

Traffic Accidents & Fines

Law Repairs

By law, no vehicle can be accepted for repair without an accident report from the Traffic Police. Insurance companies tend to have an agreement with a particular garage to which they will refer claimants. The garage will carry out the repair work and the insurance company will settle the claim for you.

Info Breakdowns

In the event of a breakdown, you will find that passing police cars stop to help, or at least to check your documents. Contact:

AAA Service Centre   285 8989

Dubai Auto Towing Services   359 4424

Vehicle Towing

By law, no vehicle can be towed by another vehicle, other than those specifically designed for that purpose. In other words, you are not allowed to tow your friend's car with a tow-rope and must instead contact a registered towing company to assist you. This, of course, does not apply to off-road driving.

Tip Bird's Eye View

Log on to www.dm.gov.ae to view current traffic patterns and hopefully avoid getting stuck in a traffic jam. 15 cameras in Deira and nine in Bur Dubai, positioned at major intersections and main roads keep track of traffic with updates every 30 seconds.

Traffic Accidents & Fines

Driving

Traffic Accidents & Fines

Paying Fines

1 Overview

The Dubai Traffic Police fine drivers for traffic infractions such as speeding, parking illegally, driving recklessly etc. Note that unless you are pulled over and fined on the spot, you will not know you have been fined, nor will you be aware of how many black points you have against your licence until you inquire with the Traffic Police.

Before renewing your vehicle registration, you will have to pay all outstanding fines. The simplest method to determine how much you owe is to log on to www.dxbtraffic.gov.ae.

2 Prerequisites

• You have been fined for a traffic infraction

3 What to Bring

☐ Vehicle registration number or driving licence number

4 Procedure

• Follow any of the methods listed below:

Fine Payment Options	Location	Comment
Walk-In		
Counter Inquiry & Payment	Traffic Police Departments or any EPPCO Tasjeel centre	14 locations in Dubai (see [p.149])
Public Inquiry & Payment Machines (touch screens)	Traffic Police offices, Dubai Courts as well as shopping malls	24-hour payment at Lamcy Plaza, Jumeirah Plaza, Union Coop Safa Park & Al Ghusais
Telephone		
Interactive Voice Response	Call 268 5555 and follow voice prompts	Pay with credit or debit card
Online		
Dubai Traffic Police Website	www.dxbtraffic.gov.ae	View and pay your fines with credit card
Bank		
Bank Counters	Emirates Bank	You may be able to pay Dubai fines while in another emirate

Traffic Accidents & Fines

Tip | Traffic Fine Notification

If you wish to be notified within 24 hours of any tickets received, fill out an application form with the Traffic Police, or log on to www.dxbtraffic.gov.ae. You will be notified either by SMS, fax or email.

Parking Subscription Card

Frequent users of public paid parking lots can purchase a subscription card from Customer Service at the Dubai Municipality Headquarters.

Towed Car

If your car is towed away, call 269 4848 and give your licence plate number. The location of your vehicle will be given to you.

Pay Fines on the Spot

Thanks to a device installed in police cars, traffic violations are registered electronically from the police car, and a credit card can then be accepted to make the payment – all on the spot!

Info | Black Points

Black points are issued to holders of a Dubai driving licence who break the law while driving. If you receive a total of 12 points within 12 months, your licence is withdrawn and you must pass a strict test before it is reissued.

See [p.166] for a listing of black points.

To determine the number of black points on your licence, look on the receipt when you pay your traffic fines or call 268 5555.

Parking Fines

Dubai Municipality has installed parking meters in many central car parks, main roads and central streets. If you do not purchase a ticket and are unfortunate enough to receive one from the police, pay the fine as follows:

- Go within 10 days from the date on the notice to the Dubai Municipality HQ (Map ref 8-H3), Counter 9
- Show the violation notice and pay the fine (cash only)
- Alternatively, pay outstanding fines plus an additional overdue fine when you renew your vehicle registration with the Dubai Traffic Police

Law | Keep Your Licence With You!

If you are pulled over and do not have your driving licence with you, you may be fined Dhs.50 – 100.

Traffic Fines & Violations

Traffic Fines & Violations		
Violations	**Charges**	**Points**
Driving a vehicle without a permit from the licensing authority	Dhs.200	3
Driving a vehicle with an expired driving licence	Dhs.100	1
Driving a vehicle not permitted on the licence	Dhs.200	3
Driving with a licence from a foreign country	Dhs.150	2
Driving a vehicle with expired registration	Dhs.100	1
Not presenting driving licence when requested	Dhs.100	1
Not presenting registration when requested	Dhs.100	1
Driving a taxi without a permit	Dhs.100	2
Exceeding speed limit (radar)	Dhs.200	1
Driving recklessly and causing danger to the public	Dhs.200	3
Jumping a red traffic signal	Dhs.500	5
Disobeying a traffic policeman's instructions	Dhs.200	1
Absconding from a traffic policeman	Dhs.200	2
Refusal to give name/address to a traffic policeman	Dhs.200	2
Failing to observe traffic signs & instructions	Dhs.100	2
Obstructing traffic	Dhs.100	1
Not giving way to emergency/official vehicles	Dhs.200	2
Not giving way to vehicles coming from the left (not yielding)	Dhs.100	1
Performing an illegal turning manoeuvre	Dhs.100	2
Overtaking on the right or dangerously	Dhs.150	3
Not giving signals when turning or changing lanes	Dhs.150	1
Reversing in a dangerous manner	Dhs.100	1
Violating a 'NO ENTRY' sign	Dhs.200	2
Stopping vehicle in pedestrian zone without keeping a safe distance from pedestrians	Dhs.100	2
Not keeping a safe distance from other vehicles	Dhs.100	1
Parking in a 'NO PARKING' area	Dhs.150	1
Parking on footways (pavement/sidewalk)	Dhs.150	1
Parking beside parked vehicles (double parking)	Dhs.150	2
Parking the vehicle on the left side of the road (hard shoulder)	Dhs.150	2
Parking which could endanger pedestrians	Dhs.100	2
Failure to take appropriate action when vehicle breaks down	Dhs.100	2
Not making sure that the car is parked safely	Dhs.150	1
Vehicle modified without permission	Dhs.400	3
Use of vehicle for purposes other than designed for	Dhs.100	1
Vehicle unfit to be driven (not road-worthy)	Dhs.150	1
Driving a vehicle which is not road-worthy	Dhs.150	2
Refusal to carry passengers in a taxi	Dhs.100	1
Carrying more passengers than permitted	Dhs.50	2
Not displaying approved tariffs in a public vehicle	Dhs.150	1
Failure to adhere to authorised tariffs	Dhs.100	1
Excess loading or load protruding more than 1.5m	Dhs.200	2
Loading a vehicle in such a way so as to cause danger	Dhs.100	2
Driving without number plates or with one number plate	Dhs.200	3
Unclear number plates	Dhs.150	1
Use of horn in restricted areas in a disturbing manner	Dhs.100	1
Driving without wearing medical glasses or lenses	Dhs.100	1
Not wearing a seat belt while driving	Dhs.100	3
Not wearing a helmet when riding a motorcycle	Dhs.200	2
Driving a vehicle emitting excessive noise	Dhs.100	1

Traffic Fines & Violations

Violations	Charges	Points
Driving at night or in fog without using lights	Dhs.150	2
Not using rear and side lights on a trailer	Dhs.150	2
Placing signs on roads which may confuse drivers	Dhs.100	2
Driving below the minimum speed limit	Dhs.100	0
Teaching driving without a teaching permit	Dhs.200	3
Teaching driving without an 'L' plate	Dhs.100	3
Not keeping the vehicle within lane lines	Dhs.100	2
Entering the road without making sure it is safe	Dhs.200	1
Sudden deviation of a vehicle (erratic driving)	Dhs.150	1
Differences between number plates for cab and trailer	Dhs.100	1
Driving in opposite direction to the flow of traffic	Dhs.200	3
Not giving way to an overtaking car	Dhs.100	2
Dangerous overtaking by truck drivers	Dhs.400	4
Overtaking where prohibited	Dhs.400	4
Vehicles entering the road in dangerous manner	Dhs.400	4
Towing a vehicle, boat or trailer improperly	Dhs.100	2
Leakage or falling of materials from vehicle	Dhs.100	2
Littering road from a vehicle	Dhs.100	2
Use of rotating multicoloured lights	Dhs.100	2
Modification to vehicle without permission	Dhs.100	1
Failing to use internal lights in buses at nights	Dhs.100	1
Not carrying driving licence or registration	Dhs.100	1
Driving a taxi with expired sponsorship	Dhs.100	2
Carrying passengers in a vehicle used for learning	Dhs.100	2
Teaching driving beyond permitted time & place	Dhs.100	2
Violating the rules of trade number plates	Dhs.100	2
Teaching driving in a vehicle not permitted to do so	Dhs.100	3
Driving with unfit tyres	Dhs.150	2
Indicators and/or lights not functioning	Dhs.100	2
Absence of red light at the rear of vehicle	Dhs.100	1
Driving a vehicle which causes pollution	Dhs.100	1
Not having vehicle inspected after modification	Dhs.300	2
Leaving vehicle on the road with its engine running	Dhs.100	2
Misuse of parking spaces	Dhs.100	3
Not fixing reflectors to the rear of the vehicle	Dhs.100	2
Attaching indecent materials on the car	Dhs.100	3
Failure to write HEAVY VEHICLE LOAD on side	Dhs.100	3
Failure to display excess permit	Dhs.100	1
Failure to attach taxi sign in appropriate places	Dhs.100	1
Not conforming to specified colour of taxi or 'L' plate	Dhs.100	1
Not conforming to loading & unloading regulations	Dhs.100	1
Opening left door of a taxi	Dhs.100	2
Not wearing specified taxi driver's uniform or unclean one	Dhs.100	1
Heavy vehicle without a vertical exhaust pipe	Dhs.200	2
Uncovered load in trucks	Dhs.100	2
Pedestrians crossing on roads or unmarked crossings	Dhs.50	0
Driving heavy vehicle in prohibited areas	Dhs.100	2
Not giving way to pedestrians	Dhs.100	1
Failing to stop after causing an accident	Dhs.100	1
Parking in front of water hydrants or handicapped zone	Dhs.100	1

Overview

Overview

Personal Life

Overview

Overview

The following personal procedures are almost always handled by the individual rather than your sponsor. Whereas in the past people have returned to their home countries to get married or give birth, it has become a lot more common to remain in Dubai for these milestones.

The procedure for getting married is different depending on nationality. Some common procedures are listed here; if you need further assistance your embassy should be able to help.

If you decide to have your baby in Dubai, there are some excellent hospitals and medical professionals here. This section outlines the procedure and all paperwork involved.

The tragic event of a death is further aggravated by the amount of bureaucracy involved; all authorities require letters of no objection for each step in the long process, along with numerous document cancellations. This is one area where you might get some help from the sponsor or your embassy, and all the procedures are listed here.

Numerous new schools have opened lately, so school places are less of a challenge. However, your school of choice may still have a long waiting list. This chapter lists the procedures involved with enrolling your child at nursery, primary or secondary school.

Finally, this chapter deals with personal banking, getting a liquor licence, and various procedures involved in bringing your pet to Dubai, registering it, sterilising it and taking it back to your home country.

Some of the procedures may require attested documents – refer to Notarising & Attesting Documents on p.11 for more information.

Overview

Personal Life

Marriage

Marriage – Overview

1 Overview

Many expats choose to get married in their home country, but this section covers Dubai-based wedding procedures for Muslim, Catholic, Anglican and Hindu ceremonies.

In a nutshell:

- If you are Muslim, you can marry at the Dubai Court
- If you are Catholic or Anglican, you can marry at a church
- If you are a Hindu (of Indian nationality), you can marry at the Hindu Temple

If you choose not to have a religious wedding, and you are not a Muslim, you may be able to get married at your embassy. Embassies that perform weddings include Germany, India, Italy, Egypt and Sri Lanka. Those that don't include USA, Canada, Australia, Lebanon and Pakistan.

Law Legal Marriages

In nearly all cases a marriage that is legally performed in Dubai will be recognised elsewhere in the world, but it's always best to check. In addition, you may need to inform your embassy of your intention to marry. The British embassy in Dubai, for example, will display a 'notice of marriage' in the embassy waiting room for 21 days prior to the marriage (along the same lines as 'the banns' being published in a parish newsletter for three successive Sundays). Afterwards, providing no one has objected, they will issue a 'certificate of no impediment' that may be required by the church carrying out your ceremony.

Getting Married

Dubai is a very popular destination for weddings - whether for tourists or residents - and there are a number of luxury hotels just waiting to play host. For more information on where to host your reception, where to get your dress and where to have your cake made see the Residents chapter of the *Dubai Explorer* (The Complete Residents' Guide) available in all leading bookshops and supermarkets.

Marriage – Hindu

1 Overview

The procedure listed below is for Indian citizens. The marriage is conducted at the Hindu Temple by the Maharaj. The temple is run in conjunction with the Indian Consulate and marriages performed here are recognised by the government of the UAE. There is no fee for this service.

2 Prerequisites

- Both parties are Hindu
- Both parties are resident in Dubai

3 What to Bring

- ☐ Completed application forms
- ☐ Both parties' passports (copy)
- ☐ Parents of both parties' passports (copy)
- ☐ Attested affidavit from the Indian Embassy that both partners are free to get married

4 Procedure

Location ❯ Hindu Temple   Map ref 8-F1

Hours ❯ Sat – Thu 09:00 – 13:00; 16:00 – 20:00

- Submit all documents to the Hindu Temple's Marriage Committee for approval
- A decision will be made within one week
- Upon approval, set a date for the ceremony when both the temple and Maharaj are available
- You may appoint a Maharaj of your choice
- After the ceremony, you will be issued with a marriage certificate
- The marriage certificate should be attested at the Dubai Court as well as at your embassy (see Notarising & Attesting Documents [p.11])

Waiting Time ❯ One week

5 Related Procedures

- Applying for a Residence Permit – Family [p.37]
- Transferring from Father to Husband Sponsorship [p.46]

Marriage

Personal Life

Marriage

Marriage – Anglican

1 Overview

Anglican marriages are conducted according to the rites and ceremonies of the Church of England, and are recognised by the UAE government. You can have an Anglican ceremony at the Holy Trinity Church (Dubai), the Christ Church (Jebel Ali) or at St Martins in Sharjah.

Anglican marriages must take place in church, but can be followed by a service of blessing in a location of your choosing (hotel, golf club, resort etc). Be sure to speak with the Chaplain prior to making any arrangements or bookings.

2 Prerequisites

- At least one partner is baptised. A baptism certificate is required.
- Neither partner is Muslim, nor should the father of either bride or groom be Muslim
- At least one partner is resident in Dubai (Banns certificate is necessary for UK citizens)
- Attested proof from the embassy that each partner is unmarried
- Minimum age: 18

3 What to Bring

- ☐ Both passports (original & copy)
- ☐ At least one residence permit (copy)
- ☐ Baptism certificates (original)
- ☐ One passport photo each
- ☐ Two witnesses over the age of 18
- ☐ If you have previously been married:
- ☐ Divorce certificate (final decree) or
- ☐ Death certificate of your previous partner
- ☐ Completed and signed forms collected from the Chaplain's office regarding the following:
  - Intent of marriage (application)
  - Confirmation that neither you nor your father is Muslim
  - Certificate from each partner stating that each is single and free to marry (can be provided by your parents or parish priest and must be attested by your embassy)

Fees ▷
- ☐ Dhs.850 – marriage conducted by the Chaplain
- ☐ Dhs.850 – celebration held outside of the Holy Trinity Church (in addition to above fee)
- ☐ Dhs.50 – marriage certificate (extra copies)

4 Procedure

Location › Holy Trinity Church (Map ref 8-E7), Christ Church (Jebel Ali),
St Martins Church (Sharjah)

Hours › Sat – Thu 09:00 – 13:00, Fri 17:00 – 19:30

- Submit all documents at the Chaplain's office
- Meet with the Chaplain to discuss your plans
- Set a date for the marriage ceremony
- The ceremony will take place at the church, or location of your choosing, where the two witnesses must sign the marriage register
- After the ceremony, you will receive two marriage certificates signed by the Chaplain
- The certificate must be translated into Arabic
- The three documents (two marriage certificates, one Arabic version of marriage certificate) should be attested at the Dubai Court as well as your embassy (see Notarising & Attesting Documents [p.11]). The Court will retain 1 English copy plus the Arabic translation and you will have one certified English marriage certificate.

Waiting Time › Up to one month

5 Related Procedures

- Applying for a Residence Permit – Family [p.37]
- Transferring from Father to Husband Sponsorship [p.46]

Web Update

While Dubai's government is committed to cutting back on the red-tape involved in setting up in Dubai, both for individuals and businesses, changes in rules and regulations are inevitable. Therefore, if there have been any changes or additions to the procedures included in this book they will appear on the Explorer website. Just log on to **www.Explorer-Publishing.com** and click on the **Red-Tape** link. This page will tell you if there have been any changes to specific procedures – giving you the heads up before you head off to plough through Dubai's administrative maze!

Marriage

Personal Life

Marriage – Muslim

1 Overview

A Muslim groom can marry a bride (Muslim or non-Muslim) at the Dubai Court, also known as the Sharia court. A non-Muslim man cannot marry in this court.

Filipino citizens should contact the embassy in Abu Dhabi before authenticating the marriage certificate at the Dubai Court.

2 Prerequisites

- Groom is Muslim
- Bride is Muslim or Christian
- Approval of the bride's father or closest male relative
- At least one partner is resident in Dubai

🗋 The father or relative must either be present, or must give official approval (see below)

🗋 Although officially a Muslim man can marry a non-Muslim woman, the local courts strongly encourage the bride to convert to Islam.

3 What to Bring

☐ Both passports (original & copy)

☐ At least one residence permit (copy)

☐ Proof that groom is Muslim (i.e. birth certificate)

☐ Two male witnesses or four female witnesses

☐ Power of attorney letter (if applicable; see below)

🗋 The father or closest male relative of the bride must attend as a witness. If the father of the bride cannot attend the ceremony, he must send a power of attorney or his approval in writing. The approval must be attested and names of the bride and groom clearly mentioned in the document.

Fees ❭ ☐ Dhs.50 – service charge

Location ❭ Dubai Court Marriage Section   Map ref 8-F6

Hours ❭ Sat – Wed 07:30 – 14:00; 17:30 – 20:30

4 Procedure

- Bring all witnesses with you
- Submit all documents for verification
- The judge will marry you immediately

5 Related Procedures

- Applying for a Residence Permit – Family [p.37]
- Transferring from Father to Husband Sponsorship [p.46]

Marriage – Roman Catholic

1 Overview

Catholic marriages are conducted at St. Mary's Church, and are recognised by the government of the UAE.

2 Prerequisites

- At least one partner is Roman Catholic, and at least one is resident in Dubai
- Proof (with seal) from home church that each partner is unmarried
- Females should be over 18 and males should be over 21

3 What to Bring

- ☐ Both passports (original & copy)
- ☐ At least one Dubai residence permit (copy)
- ☐ Baptism certificates (original)
- ☐ If one partner is not Catholic, his/her birth certificate
- ☐ A letter from the home country parish priest stating that the partner is free to marry
- ☐ If one partner is not Catholic, a statement from the embassy here or in the home country that he/she is free to marry
- ☐ If a partner is under 21, letter of consent from the parents
- ☐ Two witnesses, over 18 years old, that the bride and groom know

Fees › ☐ Church donation

4 Procedure

Location › St. Mary's Church   Map ref 8-E6

Hours › Wed – Mon 08:00 – 12:00, 16:00 – 19:00, Tue closed

- Complete the application form at the Priest's office
- Present all relevant documents
- Attend a Marriage preparation course (normally takes place at the church on Friday)
- You will receive a Marriage preparation certificate
- If no objections are registered, arrange a date for the ceremony
- Both witnesses must sign the marriage register during the ceremony
- The church will issue you with a marriage certificate
- The marriage certificate should be attested at the Dubai Court as well as at your embassy (see Notarising & Attesting Documents [p.11]

5 Related Procedures

- Applying for a Residence Permit – Family [p.37]
- Transferring from Father to Husband Sponsorship [p.46]

Marriage

Personal Life

Having a Baby

[1 Overview

Dubai residents have the choice of delivering in a public or a private hospital. You will be charged for maternity services at public hospitals, although they are less expensive than private hospitals.

In both private and public hospitals, husbands may be present during the delivery, upon approval of the attending doctor. It is also possible to have an epidural.

Health >
Insurance
Even if you are on a health insurance plan, it may not cover maternity costs. Those that do normally have a waiting period of ten months to one year before they will cover your costs. Check with your provider.

Citizenship >
Expat children born in the UAE retain the citizenship of their parents. Check with your embassy to determine regulations for citizens born abroad.

Public >
Hospitals
You must have a valid health card to deliver in a public hospital (see Obtaining a Health Card & Taking the Medical Test [p.31]). There are two public hospitals that have specially equipped maternity sections: Al Wasl Hospital and Dubai Hospital. Women living in Bur Dubai, Satwa, Jumeira, Safa, Rashidiya, Hatta and Nad Al Sheba will be assigned to Al Wasl. Women living in Deira will be assigned to Dubai Hospital. If there are any complications during your labour, you will be transferred to Al Wasl Hospital.

Antenatal >
Care
You will be encouraged to have regular antenatal check-ups in the hospital at which the delivery will take place. Public hospitals may be reluctant to reveal the baby's gender.

Info Marriage with Children

To give birth in Dubai you must be married. If you get married after conception you may need to provide hand and foot prints of the baby after it is born.

Info Terminations

Elective abortions for married or unmarried women are illegal although medical complications or abnormalities can justify a termination of pregnancy.

Birth

Personal Life

Having a Baby

1 Overview

During your pregnancy, you will need to have numerous tests, checks and scans on a regular basis (usually monthly at first; then weekly as you get nearer the birth). You can choose whether to pay for your antenatal visits as a package (upfront) or on a visit-by-visit basis.

2 Prerequisites

- Parents-to-be are married
- Parents are residents (if delivering in public hospital)

3 What to Bring

- ☐ Health card (public hospitals)
- ☐ Registration card (private hospitals)
- ☐ Passport copy of both parents
- ☐ Marriage certificate
- ☐ Fees (see fee structure)

4 Procedure

Public > Hospital
- Call or visit for an appointment
- On the day of your visit, submit your passport copy and health card
- Pay the package fees (see fee structure)
- You will be assigned to a gynaecologist and given an appointment card that you have to bring with you on every visit
- After your initial consultation you will have regular check-ups (up to 12 visits). At each visit you will have the necessary prenatal tests and checks
- The doctor will advise you of your approximate due date, and closer to that date you will be given an admission date. You will also be given a list of things to bring at time of admission.
- After the birth, you will be given a date for a follow-up check for both you and your baby

Private > Hospital
- Upon your first visit at the private hospital, you will be given a registration card that you should bring with you on each subsequent visit.
- After the baby is born, the hospital will require the necessary documentation to prepare the baby's notification of birth – you should bring these documents with you to the hospital (passport copy of mother and father, and marriage certificate).

5 Related Procedures

- Obtaining a Birth Certificate [p.181]

Birth

Personal Life

Antenatal Package Prices

[1 Overview

Prices for antenatal and delivery packages vary greatly depending on circumstances, and therefore the figures provided below should be for guidance only.

Public Hospital **Antenatal care package price:** Dhs.2,500 (includes 12 scheduled visits and all routine tests. You will be charged extra for any additional services or tests).

Normal delivery package price: Dhs.2,000 (Dhs.3,000 if you want a private room. Fee includes routine delivery and tests, two days in hospital, plus a follow-up with gynaecologist and paediatrician).

Caesarean section package price: Dhs.4,000 (Dhs.5,000 if you want a private room. Fee includes surgery and anaesthetist fees, routine tests, four days in hospital, plus follow-up with gynaecologist and paediatrician).

Other costs: In the case of a twin pregnancy, an additional Dhs.1000 is charged for the second twin. Circumcision is charged at Dhs.500.

Private Hospital **Antenatal care package price:** Dhs.3,250 (includes 12 scheduled visits and all routine tests. You will be charged extra for any additional services or tests).

Normal delivery package price: Dhs.7,900 (Fee includes routine delivery and tests, two days in private room, plus a follow-up with gynaecologist and paediatrician as well as a visit from the paediatrician one week after delivery, and a post-partum visit with the gynaecologist). Epidural is NOT included in the package, and is charged at Dhs.2,200.

Caesarean section package price: Dhs.16,800 (Fee includes surgery and anaesthetist fees, routine tests, four days in a shared room, plus follow-up with gynaecologist and paediatrician, as well as a visit from the paediatrician one week after delivery, and a post-partum visit with the gynaecologist).

Other costs: In the case of a twin pregnancy, an additional Dhs.1000 is charged for the second twin. Circumcision is charged at Dhs.1,100. If your husband stays in the room with you overnight, there is an extra charge of Dhs.60 per night, plus costs of any additional meals.

Doctor, Doctor

One of the hardest things about moving to a new country is getting familiar with your surroundings and finding new professionals that you can trust. Whether you are looking for a GP, gynecologist or pediatrician the Residents chapter of the *Dubai Explorer* (The Complete Residents Guide) available in all leading bookshops and supermarkets, can point you in the right direction.

Obtaining a Birth Certificate

1 Overview

If your child is born in Dubai, you will automatically get a birth notification letter (in Arabic) from the hospital. You will need to get this stamped by the Ministry of Health before you can apply for the birth certificate.

Note that non-Emirati children born in the UAE are not eligible for a UAE passport. Children born here assume their parents' nationality.

It is a good idea to get the birth certificate translated into English.

2 Prerequisites

• The child was born in Dubai

3 What to Bring

☐ Both parents' passports (original & copy)

☐ Both parents' residence permits (original & copy)

☐ Attested marriage certificate

☐ Hospital birth records ('birth notification') stamped by Ministry of Health

Fees › ☐ Dhs.50 – Arabic birth certificate

☐ Dhs.10 – translation fee

☐ Dhs.50 – English birth certificate

☐ Dhs.10 – birth certificate attestation fee

4 Procedure

Birth
icate › • The hospital in which the baby was delivered will issue a notification of birth certificate

• Some public hospitals, such as the Dubai Hospital, have a Ministry of Health Counter which will issue the Arabic birth certificate.

ation › Preventive Medicine Department, Al Baraha Hospital   Map ref 9-B2

Al Bahara Hospital is commonly referred to as the Kuwaiti Hospital

lours › Sat – Wed 08:00 – 14:00

• Submit the birth notification and all documents at the Birth Certificate Office

• Pay the fees at the same office

• The UAE birth certificate will be ready for pickup one to two days later

• Have the Arabic spelling of the name checked for errors

Birth

Personal Life

English Birth Certificate >
- Collect an application form from the Birth Certificate Office (first floor of Building 2)
- Have it typed in English at one of the typing booths within the hospital grounds
- A Birth Certificate Office official can direct you to the typing booths
- Submit the translated document to the Birth Certificate Office at the Preventive Medicine Department.
- The official birth certificate will be endorsed immediately

Attestation >
- Submit both the Arabic and English birth certificates to the doctor in charge of attestation
- The certificate will be stamped and signed, then must be countersigned by another official
- A Birth Certificate Office official can direct you to both offices
- Pay the attestation and translation fees at the Attestation Counter
- You will be given the attested English and Arabic birth certificates immediately

Waiting Time > 2 – 3 days

5 Related Procedures

- Registering a Newborn Child [p.48]
- Applying for a Residence Permit – Family [p.37]

Public vs Private

When you become a resident in Dubai you will be issued with a health card (see page 31) and therefore entitled to treatment at the public hospitals, for an affordable fee. However there are also a number of private hospitals that offer an excellent level of care. For more information on the various hospitals in Dubai refer to the Health section of **Dubai Explorer** (The Complete Residents Guide) available in all leading bookshops and supermarkets.

1 Overview

There is unfortunately a great deal of paperwork surrounding a death. It should be decided as soon as possible whether the body will be buried in Dubai or in the deceased's home country. If the body is to be flown out of the UAE, additional permits are necessary before departure.

You will need to get numerous no objection certificates (NOCs) from government officials – these are needed mostly to show that the deceased had no pending legal or civil actions, and that all financial obligations have been settled. You will have to get NOCs from the deceased's sponsor, the Dubai Police, Immigration, the Labour Department, the embassy and the Dubai Municipality.

Web Update

While Dubai's government is committed to cutting back on the red-tape involved in setting up in Dubai, both for individuals and businesses, changes in rules and regulations are inevitable. Therefore, if there have been any changes or additions to the procedures included in this book they will appear on the Explorer website. Just log on to **www.Explorer-Publishing.com** and click on the **Red-Tape** link. This page will tell you if there have been any changes to specific procedures – giving you the heads up before you head off to plough through Dubai's administrative maze!

Death

Personal Life

In case of Death

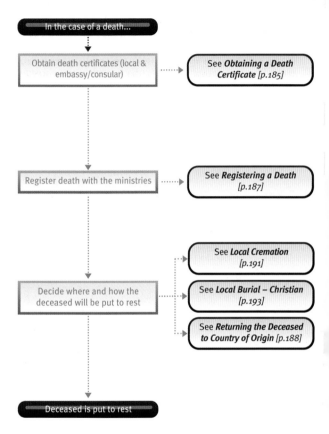

In the case of a death...

Obtain death certificates (local & embassy/consular) ·····▶ See *Obtaining a Death Certificate* [p.185]

Register death with the ministries ·····▶ See *Registering a Death* [p.187]

Decide where and how the deceased will be put to rest ·····▶ See *Local Cremation* [p.191]

·····▶ See *Local Burial – Christian* [p.193]

·····▶ See *Returning the Deceased to Country of Origin* [p.188]

Deceased is put to rest

Death

Personal Life

Obtaining a Death Certificate

1 Overview

The first administrative step in dealing with a death is to get a death certificate. This document is required before you can send the body home or arrange a local burial.

If the death occurs in a hospital, they will arrange for the transport of the body to Rashid hospital. You will have to continue the procedure from there on.

2 Prerequisites

- A death has occurred

3 What to Bring

☐ Passport and visa/residence permit of the deceased (original & copy)

☐ Police report

☐ Death report from the hospital

☐ Death Certificate Declaration

Fees › ☐ Dhs.50 – death certificate fee

☐ Dhs.100 – English translation fee (optional)

☐ Up to Dhs.700 – embassy/consular certificate and registration fee

4 Procedure

cation › District Police, Various (see directory)   Map ref Various

Hours › 24 hours

cation › • Notify the police of your district
- On arrival, the police will make a report
- The police will arrange for an ambulance
- The body will be transported to Rashid Hospital (free of charge)

cation › Rashid Hospital Mortuary   Map ref 8-F6

Hours › Sun – Sat 07:00 – 15:30 (in some cases until 22:00)

Death › • The hospital will determine the cause of death and issue a report, confirming the death. A post-mortem examination is not routinely performed unless foul play is suspected. If the family wants there to be a post-mortem, a written request should be submitted to the Medical Superintendent at the Police HQ

- Submit all documents (original passport and copy) & fee
- The hospital will issue a 'Death Certificate Declaration' (not to be mistaken for the Death Certificate itself).

- Ensure the actual cause of death is stated on the declaration and that the police stamp the declaration at the hospital

Location > District Police, Various (see directory)   Map ref Various

Hours > 24 hours

Police NOC >
- Submit all documents
- The police will issue a no objection letter addressed to Al Baraha Hospital – Preventive Medicine Department
- If the deceased will be sent to the home country, request no objection letters addressed to the airport, the mortuary and the hospital at this time (see Returning the Deceased to Country of Origin [p.188])

Location > Al Baraha Hospital Preventive Medicine Department   Map ref 9-B2

Hours > Sat – Wed 08:00 – 14:00

Death Certificate >
- Submit all documents
- A death certificate will be issued in Arabic.
- If the deceased is being sent home, the death certificate must be translated into English or the language required by the home country, speak to someone in the legal translation profession. See directory for legal translators

Location > Embassy/Consulate, Various (see directory)

Hours > Sat – Wed 08:00 – 13:00 (varies)   Map ref Various

Embassy Death Certificate >
- Notify the embassy or consulate of the death
- The embassy will cancel the passport and register the death in the deceased's country of origin
- An 'Embassy Death Certificate' will be issued
- If you wish to fly the deceased home, request an NOC for this purpose

[5] Related Procedures

- Registering a Death [p.187]

Registering a Death

[1] Overview

Once the official and embassy death certificates have been issued, the death must be registered with the concerned authorities in Dubai.

Keep copies of documents, including the deceased's cancelled passport, with you for this and all following procedures.

[2] Prerequisites

- Death certificates have been collected (see Obtaining a Death Certificate [p.185])

[3] What to Bring

☐ Original cancelled passport

☐ Local death certificate (Arabic) (original & copy)

☐ Embassy/consular death certificate (original & copy)

Fees ❯ ☐ Dhs.10 (approx) – Ministry of Health registration fee

☐ Dhs.50 (approx) – Ministry of Foreign Affairs attestation fee

☐ Dhs.100 (approx) – Immigration Department cancellation fee

[4] Procedure

cation ❯ Ministry of Health   Map ref 7-D4

Hours ❯ Sat – Wed 08:30 – 14:30

- Submit all documents and pay the fee
- The Ministry will register the death

cation ❯ Ministry of Foreign Affairs   Map ref 8-H3

Hours ❯ Sat – Wed 08:30 – 12:00

- Submit all documents and pay the fee
- The original certificate will be attested and handed back to you

cation ❯ Immigration Department   Map ref 7-B4

Hours ❯ Sat – Wed 07:30 – 14:30

- Submit all documents and pay the fee
- The deceased's visa will be cancelled immediately

[5] Related Procedures

- Returning the Deceased to Country of Origin [p.184]
- Local Cremation [p.191]
- Local Burial – Christian [p.193]

Death

Personal Life

Death

Returning the Deceased to Country of Origin

1 Overview

If you are sending the body back home, you will need to think about transport arrangements, getting the necessary paperwork in order and embalming the body. Embalming is done at Maktoum Hospital.

Your embassy or consulate may offer assistance with parts of this procedure.

Dnata (211 1111) is currently the only handling agent who can make the necessary transport arrangements for you. If desired, a family member can accompany the body, although this is not required by Dnata.

In most cases, all documentation must be translated into English (unless body is being transported to an Arabic-speaking country).

2 Prerequisites

- All relevant certificates have been collected (see Obtaining a Death Certificate [p.185])
- The death has been registered with the concerned authorities (see Registering a Death [p.187])

3 What to Bring

- ☐ Original cancelled passport & 7 copies
- ☐ Local death certificate (original & 7 copies)
- ☐ Embassy/consular death certificate (original & 7 copies)
- ☐ Police Clearance certificate (original & 7 copies)
- ☐ NOC to embalm body (original & 7 copies)
- ☐ Embalming certificate (original & 7 copies)
- ☐ Accompanying Passenger Confirmed Ticket & 2 copies
- ☐ Accompanying Passenger Passport Photo Copy (1 copy)

Fees ›
- ☐ Dhs.1,000 – 3,000 (average cargo fees – can be up to Dhs.10,000) (cash)
- ☐ Dhs.1,000 – embalming fee (cash)
- ☐ Dhs.750 – coffin (approx)
- ☐ Dhs.100 – Transportation fee (Al Maktoum to Cargo Village)

4 Procedure

Location › DNATA Export Office, Cargo Village   Map ref 9-A7

Hours › 24 hours

Transport Arrangements ›
- Contact the cargo department of the desired airline to reserve space

- If the deceased will be accompanied, a flight ticket should be purchased at the same time
- Contact the DNATA Export Supervisor to determine cargo fees
- If the casket will be unaccompanied, make arrangements for it to be collected at the destination. The person or undertaker in charge must confirm acceptance by fax (282 2683) directly to DNATA prior to shipment.

Location › Cargo Village Police Station   Map ref 9-A7

Hours › 24 hours

ice NOC ›
- Request an NOC to send the deceased out of the country
- Make 7 copies of this letter

Location › Embassy/Consulate, Various   Map ref Various

Hours › Sat – Wed 08:00 – 13:00 (Varies)

ssy NOC ›
- Request an NOC to send the deceased out of the country
- Make 7 copies of this letter

Location › DNATA Export Office, Cargo Village   Map ref 9-A7

Hours › 24 hours

mation ›
- Submit all documentation, including two copies of the confirmed flight ticket of accompanying person

Location › District Police, Various (see directory)   Map ref Various

Hours › Sat – Wed 07:30 – 14:30

balming ›
NOC
- Request an NOC to embalm the body

Location › Al Maktoum Hospital Mortuary   Map ref 8-H3

Hours › Sat – Wed 07:00 – 18:00; Thu 08:00 – 13:00

alming ›
- Submit the NOCs from the police and the embassy, the death certificate and a passport copy
- An NOC will be issued to the hospital housing the deceased
- The deceased will be transported to Al Maktoum Hospital Mortuary
- The body must be identified before and after embalming by the person making all arrangements and signing the various documents
- The embalming process takes 2 – 4 hours
- The same person must collect the embalming certificate and wait at the Mortuary until the body has been transferred to the Cargo Village
- The Hospital will arrange for transportation to the Cargo Village

Location › Cargo Village   Map ref 9-A7

Hours › 24 hours

Flight ›
- Delivery must take place at least four hours prior to departure
- The casket is weighed in the Export Cargo Department and all paperwork processed in the office next door
- Pay the cargo fees (cash only)

Death

Personal Life

Death

- Ensure the following documents (original) are accompanying the deceased:
  - Cancelled passport
  - Local death certificate
  - Translation of death certificate
  - Embassy/consular death certificate
  - Police NOC
  - Embassy NOC
  - Embalming certificate
- All documents must be translated into English (unless body is being transported to an Arabic country).

5 Related Procedures

- Obtaining a death Certificate [p.185]
- Registering a death [p.187]

Info Transporting Ashes back to Home Country

If the deceased has been cremated in Dubai, the ashes can be sent to the home country. Contact DNATA cargo on 04 282 2101 for further assistance or information

Info Still Birth

In the case of a still birth the process of registering the child's birth and death can be a very emotional task. There is, however, a support group in Dubai – The Still Birth & Neo Natal Death Society who can be contacted on 348 2801.

Local Cremation

1 Overview

Deceased of any nationality or religion may be cremated in Dubai, but only in the Hindu manner.

2 Prerequisites

- The deceased must have been resident in Dubai
- All relevant certificates have been collected (see Obtaining a Death Certificate [p.185])
- The death has been registered with the concerned authorities (see Registering a Death [p.187])
- All financial obligations have been settled

3 What to Bring

- ☐ Death certificate
- ☐ Original cancelled passport and residence permit
- ☐ Written permission from the next of kin or sponsor
- ☐ Next of kin's passport (proof of relation)
- ☐ NOC from sponsor that all financial obligations have been settled
- ☐ NOC from sponsor that all financial obligations have been settled

Feea ▸
- ☐ Dhs.2,000 – cremation fee
- ☐ Dhs.500 – deposit, paid upon submission of application and reimbursed on the collection of the ashes

4 Procedure

Location ▸ Hindu Temple — Map ref 8-F1

Hours ▸ Sat – Thu 09:00 – 13:00; 16:00 – 20:00

lication ▸
- Collect a cremation application form
- Pay the cremation fee and a vessel will be arranged

Location ▸ Embassy, Various — Map ref Various

Hours ▸ Sat – Wed 08:00 – 13:00 (Varies)

sy NOC ▸
- Submit all documents
- The embassy may require an NOC from the relatives of the deceased
- The embassy will issue an NOC for cremation

Location ▸ District Police, Various (See directory) — Map ref Various

Hours ▸ Sat – Wed 7:30 – 12:00

ce NOC ▸
- Submit all documents and request an NOC for cremation

Death

Personal Life

Location> Dubai Municipality Cemetery   Map ref 6-H5

Hours> Sat – Wed 06:00 – 21:00

Cremation> • Submit all documents and request an NOC for cremation
NOC

Location> New Sonapur (Hindu Cremation Ground)   Map ref na

Hours> Sat – Wed 09:30 – 15:00

Cremation> • Once all documentation is complete, the cremation will be organised within one day

• Either the relatives or the embassy may collect the ashes within one day

5 Related Procedures

• Obtaining a death Certificate [p.185]
• Registering a death [p.187]

Info Where is Sonapur Crematorium?

There is a crematorium in the municipality area called Muhaisnah (known locally as Sonapur, not to be confused with 'New Sonapur') it is situated between the Dubai Municipality labour accommodation and the Al Qusais labour accommodation.

There is also another crematorium and a Christian cemetery situated at New Sonapur, which is about 45kms from Dubai World Trade Centre. Follow Sheikh Zayed Road (towards Abu Dhabi) and take Exit 13 (before the ninth bridge). When the road splits into two, keep left. After looping back round to go over the bridge, you will see signs for the Medical & Hazardous Waste Disposal Plant. Turn right just before the plant and you'll see the cemetery on your left after half a kilometre.

Death

Personal Life

Local Burial – Christian

[1] Overview

A local burial can be arranged at the Christian cemetery in Dubai. The cemetery, financed by charity, will assist you with burial arrangements. The graveyard is located at Jebel Ali and the land is provided by the Dubai Government.

[2] Prerequisites

- Deceased was a member of any Christian community
- Deceased was resident in Dubai
- All relevant certificates have been collected (see Obtaining a Death Certificate [p.185])
- The death has been registered with the concerned authorities (see Registering a Death [p.187])

[3] What to Bring

- ☐ Cancelled passport and residence permit (original & copy)
- ☐ Death certificate (original & copy)
- ☐ NOC from sponsor that all financial obligations have been settled (original & copy)
- ☐ Dubai Police NOC (see below)
- ☐ Dubai Municipality Clearance letter (see below)
- ☐ Dubai Municipality Fees Dhs.1,000

Burial Fees > ☐ Dhs.1,100 – adult burial; Dhs.350 – child burial

[4] Procedure

Location > Dubai Police Headquarters Map ref 10-E7

Hours > Sat – Wed 07:30 – 14:30

Police NOC > • Submit all documents
- The police will issue an NOC requesting that Dubai Municipality clears the burial

Location > Dubai Municipality Cemetery Office Map ref 6-H7

Hours > Sat – Wed 06:00 – 21:00

Municipality Clearance Letter > • Submit all documents
- Collect a clearance letter from the Municipality permitting the burial

Location > Christian Cemetery Office Map ref na

Hours > Sun – Thu 09:00 – 18:00

Burial > • Submit all documents
- Contact the cemetery caretaker

Death

Personal Life

- The caretaker will assist you in arranging a funeral
- Contact an undertaker or a carpenter to prepare a coffin
- If you wish, you may arrange for a gravestone to be prepared, but only after six months.
- Contact your church if you wish to hold a memorial service

5 Related Procedures

- Obtaining a death Certificate [p.185]
- Registering a death [p.187]

Info | Christian Cemetery in New Sonapur

The Christian cemetery is situated at New Sonapur, about 45kms from Dubai World Trade Centre. Follow Sheikh Zayed Road (towards Abu Dhabi) and take Exit 13 (before the ninth bridge). When the road splits into two, keep left. After looping back round to go over the bridge, you will see signs for the Medical & Hazardous Waste Disposal Plant. Turn right just before the plant and you'll see the cemetery on your left after half a kilometre.

Info | Support Needs

Culture shock and feeling miles away from home can make settling into your new life in Dubai somewhat challenging but there are a number of networks in Dubai set up to make the transition easier. Similarly if you have to cope with a bereavement help is at hand. For more information on support groups refer to the Residents chapter of the *Dubai Explorer* (The Complete Residents Guide) available in all leading bookshops and supermarkets.

Local Burial – Muslim

1 Overview

Burial procedures for a Muslim have to be done quickly. Formalities such as getting the death certificate and cancelling the visa can be done after the burial takes place (within one month of the death). The original passport of the guarantor or next of kin will be held by the Dubai Police until all pending formalities have been completed. Graveyards are situated in Sonapur, Al Qusais, Bur Dubai and Al Quoz.

2 Prerequisites

- Deceased is a Muslim
- Deceased was resident in Dubai
- All relevant certificates have been collected (see below)
- Original passport of the deceased and two copies
- Death notification certificate (original & copy) from the hospital where the body is being kept

3 What to Bring

☐ Original passport (and photocopy) of guarantor or next of kin

☐ No Objection Certificate (NOC) from Dubai Police

4 Procedure

Location › Dubai Police Headquarters   Map ref 10-E7

Hours › Sat – Wed 07:30 – 14:30

Police Clearance Letter ›
- Submit all documents
- Original passport of the guarantor or next of kin will be retained by the police, and can only be collected after the rest of the documentation is complete (within one month of death)
- The police will issue a letter (in quadruplicate) requesting Dubai Municipality to clear the burial

Location › Dubai Municipality Cemetery   Map ref 6-H7

Hours › Sat – Wed 06:00 – 21:00

Dubai Municipality Permission ›
- Submit a copy of the police letter – this is to obtain permission to dig the grave for burial
- The Kafan/Dafan Committee (at the Dubai Municipality) will make arrangements for digging the grave, as well as prayers, kafan (coffin) and dafan (burial)
- Dubai Municipality will also advise you when to release the body from the hospital

Death

Personal Life

5 Related Procedure s

- Getting a Death Certificate [p.185]
- Registering a Death [p.187]
- Registering a Death with your embassy or consulate [p.186]

Info Muslim Burial Customs

According to Islamic custom, the quicker a body is buried after death occurs, the better. In the UAE, a deceased Muslim person is often buried within 24 hours, although there are no hard and fast rules about the time limit.

Factors such as repatriation of the body to the home country, or the need for an autopsy after death, can be taken into consideration and allow for a delay in burial.

Web Update

While Dubai's government is committed to cutting back on the red-tape involved in setting up in Dubai, both for individuals and businesses, changes in rules and regulations are inevitable. Therefore, if there have been any changes or additions to the procedures included in this book they will appear on the Explorer website. Just log on to **www.Explorer-Publishing.com** and click on the **Red-Tape** link. This page will tell you if there have been any changes to specific procedures – giving you the heads up before you head off to plough through Dubai's administrative maze!

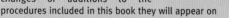

Enrolling in a School

1 Overview

There are no English-speaking government schools, and therefore expat children must attend private school. Certain organisations offer a schooling allowance as part of the remuneration package.

The year is split into three school terms: Autumn (mid-September – mid-December), Spring (early January – early April) and Summer (mid April – early July). Most schools operate Saturday to Wednesday from 08:00 – 13:00 or 15:00.

One of the biggest hindrances to enrolling your child in the school of your choice is long waiting lists. Enrol early and follow up regularly.

2 Prerequisites

• Student is between 3 and 18 years of age

3 What to Bring

For the **>** School
- ☐ Student's and parents' passports (copy)
- ☐ Residence permit (copy)
- ☐ Student's birth certificate (copy)
- ☐ Eight passport sized photographs
- ☐ School records for the past two years (original & copy)
- ☐ Current immunisation record and medical history (copy)
- ☐ Character reference from the previous school (if necessary)

UAE **>** plicants
- ☐ Transfer certificate from the previous school

You will need an original certificate from the old school addressed to the new school

External **>** plicants
- ☐ An official transfer certificate from the student's previous school detailing his/her education to date (original & 2 copies)

⚠ Original transfer certificates from any country other than UAE, Australia, Canada, USA, or western Europe must be attested by the Ministry of Education, Ministry of Foreign Affairs and the UAE Embassy in that country

- ☐ The original document must contain the following details:
  • Date of enrolment
  • Year placement
  • Date the child left the school
  • School stamp
  • Official signature

For the **>** Ministry
- ☐ Original official transfer certificate
- ☐ The most recently issued report card (original)

Education

Personal Life

4 Procedure

- Contact school, ask about waiting list
- If you have to put your child on a waiting list, investigate some alternative schools just in case
- Fill in the application form
- Fill in the student questionnaire (if applicable)
- Pay the required deposit
- If the student is accepted, pay the school registration fee
- Some schools require that prospective students sit an entrance exam, have a Ministry of Health physical examination, and undergo a family interview

5 Related Procedures

- Applying for a Residence Permit – Family [p.37]

Info Special Needs

If your child has physical or learning disabilities, there are several organisations you can contact in order to find out what activities or facilities are available to suit the special needs of your child. Some mainstream schools will try to accommodate children suffering from dyslexia, ADHD and other more manageable challenges but you will need to discuss this with the school's administration. The Al Noor Centre for Children with Special Needs (394 6088, www.alnooruae.org) provides therapeutic support and comprehensive training to special needs children of all ages. The Dubai Centre for Special Needs (344 0966) currently has around 130 students each with their own individual programme including physiotherapy, speech therapy and/or occupational therapy. The Rashid Paediatric Therapy Centre (340 0005) includes physical, occupational and speech therapy. Other support/activity groups include Riding for the Disabled (rdaddubai@hotmail.com), Dubai Autism Centre (398 6862) and the Dyslexia Support Group (334 6657).

Picking a nursery or school

The level of education in Dubai is excellent - whether you are looking for a nursery, primary school or secondary school. Making the choice of which school to opt for is the biggest challenge with various factors to consider such as location, fees, number of children in the class, hours etc. For more information on specific schools and nurseries check out the Residents chapter of the *Dubai Explorer* (The Complete Residents Guide) available in all leading bookshops and supermarkets.

Education

Personal Life

Enrolling at Nursery / Pre-school

1 Overview

Most pre-schools accept children from the age of three. Nursery schools may take babies as young as three months, although most will only admit children once they are walking. Nurseries are generally open from 08:00 to 12:30 or 13:00, but many offer late hours (some even up to 19:00) and early drop-offs (07:30). Most nurseries are open five days a week.

2 Prerequisites

- Residency visa
- Child is of the right age

3 What to Bring

☐ Completed registration forms

☐ Photocopy of child's passport with valid residence visa (two copies)

☐ Photocopy of birth certificate (two copies)

☐ Passport photos (up to eight)

☐ Completed medical form

☐ Copy of immunisation records

☐ Registration fees (from Dhs.100 – Dhs.500, non-refundable)

☐ Medical fees (from Dhs.100 – Dhs. 500, payable once a year)

☐ Term fees (from Dhs.3,000 – Dhs.7000 per term

4 Procedure

- Contact the nurseries you are interested in
- Find out if there is a waiting list, and put your child's name on it if there is
- Fill in the application/registration form
- Fill in the student questionnaire (if applicable)
- Pay the necessary deposit
- Upon confirmation, pay the term fees

Education

Personal Life

Education

Enrolling in University

1 Overview

More school-leaving students are choosing to remain in the UAE to study tertiary courses. The opening of Knowledge Village (www.kv.ae) in 2004 saw an influx of international educational organisations offering various courses.

One of the important factors to consider is the residency of the student: girls can remain on their father's sponsorship while they study, but boys may not be sponsored by their fathers after their 18th birthdays, and therefore have to apply for a student visa (see below).

2 Prerequisites

- Residency visa
- School leaving certificate from a UAE school or a recognised international equivalent
- Successful completion of the University's entrance assessment (if applicable)
- TOEFL certificate if English is not the first language

3 What to Bring

- ☐ Completed application form
- ☐ Passport photographs (up to eight)
- ☐ Passport copy with valid residence visa page
- ☐ Non-refundable application fee
- ☐ High school certificate and academic record covering the last three years of school
- ☐ Letters of recommendation from teachers (stamped and sealed)

4 Procedure

- Visit the university to discuss entrance requirements and available courses
- Select courses and fill out registration form
- Pay the fees

Info Student Visa

For students coming to Dubai to study from outside the country, or for male students resident in Dubai over the age of 18, universities usually offer sponsorship and provide a residence visa. This is only valid while the student is studying, and does not permit employment. Cost of this visa is around Dhs.1000, which is borne by the student.

Importing Pets

1 Overview

Pets may be brought into the UAE without quarantine as long as they are microchipped and vaccinated with verifying documentation, including a government health certificate from the country of origin (not from a private vet). The limit, although not official, is three pets per person and if documents are incorrect the animal will be confiscated and quarantined.

2 Prerequisites

- Last rabies vaccination should have been done not less than 30 days and not more than one year before application.
- Animals should be microchipped in order to enter Dubai and must have verifying documentation.

3 What to Bring

- ☐ Owner's passport (copy)
- ☐ Owner's residence permit or visit visa (copy)
- ☐ Owner's contact details: company name, telephone & fax numbers, PO Box number
- ☐ Vaccination card (copy)
- ☐ Government health certificate from country of origin (copy)

Fee › ☐ Handling fee – Dhs.200, payable only with e-dirham card

4 Procedure

ocation › Ministry of Agriculture & Fisheries   Map ref 8-H5

Hours › Sat – Wed 07:30 – 14:30

Import › • At the Ministry, fill in an application form for an import permit
Permit
- Submit all relevant documents
- Either pick up the import permit the following day, or the Ministry will send it to you within one week
- The import permit is valid for one month only
- Make flight arrangements with the airline

ocation › Cargo Village (arriving as manifested cargo)   Map ref 9-A7

Hours › 24 hours

Arrival › • Submit the import permit (copy) to the Import Office
Arrival
- The airline will send a telex to the Cargo Village prior to the pet's arrival
- When clearing your pets, you must be able to produce owner's passport (copy)
- Clearance can take between two and four hours

Education

Personal Life

- A customs fee of Dhs.90 is payable

Permit Validity > One month

5 Related Procedures

- Vaccinating and Registering Pets [p.204]
- Sterilising Pets [p.205]

Info K9 Friends and Feline Friends

The tireless efforts of these two non-profit organisations have improved the lives of many lucky dogs and cats in Dubai. If you would like to lend a hand, make a donation (cash, jumble or even time), or adopt a pet of your own, you can get more information on their websites:

www.K9Friends.com

www.felinefriendsuae.com

Cats and Dogs

If you are considering getting a cat or dog while you live in Dubai then K9 and Feline Friends (see above) is the best bet. For more information on these associations as well as pet services check out the Residents chapter of the *Dubai Explorer* (The Complete Residents Guide) available in all leading bookshops and supermarkets.

Pets

Personal Life

Exporting Pets

1 Overview

A pet can be sent out of Dubai either accompanied by a person on the same flight, or unaccompanied as cargo depending on the airline and destination. Below is the basic procedure as required by the government and Dnata, the only cargo-handling agent in Dubai. Dubai kennels & cattery offer an export service (285 1646).

2 Prerequisites

• As per the laws of the country to which you are sending the pet

3 What to Bring

☐ A vaccination card, showing a rabies vaccination not older than one year and not less than 30 days

☐ A travel box, normally wooden or fibreglass, that meets airline specifications

Fee > ☐ Variable

4 Procedure

Flight > • Contact the airline cargo department and inquire about country-specific pet import regulations

• Book passage for the pet

ocation > Dubai Cargo Village   Map ref 9-A7

Hours > Sat – Wed 07:30 – 14:30

Export > • No more than seven days prior to departure, take the vaccination
Permit   records and health certificate to the Ministry of Agriculture & Fisheries veterinarian at the Cargo Village

• Pay Dhs.100

• You will be given an export permit, valid five days only

ocation > DNATA Export Office, Cargo Village   Map ref 9-A7

Hours > 24 hours

ipment > • Book flight with airline

• Take the pet, travel box and all documents to the Export Office

• Fill in a Live Animal Declaration form

• The animal will be weighed and measured, and the export fee calculated

• Pay the fee (cash only)

• Collect the airway bill

• At least 4 hours before departure, take the pet and travel box to the Export Office

ocedure > Ten days
Timings

Pets

Personal Life

Vaccinating and Registering Pets

1 Overview

Dogs and cats should be vaccinated annually. After vaccination you will be given a Municipality ID disc, which should be worn on the collar at all times. Vaccinations can be done either by a private vet or by the Dubai Municipality Veterinary Section (289 1114).

⚠ The Municipality controls the stray population by trapping and euthanasing cats and dogs. Pets without an ID disc, or without a current ID disc are treated as strays.

2 Prerequisites

- Pet is not yet vaccinated or registered

3 What to Bring

Fees >
- ☐ Dhs.350 – vaccination at private veterinary clinic (approx)
- ☐ Dhs.50 – vaccination at the Dubai Municipality Vet

4 Procedure

Location > Dubai Municipality Veterinary Section/private clinic   Map ref 6-G9

Hours > Sat – Wed 07:30 – 14:30

- Go to a veterinary clinic in Dubai or to the Municipality's Veterinary Section
- Your pet will be vaccinated
- Collect the vaccination certificate and a red Municipality number disc
- Attach the tag to the pet's collar
- Ensure the pet wears the tag at all times to protect it from being collected as a stray
- If your pet is wearing its tag and the Municipality finds it, they will contact you immediately

Sterilising Pets

1 Overview

Sterilising (or 'desexing') your pets is strongly recommended, especially in this part of the world where there is a problem with strays and unwanted animals. Female pets are spayed (womb and ovaries are removed) and male pets are castrated (testicles are removed). Both operations are straightforward, carried out under general anaesthetic, and your pet will recover quickly. It is recommended to have your pets sterilised to prevent them from breeding. Once sterilised, your pet will also probably wander less, and therefore be less exposed to the dangers of traffic and disease.

You can choose to have your pet sterilised either at a private veterinary clinic or at the Dubai Municipality Clinic (289 1114).

2 Prerequisites

- Pet is not yet sterilised
- Pet is the appropriate age (approximately six months for dogs, and five months for cat or dog, although your vet will be able to recommend the best age for your pet)

3 What to Bring

☐ **Dubai Municipality Vet** – Dhs.50 (regardless of size or gender of cat or dog)

☐ **Private veterinary clinic** (price depends on weight and sex):
- Dogs: Dhs.450 – 760 (female); Dhs.300 – 450 (male)
- Cats: Dhs.300 – 380 (female); Dhs.195 – 265 (male)

4 Procedure

- Make an appointment
- Take your pet to the vets at the appointed time (will usually be in the morning)
- The animal will have a pre-op check (if you are at a private vet, at this stage they may ask you if there are any other minor procedures you want to have done while your pet is under general anaesthetic. Such procedures might include nail clipping or teeth cleaning, and will be charged extra)
- Leave your pet at the vets for the operation
- Pick them up in the afternoon – at this point the vet will give you clear instructions for care during recovery

Pets

Personal Life

Banking

Opening a Bank Account

[1 Overview

A Dubai bank account is a requirement for most residents and each bank has specific prerequisites, general banking hours are Saturday to Wednesday 08:00 – 15:30 and Thursday 08:00 – 14:00.

- Residence permit or residency application in process (if applying for a savings account)

[2 Prerequisites

- If residency application is in process, applicant is permitted to open a savings account, if the sponsoring company confirms his/her employment and the branch manager signs the application
- Most banks set a minimum account/balance limit – normally Dhs.5,000 for a savings or current account. If the balance drops below the minimum set by the bank, a fee of Dhs.30 – 100 is charged per month (depending on bank and account type)

[3 What to Bring

As all banks have different procedures the following is a general overview.

Private > Account
- ☐ Passport (original & copy)
- ☐ Residence permit (copy)
- ☐ One form of local ID (copy)

Corporate > Account
- ☐ Minimum balance amount (varies from bank to bank)
- ☐ Valid trade licence
- ☐ Proof of membership with the Dubai Chamber of Commerce & Industry

New > Company
- ☐ Board resolution authorising the opening of the account
- ☐ Certified copies of the memorandum and articles of association
- ☐ List of directors
- ☐ Registration certificate from the Ministry of Economy & Commerce
- ☐ Passport copies of company owner(s)
- ☐ If you are about to establish your company in Dubai and you do not yet have all of the above documents, you will need a letter from the Dubai Department of Economic Development.

[4 Procedure

Location > Various (see [p.273])   Map ref Various

Hours > Sat – Wed 08:00 – 15:30; Thu 08:00 – 14:00

As both procedures and timings differ from bank to bank, please check with your bank for more information on a particular procedure.

Applying for a Good Conduct Certificate

[1] Overview

The two main reasons for needing a good conduct certificate are employment and emigration. This certificate is provided by the Criminal Investigation Department (CID) and confirms that you have no criminal record in the UAE.

Future potential employers may request that you supply this certificate before completing the recruitment process, and certain countries (USA, Canada, Australia, etc) require this as part of the application for immigration process.

[2] Prerequisites

• Applicant has been resident in Dubai at least 6 months

[3] What to Bring

☐ Passport (original & copy)

☐ Residence permit (copy)

☐ 2 passport sized photos

Hours > ☐ Dhs.100 – service charge

[4] Procedure

Location > CID, Dubai Police Headquarters   Map ref 10-E7

Hours > Sat – Wed 07:30 – 14:00

• Pick up the application form from the CID

☐ This form is in Arabic only, but a police officer will type it up for you

• Submit all documents with the application form

• Give one set of fingerprints

• If you pass the background check, the certificate will be ready for pickup after three days

Waiting > Three days
Time

Work

Personal Life

Liquor Licence

Applying for a liquor Licence

1 Overview

The sale of alcohol is strongly controlled in the UAE. In order to purchase alcohol for home consumption, you first have to have a liquor licence. With your licence, you can buy a limited quantity of alcohol per month from one of two licensed companies; African and Eastern (A & E), or Mercantile Maritime International (MMI). Both have numerous branches around Dubai. For a list of locations, see p.282.

Whereas before you had to apply for your liquor licence at the Dubai Police Headquarters, you now do it at any branch of A & E or MMI.

Monthly Quota › When you get your licence, you will be given a 'monthly quota' – the amount of alcohol you are allowed to buy in one month. The quota is based on your salary, age, job and size of your family. It usually ranges from Dhs.500 upwards.

Licence Transfer › Liquor licences are not transferable, so your friends are not permitted to buy alcohol using your licence. It is possible for a wife to buy alcohol on her husband's licence, but only after permission to do so is granted See the Info box opposite.

Validity › One year

2 Prerequisites

- Applicant must be non-Muslim
- Applicant must be resident in Dubai
- Minimum monthly salary of approximately Dhs.3,500
- Minimum age of 21 years
- Married couple: only the husband may apply

The wife may only apply with written agreement from the husband if the husband is Muslim and the wife is non-Muslim, or if the husband's sponsoring company does not support its employees applying for liquor licences due to religious reasons

3 What to Bring

☐ Completed application form from any of the above liquor stores, signed and stamped by your employer. The application must be signed by the applicant, and it should bear the stamp of the company.

☐ Passport (valid for at least six months) and copy

☐ Residence permit (valid for at least three months) and copy

☐ One passport photo, with your full name written on the back

☐ One passport photo of wife (optional) – see Info box below

☐ Tenancy contract (copy)

☐ Employment contract showing your monthly salary (copy)

☐ Letter of no objection from your employer (original)

Fee> ☐ Dhs.150 – application fee (cash & exact change only if applying through Police).

4 Procedures

Location

Any A&E or MMI store   Map ref Various

- Get an application form from any A&E or MMI store

- Submit all documents

- Pay the fee

- The store will then process the application for you

- You will be given a date to return for the licencer

Waiting Time   One week

Law   Alcohol Use

- It is against the law to sell or offer alcoholic beverages to Muslims

- It is illegal to consume alcohol in public places, including in the desert or at the beach

- Driving under the influence of alcohol and public drunkenness are punishable offences; there is a ZERO TOLERANCE policy in effect and breaking the law can end in a stint in jail.

- During Ramadan, only tourist establishments are permitted to serve alcohol, and only after 18:00

Duty Free
This allowance is for non-Muslims only and is a generous two litres of spirits **and** two litres of wine.

Info   Liquor Licence – Wife

Submit a letter to either MMI or A & E requesting that your wife be permitted to purchase alcohol on your licence. The letter will be stamped and signed by the manager. Within three days, you can pick it up and attach it to the original licence. Both the letter and licence must be shown in order to purchase alcohol. Alternatively, at time of new application, attach a passport photo of your wife so that she can buy alcohol on your licence.

Liquor Licence

Personal Life

Overview

Overview

Business

Overview

In this chapter, various options for opening a business are outlined with a focus on the expat entrepreneur. A step-by-step guide through the trade licence application procedure is also included.

Overview & Main Institutions

Red-Tape gives a short introduction to business in Dubai, as well as the organisations you need to deal with, like the Department of Economic Development (DED), the Federal Ministry of Economy and Planning, the Dubai Chamber of Commerce & Industry (DCCI) and the Dubai Municipality.

Preparation & Selection

Outlines the different company forms that can be set up here and lists things to consider before applying for a trade licence.

Setting Up

Covers how to set up an LLC, a branch or representative office of a foreign company, a sole proprietorship and a professional civil company.

Immigration & Labour

How to open company files with the Ministry of Labour and Immigration. More info on applying for visas is in the Visas Section.

Commercial Agent

In most cases, a foreign company may have to appoint a commercial agent. This section explains how to do this.

Free Zones

Free zone regulations differ greatly from the rest of Dubai. There is an increasing number of free zones in Dubai, but we have focused on the main ones.

E-Government

The Dubai government means and supports business. For more information on the new 'e' drive, see [p.viii] in the introduction.

Web Update

While Dubai's government is committed to cutting back on the red-tape involved in setting up in Dubai, both for individuals and businesses, changes in rules and regulations are inevitable. Therefore, if there have been any changes or additions to the procedures included in this book they will appear on the Explorer website. Just log on to **www.Explorer-Publishing.com** and click on the *Red-Tape* link. This page will tell you if there have been any changes to specific procedures – giving you the heads up before you head off to plough through Dubai's administrative maze!

Overview

Business

Business Environment

1 Overview

Financial Benefits >
- No personal income tax
- No foreign exchange controls
- No restrictions on repatriating capital and/or earnings
- No corporate tax except for branches of foreign banks, courier companies and oil companies

Ownership > At least 51% participation by UAE nationals is the requirement for all UAE-established companies. See below for exceptions.

Exceptions > 100% foreign ownership is permitted in the following cases:
- Companies located in UAE free zones
- Companies with activities open to 100% AGCC ownership
- Companies where wholly owned AGCC companies enter into partnership with UAE nationals
- Branches and representative offices of foreign companies registered in Dubai
- Professional or artisan companies practising business activities that allow 100% foreign ownership

Land Ownership > Currently, foreign companies and non-Nationals are not permitted to own commercial land in the UAE other than in free zones, where lease-hold ownership is offered. Commercial property must be either rented or leased, and rates tend to be high.

Labour Law > The UAE Labour Law deals with working hours, termination rights, benefits and repatriation, but is considered employer friendly in some aspects. Labour issues are administered by the Federal Ministry of Labour and Social Affairs. Trade unions do not exist and strikes are forbidden.

Copyright Law > Introduced in 1993, the UAE Copyright Law was most recently updated in 2002 with the development of Federal Copyright Law No.7. It protects the rights of creators, performers, producers of audio recordings and broadcasting/recording corporations.

Trademark Law > Trademark law was introduced in 1974 and updated in 1993. Trademark registration in the UAE is done through the Ministry of Economy & Planning and takes between 12 to 18 months.

Work Permits > The employer is responsible for all work permits and related immigration procedures for their employees including any costs. In a free zone, the free zone authority will handle all immigration procedures.

Employment Contracts > The Ministry of Labour provides a model labour contract in Arabic, but employers tend to draft an English version stating employment and benefit details, particularly for senior staff. The Arabic labour contract is enforceable in a court of law.

Employees > The Ministry sets a maximum number of expatriate staff that may be hired according to the size of the business and the business activity.

Overview

Business

Main Institutions

1 Overview

The Department of Economic Development (DED), the Federal Ministry of Economy & Planning, and the Dubai Chamber of Commerce & Industry (DCCI) are the main authorities involved when setting up a company in Dubai.

Dubai Department of Economic Development (DED)

This is the first port of call when setting up a business in Dubai, the Economic Department, as it is known, issues the trade licence and is an integral authority for businesses. Their office is always extremely busy, but there is an efficient queuing system. They have a comprehensive website (www.dubaided.com) that's worth checking out.

Ministry of Economy & Planning

The Ministry of Economy & Planning is the federal institution overseeing all economic activity in the UAE. It plays a supervisory and regulatory role in setting up all commercial companies. The head office is located in Abu Dhabi and while there is a Dubai office few new companies will need to make a visit. Foreign companies wanting to set up a branch in Dubai, as well as insurance companies, agents and brokers, must obtain approvals from this Ministry.

The Ministry of Economy also handles the registration of commercial agents/agencies. Other responsibilities include issuing certificates of origin for National exports and the protection of trademarks.

Dubai Chamber of Commerce & Industry (DCCI)

The Dubai Chamber of Commerce promotes commerce through various means, both locally as well as internationally. The Chamber also compiles all business-related data for the emirate, issues certificates of origin of commodities and other goods, nominates experts for goods surveying, receives commercial complaints, states and sets standards, defines commercial usage and terminology, and holds economic and commercial conferences.

stration > Every commercial, professional and industrial company must register with the Chamber (very small businesses may be the exception).

Dubai Municipality

All companies outside of a free zone must gain approval from the Municipality for their premises before setting up; zoning regulations are both devised and enforced here.

The Municipality is responsible for Dubai's infrastructure and urban landscaping.

Free Zones

Free Zones are designed to encourage foreign investment and the rules and procedures for establishing companies differ from the rest of Dubai, particularly with regard to foreign ownership. Both labour and immigration laws vary slightly as well, easing requirements and reducing headaches for business owners, see [p.254].

Overview

Business

Setting up a Company

[1] Overview

Variable Rules

While the information gathered in this book is as accurate as possible, anyone setting up a business in Dubai needs to be prepared for the unpredictable. Rules can vary and depend on nationality, business activity, capital amounts, partners and products, and the laws and/or regulations change on a regular basis.

Guidance

The procedures outlined in the following pages provide a guidance as to the types of red-tape and formalities required when setting up various kinds of businesses in Dubai. Four options for non-GCC nationals have been covered alongside free zone set up: setting up an LLC, a branch of a foreign company, a sole proprietorship and a professional company.

First Steps – Helping Hand

In addition to the information in this book the Department for Corporate Relations and the Investment Promotion Centre at the DED will lend an essential helping hand. In an effort to promote investment, particularly foreign investment, they will assist with the paperwork involved in obtaining a trade licence – the first step in setting up a business. For a commercial service fee of between Dhs.200 – 500, depending on the licence type, this very friendly, helpful and efficient department will guide you through the trade licence application procedure. This can significantly speed up the process and save a few headaches. The office is located in the DED head office, on the first floor.

How to succeed in Business

Doing business in Dubai is a whole new ball game for new residents and learning the dos and don'ts of business etiquette is a must before you step into the boardroom. For more information on working and doing business in Dubai check out the Residents chapter of the *Dubai Explorer* (The Complete Residents' Guide) available in all leading bookshops and supermarkets.

Overview

Business

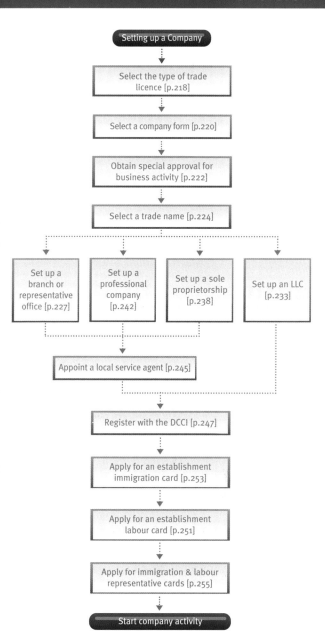

Setting up a Company

Select the type of trade licence [p.218]

Select a company form [p.220]

Obtain special approval for business activity [p.222]

Select a trade name [p.224]

Set up a branch or representative office [p.227]

Set up a professional company [p.242]

Set up a sole proprietorship [p.238]

Set up an LLC [p.233]

Appoint a local service agent [p.245]

Register with the DCCI [p.247]

Apply for an establishment immigration card [p.253]

Apply for an establishment labour card [p.251]

Apply for immigration & labour representative cards [p.255]

Start company activity

Overview

Business

Selecting a Trade Licence Type

1 Overview

Trade > Licence
All companies in Dubai must have a trade licence, as it determines which specific business activities a company is permitted to practise.

Licence > Type
Three types of trade licence exist:

- Commercial Licence: Issued for all business activities in general
- Professional Licence: Issued for services as well as different professions
- Industrial Licence: Issued for manufacturing activities

DED >
The institution responsible for this stage of company establishment is the Dubai Department of Economic Development (DED), as it issues the trade licence.

Free Zones >
All free zone companies have trade licences provided by their free zone authority.

Special > Approval
Depending on the business activity and the company form, approvals from other ministries may be necessary before the DED issues the trade licence (see Business Activities Requiring Special Approval table [p.222]).

Company > Forms
Before setting up a company, you will first have to decide which legal company form you would like. The form will depend on the business activity and the ownership of the company. For more information on the various options available, see Selecting a Company Form [p.214]. The company form will influence which type of trade licence can be applied for.

Categories >
All business activities in Dubai fall into one of the three categories of licence as listed above. The Licence Categories table on the facing page will assist you in determining into which category your company will fall.

Licence Categories

Licence	Business Activity
Commercial Licence	All trading activity (ie. buying and selling goods) for the purpose of profit • Banks • Media companies • Contractors • Insurance Agencies • Real Estate • Retail Companies • Supermarkets • Transport Companies
Professional Licence	Professions, services, craftsmen and artisans who practice a profession in which the service depends on physical or mental efforts rather than on capital. • Accountants • Advertising Agencies • Architectural Consultants • Auditors • Education and Welfare • Engineering Consultants • Exhibition Organisers • Legal Consultants • Medical & Health Services • Secretarial Services • Social Services • Technical Consultants • Translation Services • Veterinary Services
Industrial Licence	Industrial or manufacturing activity: any investment activity in order to discover natural resources or to transform raw material into fully manufactured or semi-manufactured products, or transform semi-manufactured products into fully manufactured products using mechanical power. • Agriculture • Building & Contracting • Construction • Discovery of Natural Resources • Electricity-related • Fishing • Gas & Water • Industrial

Preparation & Selection

Business

Selecting a Company Form

1 Overview

Legal Status ▸ In order to practice an activity, the company must first have legal status. There are several company form options with corresponding legal status, and therefore different requirements. These differences are particularly important for foreign nationals wanting to start a business in the UAE, as they are restricted by the company form they are permitted to own and business activities they are allowed to practise.

Company Forms ▸ Under UAE commercial law, there are seven broad company types, with different specifications in terms of shareholders, directors, minimum capital and corporate procedures. In general, for most forms, 51% UAE National participation is required.

Sole proprietorship and branches of foreign companies are also covered by commercial law, unlike professional companies, considered to be civil companies and falling under civil transactions law.

Free zone companies follow rules and regulations as set by the various free zone authorities.

Listed below are the main company forms available:

- Commercial companies:
  - General Partnership
  - Joint Participation
  - Limited Liability Company (LLC)
  - Partnership Limited By Shares
  - Private Joint Stock Company
  - Public Joint Stock Company
  - Simple Limited Partnership
- Professional Company
- Sole Proprietorship
- Branch or Representative Office of a Foreign Company
- Free Zone Companies:
  - Branch or Representative Office of a Foreign Company
  - Free Zone Establishment

In this book, those company forms which are of most interest to expats have been described. Those which are described/outlined are highlighted in blue in the table on the facing page.

Limitations ▸ Limitations depend upon nationality:

- UAE Nationals: may conduct all commercial, professional and industrial activities
- GCC Nationals: may conduct most commercial, professional and industrial activities except the reserved activities for Nationals (according to Cabinet decision 6 of 2004)
- Other Nationals: limitations exist (see table)
- Foreign Companies: limitations exist (see table)

Preparation & Selection

Business

◻ Permission to set up such companies is subject to approval of the concerned authorities, depending upon the business activity. For example, media activities require approval of the Ministry of Information & Culture (see Business Activities Requiring Special Approval [p.222]).

Joint Venture › A foreign party may enter a joint venture agreement for a specific one-off project without needing a separate licence. Business will be conducted under the name of the local entity holding a licence for this activity. Local participation must be greater than 51%, but profit and loss can be distributed according to the agreement signed.

Options According to Nationality	
Nationality	**Permissable Company Forms**

UAE National	• Sole Proprietorship (Individual Establishment)
	• Commercial Companies:
	  • General Partnership Company
	  • Simple Limited Partnership Company
	  • Particular Partnership
	  • Public Joint Stock Company
	  • Private Joint Stock Company
	  • Limited Liability Company (LLC)
	  • Partnership Limited By Shares
	• Professional Company

GCC National	• Sole Proprietorship • Joint Participations • Limited Liability Company • Private Joint Stock Company • Public Joint Stock Company • Professional Company: may practise a specific profession without a local service agent
Non-GCC National	• Sole Proprietorship: may only practise professional activities with the assistance of a UAE National local service agent except in cases of legal, engineering or auditing consultancies. • Limited Liability Company: may practise any commercial or industrial activity with one or more UAE National partners who own at least a 51% share of the company, except for the reserved activities of insurance, banking and investment. • Private Joint Stock Company: may practise any commercial or industrial activity, with one or more UAE National partners who own at least a 51% share of the company • Professional Company: may practise a profession with a UAE service agent or a UAE National partner • Public Joint Stock Company: Shareholders may decide to allow non-UAE nationals to become shareholders
Foreign Company	• Branch of a Foreign Company • Limited Liability Company: may practise any commercial or industrial activity, with one or more UAE National partners who own at least a 51% share of the company, except for the reserved activities of insurance, banking and investment. • Private Joint Stock Company: may practise any commercial or industrial activity, with one or more UAE National partners who own at least a 51% share of the company • Public Joint Stock Company: Shareholders may decide to allow non-UAE nationals to become shareholders

Obtaining Special Approval for Business Activity

1 Overview

Certain business activities require additional approval from various ministries and/or other authorities. You will need a no objection letter (NOC) from the ministry before applying for a trade licence with the DED.

- Some business categories (eg. businesses engaged in oil or gas production and related industries) require more detailed procedures than a simple NOC letter.
- Some trade activities (eg. jewellery and insurance) require the submission of a financial guarantee issued by a bank operating in Dubai.

For more information, call DED Customer Service on 222 5000, or the Call Centre on 202 0200 or 7000 40000 to be connected to the relevant department (working hours: Sat – Wed 07:30 – 14:30; 18:00 – 20:00).

Business Activities Requiring Special Approval	
Activity	**Authority**
Pharmacies	Ministry of Health
Music & Video Shops, Bookshops, Publishers and Printers, Newspapers, Magazines, Advertising and Translation Offices, News Agencies, Party Contractors, Calligraphers, Photographers, Computer Software Importers	Ministry of Information
Explosives & Arms	Ministry of Defence
Telecommunication & Wireless Systems	Ministry of Communication
Financial & Banking Institutions, Exchange Establishments, Money Brokers, Financial Investment Consultants, Investment Firms, Banking Investments	Central Bank
Private Clinics	Department of Health & Medical Services (Medical Committee)
Contracting Companies, Engineering Consultants, related Technical Services, Laboratories	Dubai Municipality
Travel Agents and Air Cargo Offices	Civil Aviation Department
Sea Freight, Passenger Charters, Cargo, Packing, Forwarding & Clearing Services	Seaports & Customs Authority
Lawyers, Legal Consultants, Fuel Stations	Ruler's Court
Nurseries, Private Schools, Institutes	Ministry of Education (Private Education Department)
New Industrial Projects and Expansions	Ministry of Finance & Industry (Industrial Directorate)
Chartered Accountants, Auditors	Ministry of Economy & Planning

Preparation & Selection

Tip Get the Business Activity Right the First Time Around!

Once the Ministry of Economy & Planning has approved an activity, the DED will examine the activity according to its own guidelines. If incompatibilities exist, changes to the Ministry's certificate may be necessary before you will be given the trade licence.

As this can become costly, it is advisable to decide from the beginning exactly which activity the company is applying for, and verify that it is acceptable. Also keep long-term plans in mind. If the company will add a new activity at a later stage, it must provide proof that it has experience in that field, and further approval and payment will be necessary once again.

For additional information, have a look at the *Standard Classification of Economic Activities*, published by the DED & DCCI, listing the various acceptable business activity categories and their codes.

Web Update

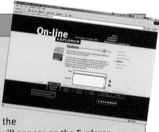

While Dubai's government is committed to cutting back on the red-tape involved in setting up in Dubai, both for individuals and businesses, changes in rules and regulations are inevitable. Therefore, if there have been any changes or additions to the procedures included in this book they will appear on the Explorer website. Just log on to **www.Explorer-Publishing.com** and click on the *Red-Tape* link. This page will tell you if there have been any changes to specific procedures – giving you the heads up before you head off to plough through Dubai's administrative maze!

Preparation & Selection

Business

Selecting a Trade Name

1 Overview

If you are setting up a Dubai-based company outside a free zone, approval for the company name by the DED must first be obtained. A trade name can be reserved as part of the setting up procedure. Have a look at the various flowcharts in this section to determine the best time to apply for the trade name (see [p.220,222, 238]).

⚠ The DED has the right to reject a proposed trade name if the name does not comply with their prerequisites. Even if the trade name has already been reserved, the DED can request a name change if they feel it is not indicative of the type of activity declared.

- The name should be translated into Arabic

2 Prerequisites

- It should be indicative of the business activity (but not always enforced)
- It should not conflict with Arabic and Islamic traditions and values
- It should not involve any of God's names and descriptions, or have any Islamic indication
- It should be consistent with true state of affairs

3 What to Bring

☐ Completed Trade Name Application Form ('BR/1') collected from the DED reception desk. Alternatively, you can download the form from their website: www.dubaided.gov.ae

Fees › ☐ Dhs.2,000 per year, if a local company chooses a foreign trade name

☐ Dhs.1,000 additional per year to add the word(s) 'International', 'Middle East' or 'Global'

☐ Dhs.2,000 additional per year to add the word(s) 'Dubai', 'UAE' or 'Gulf'

☐ Dhs.2,000 per year for name including abbreviations

☐ Dhs.1,000 per year to use a foreign name of a company using a trade name or trade mark of an international company

🗋 There is no fee for a foreign trade name given to branches of foreign companies & representative offices, or to Arabic trade names

🗋 Fees referred to above apply to new licences and to changes of trade names

☐ Dhs.100 – trade name registration fee

☐ Dhs.200 per year – trade name reservation

4 Procedure

Location > **DED**   Map ref **8-H4**

Hours > Sat – Wed 07:30 – 14:30

- Submit the application form at the Licensing Department and collect a receipt with a collection date
- Return to the same department on the specified date; if the name is approved, collect payment voucher
- Pay the application fees at the Cashier
- Return to the Licensing Counter and collect the approval receipt

5 Related Procedures

- Setting up a Company [p.216]
- Setting up a Branch or Representative Office of a Foreign Company [p.227]
- Setting up a Limited Liability Company (LLC) [p.233]
- Setting up a Sole Proprietorship [p.238]
- Setting up a Professional Company [p.242]
- Free Zone Overview [p.262]

Tip Selecting an Office or Warehouse

When applying for a trade licence, the rent agreement is normally required as part of the documentation. Ensure you select a location for your premises in an area in which you are permitted to perform your business activity. Dubai has strict zoning rules which restrict where a company may open up an office or warehouse. Approval must be gained from the Planning Department and will depend on your business activity. To have a warehouse you must have an industrial licence.

Tip Don't Sign Yet!

Don't sign a tenancy agreement for a warehouse or office before the DED has contacted the Municipality and approved it.

For more information, contact the Municipality's Planning Department in the DED Building (202 0105), or the Planning Department in the Dubai Municipality Building (206 3788).

If the property is leased from or granted by the Government of Dubai, you will also need a sub-lease no objection letter from the Real Estate Department.

Preparation & Selection

Business

Setting Up

Options for Non-Nationals & Foreign Companies

[1] Overview

Foreign > Company
The most common ways a foreign company may enter the Dubai market are as follows:

- Give the 'agency' for its products/services to an agent (see Appointing a Local Service Agent [p.245])
- Set up a branch office or a representative office in Dubai (see Setting up a Branch or Representative Office of a Foreign Company [p.227])
- Set up a branch or representative office in a free zone (see Free Zone Overview [p.262])

Regional > Head
Some foreign companies choose to set up a free zone branch as the regional head office, plus have an agent in Dubai cover a specified region, such as Dubai, the Northern Emirates, or the entire UAE (see Appointing a Local Service Agent [p.245]).

More > Presence
On the other hand, if a physical presence is necessary, options range from the establishment of a representative or branch office with 100% foreign ownership, an LLC with a maximum of 49% foreign equity, or the establishment of a professional or consultancy business under a local licensing regulation issued by the Dubai Government.

Setting up a Company in Dubai

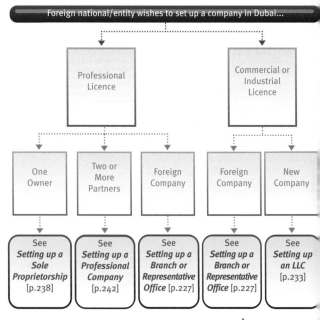

Foreign national/entity wishes to set up a company in Dubai...

Professional Licence			Commercial or Industrial Licence	
One Owner	Two or More Partners	Foreign Company	Foreign Company	New Company
See *Setting up a Sole Proprietorship* [p.238]	See *Setting up a Professional Company* [p.242]	See *Setting up a Branch or Representative Office* [p.227]	See *Setting up a Branch or Representative Office* [p.227]	See *Setting up an LLC* [p.233]

Setting up a Branch Office

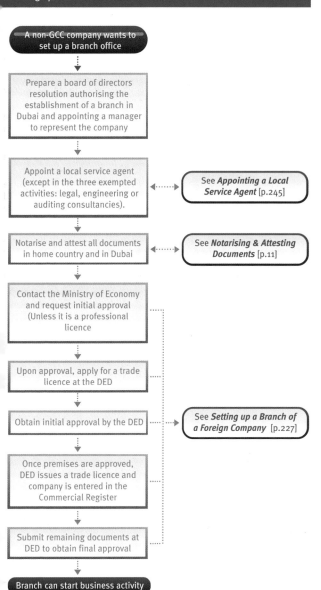

A non-GCC company wants to set up a branch office

↓

Prepare a board of directors resolution authorising the establishment of a branch in Dubai and appointing a manager to represent the company

↓

Appoint a local service agent (except in the three exempted activities: legal, engineering or auditing consultancies). ┈┈▶ See **Appointing a Local Service Agent** [p.245]

↓

Notarise and attest all documents in home country and in Dubai ┈┈▶ See **Notarising & Attesting Documents** [p.11]

↓

Contact the Ministry of Economy and request initial approval (Unless it is a professional licence

↓

Upon approval, apply for a trade licence at the DED

↓

Obtain initial approval by the DED ┈┈▶ See **Setting up a Branch of a Foreign Company** [p.227]

↓

Once premises are approved, DED issues a trade licence and company is entered in the Commercial Register

↓

Submit remaining documents at DED to obtain final approval

↓

Branch can start business activity

⚠ As this procedure depends on many variables, and rules and procedures change, visit the Corporate Relations Department at the DED for assistance (see [p.215]).

Setting Up

Business

Setting Up

[1] Overview

Established foreign companies may set up a branch or a representative office of their firm in Dubai. The branch will be considered a part of the parent company, and not a separate legal entity.

The branch office is technically allowed to trade, but it will not always receive permission to import and export the company's products. The company will be encouraged to select a local distributor/agent to distribute its goods (see Appointing a Local Service Agent [p.245]).

Service Agent > If the branch is 100% foreign owned, the company must appoint a local service agent (see Appointing a Local Service Agent [p.245]). Exceptions to this rule are legal, engineering or auditing consultancies.

Company Register > In addition to having to find a sponsor, foreign companies setting up a branch in the UAE must gain approval from the Ministry of Economy & Planning and be registered in their Register of Foreign Companies before applying for a trade licence.

A representative office does not need to register with the Ministry of Economy & Planning.

All documents submitted to the Ministry of Economy must be in sets of two. One set will remain in the office in Dubai; one will be sent to the head office in Abu Dhabi.

Charges > Dhs.2,000 – any amendments in documentation

Documents produced outside the GCC must be authenticated by the UAE or GCC consulate or embassy in the company's home country, and notarised by the Ministry of Foreign Affairs in the UAE (see Notarising & Attesting Documents [p.11]).

All documents should be submitted in Arabic. If written in a foreign language, an attested Arabic translation should be attached.

Before a brand of a foreign company may commence operations, it must do the following:

- Register in the Ministry's Register of Foreign Companies
- Be inscribed in the DED Commercial Register
- Obtain a trade licence from the DED

Representative Office > Unlike a branch office, a representative office is allowed to promote the activities of the parent company only, and not sell products itself

It is permitted to practice promotional services towards the company and the products, and also facilitate contacting potential customers

2 Prerequisites

- The branch may only engage in similar activities as the parent company, and only as stated in the licence

- Industry restrictions apply for companies practising the following business activities:
  - General trading
  - Import/export
  - Manufacturing
  - Insurance
  - Banking & other financial activities

- If the foreign company (without any registration in the UAE) is engaging in any commercial activity, it must appoint a local trade agent to import, export or sell its products in the UAE (see Appointing a Local Service Agent [p.245])

- The branch may not import parent company products

- Depending on the activity, additional special approval from the concerned authorities may be necessary (see Obtaining Special Approval for Business Activity [p.222])

- Trade Name must be the same as the name of the parent company (See Selecting a Trade Name [p.224])

3 What to Bring

Initial approval ▸ Ministry of Economy & DED

(Ministry of Economy: branch office applications only)

☐ Articles and memorandum of association of parent company (copy)

☐ Board of Directors' resolution from parent company authorising establishment of a branch office in Dubai and appointing the branch office manager

☐ Power of attorney from parent company authorising branch office manager to conduct all affairs of the branch office and sign on the behalf of the branch office

☐ Audited financial statements of the parent company for the past two years

☐ Certificate of corporation stating company's form and capital (certificate of registration of parent company from the authority that regulates registration and incorporation of companies in that country, stating the company is validly incorporated and continues to exist)

☐ If applicable, a list of parent company's branches in the UAE and name of the local agent for each branch

☐ If the company has no other branches in the UAE, a letter certifying this

☐ Manager's passport (copy)

Setting Up

Business

Initial Approval **>** Ministry of Economy (in addition to above)

(Branch office applications only)

☐ Application form in Arabic (typed)

☐ Local service agency agreement and documents proving the agent is a UAE national or the company is fully UAE owned (see Appointing a Local Service Agent [p.245])

☐ Profile of the company – list of previous experience and activities in the field in which it is applying for in the UAE

☐ Licence issued and ratified by licensing authority in home country (copy)

Fee **>** ☐ Dhs.5,000 (e-Dirham) – application fee

Additional Costs **>** ☐ Dhs.50,000 Bank Guarantee

Initial Approval **>** DED (in addition to above)

(Branch & representative office applications)

☐ Registration & Licensing Application Form ('BR/1') (typed)

☐ Trade Name Application Form if not already applied for ('BR/2') (typed) (see Selecting a Trade Name [p.224])

☐ Ministry of Economy & Planning Initial Approval Form (NOC)

☐ For representative office, certificate from the competent authority in the parent company's home country stating that the company has been registered for at least two years (translated by a certified legal translator)

☐ If an establishment or company was incorporated in the Jebel Ali Free Zone, certificate of formation (copy)

☐ If company was incorporated in another emirate, trade licence (copy) and Chamber certificate of all company branches (copy)

☐ If applicable, no objection certificate from the government authorities according to the type of commercial activity (see Obtaining Special Approval for Business Activity [p.222]

Fees **>** ☐ Dhs.100 – initial approval fee

☐ Dhs.200 – trade name registration fee

Optional Fees **>** ☐ Dhs.500 – express service fee

☐ Dhs.5,000 – representative office registration fee

Final Approval **>** DED (in addition to above)

(Branch and representative office applications)

☐ DED initial approval

☐ DED trade name approval

☐ Ministry of Economy initial approval

☐ Tenancy contract of office premises including plot number (copy) (see Selecting an Office or Warehouse [p.225])

☐ If premises will be leased from or granted by the Dubai Government, a sublease no-objection letter from the Department of Real Estate

☐ Company cheque (or personal cheque if the partner/owner is named on the trade licence) with the licence number and establishment's trade name on the back

Fee > ☐ Dhs.200 – 'local fee'

☐ Dhs.500 – 'wastage fee'

☐ Dhs.3,000 – Ministry of Economy fee

☐ 5% of tenancy contract – Municipality tax

Final > Ministry of Economy
approval
(Branch office applications only)

☐ Trade licence (original & copy)

☐ Commercial registration certificate (original & copy)

Fee > ☐ Dhs.10,000 (e-Dirham) – registration fee

4 Procedure

Location > Ministry of Economy & Planning   Map ref 9-A5

Hours > Sat – Wed 07:30 – 14:30

📄 This section applies to branch office applications only

Initial > • Collect an application form from the Department of Commercial
approval   Affairs

• Complete the form, specifying the activity that the office or branch will undertake in the UAE

• Submit all documents for approval; pay the application fee at the same office

• Within one week the Federal Foreign Companies Committee will approve or decline the application

• If approved, an NOC (valid three months) will be issued specifying the approved activities

• Within these three months, the company must apply for the trade licence and commercial registration

Location > DED Licensing Department   Map ref 8-H4

Hours > Sat – Wed 07:30 – 14:30

Initial > • Submit all documents in order that the company be entered into
approval   the Commercial Register

• Go to the Licensing Counter on the first floor; take a ticket and wait for your number to be called

• Submit all documents and collect the application receipt (cash payment voucher) that will specify a date

• Return to the Licensing Counter on the specified date to check if the application received initial approval

• If it was approved, go to the Cashier and pay the fee

• Return to the Licensing Counter and collect the initial approval receipt and all documents submitted

Setting Up

Business

- If the department rejects the application, you have 15 days from the notification date to submit a grievance

📑 Initial approval is valid 6 months from date of approval. If you fail to renew the initial approval, it will expire within 10 days of the expiry date.

Final **>** Approval
- Go to the Dubai Municipality Planning Department Counter (first floor, DED) and request approval for the business premises

- Submit all required documents at the Licensing Counter; you will be given an application receipt and a date on which to return

- Return on the specified date to collect the 'fee payment voucher'

- Pay the fee at the Cashier and collect the licence

📑 You will receive two sealed copies of the licence, one to be used for inscription in the Commercial Register and the other for registration with the Dubai Chamber of Commerce (see Registering with the DCCI [p.211])

Commercial **>** Register
- Commercial and industrial companies must register with the DED at the Commercial Registry; the charge varies from Dhs.700 to 1,200 (depending on the company type)

Location **>** Ministry of Economy & Planning   Map ref 9-A5

Hours **>** Sat – Wed 07:30 – 14:30

📑 This section applies to branch office applications only

Final **>** Approval
- Submit all documents and pay the certificate fee at the Commercial Affairs Department

- The certificate will be given to you within days

5   Related Procedures

- Applying for an Establishment Immigration Card [p.253]
- Applying for an Establishment Labour Card [p.251]
- Applying for Immigration & Labour Representative Cards [p.255]
- Registering with the DCCI [p.247])

Setting Up

Business

Setting up an LLC

A non-GCC national wants to set up an LLC

↓

Find UAE partner(s)

↓

Select an appropriate trade name ◄······ See *Selecting a Trade Name* [p.224]

↓

Select appropriate premises ◄······ See *TIP* [p.225]

↓

If applicable, obtain special approval ◄······ See *Obtaining Special Approval for Business Activity* [p.222]

↓

Decide which business activities will be conducted ◄······ See Business Activities Requiring Special Approval [p.222]

↓

Apply for trade name and initial approval at DED

↓

Request entry in Commercial Register

↓

Appoint an auditor ······ See *Setting up a Limited Liability Company* [p.234]

↓

After initial approval, deposit capital in bank

↓

Once premises are approved, DED will issue trade licence and company is entered in the Commercial Register

↓

Commercial licence must be registered with the DCCI ◄······ See *Registering with the DCCI* [p.247]

↓

LLC can start business activity

⚠ As this procedure depends on many variables, and rules and procedures change, visit the Corporate Relations Department at the DED for assistance (see [p.215]).

Setting Up

Business

Setting Up

Setting up a Limited Liability Company (LLC)

1 Overview

An LLC is a business structure that is a hybrid of a partnership and a corporation. Its owners are shielded from personal liability; the liability of the shareholders is limited to their shares in the company's capital.

Limitations >
- Formed by minimum of two, maximum of 50 people whose liability is limited to their shares in the company's capital
- Minimum share capital: currently Dhs.300,000 (US$ 82,000), contributed in cash or in kind, unless the activity is investment in and management of commercial, industrial and agricultural projects (when the minimum share capital is Dhs.3 million).
- Maximum foreign equity in the company: 49%
- Selling shares publicly is not permitted

2 Prerequisites

- Company auditor must be UAE accredited
- Trade name (ending with 'LLC') has been approved (see Selecting a Trade Name [p.224])
- Appropriate premises have been selected (preferably contract has not yet been signed)
- Depending on the activity, additional special approval from the concerned authorities may be necessary (see Obtaining Special Approval for Business Activity [p.222])

3 What to Bring

- ☐ Registration & Licensing Application Form ('BR/1') (typed)
- ☐ Trade Name Application Form if not already applied for ('BR/2') (typed) (see Selecting a Trade Name [p.224])

Initial > Approval
- ☐ If the LLC is established by a company, the company's memorandum (authenticated by notary public) containing objectives and provisions for management, capital and distribution of company profits

☐ No memorandum needed if established by an individual

- ☐ If applicable, no objection certificate from the government authorities according to the type of commercial activity (see Obtaining Special Approval for Business Activity [p.218])
- ☐ Bank certificate certifying that all shares have been deposited

Fees >
- ☐ Dhs.100 – initial approval fee
- ☐ Dhs.200 – trade name registration fee

Commercial > Register
- ☐ DED initial approval

- ☐ Application form signed by manager/representative (two originals)
- ☐ Certificate (two copies) issued by manager and signed by company auditors stating that all shares are fully paid, their value has been deposited in a UAE bank, the shares have been valued and their value has been credited to the company assets
- ☐ Memorandum of association (original & copy – both authenticated)
- ☐ Auditors' trade licence
- ☐ Letter from the company's auditors stating that they are willing to act as auditors for the company

Fees ▶ ☐ Dhs.500 – licence registration fee

Document notarisation charges range from Dhs.750 (Export/Import LLC) to Dhs.7,500 (General Trading LLC) depending on business activity

Final ▶
Approval
- ☐ DED initial approval
- ☐ DED trade name approval
- ☐ All documents mentioned above
- ☐ Tenancy contract of office premises including plot number (copy) (see Selecting an Office or Warehouse [p.221])
- ☐ If premises will be leased from or granted by the Dubai Government, a sublease no objection letter from the Department of Real Estate
- ☐ Memorandum of Association Form ('Form 4') collected from the DED, signed by the company's shareholders and notarised at the Dubai Court
- ☐ A certificate from a UAE-licenced bank certifying that all the shares of the company have been deposited in cash
- ☐ If industrial activity, Ministry of Finance & Industry approval
- ☐ Notarised memorandum of association (copy)
- ☐ Application for entry in the Commercial Register (copy)
- ☐ Certificate issued by manager (as above), with date and number of commercial registration (copy)
- ☐ Manager's passport (copy)

Fees ▶
- ☐ Dhs.200 – local fee
- ☐ Dhs.500 – wastage fee
- ☐ Dhs.3,000 – Ministry of Economy fee
- ☐ 5% of tenancy contract – Municipality tax
- ☐ Dhs.1,000 – charge per foreign partner
- ☐ Dhs.500 – DED express service fee (optional)

4 Procedure

DED Licensing Department   Map ref 8-H4

Location ▶ Sat – Wed 07:30 – 14:30

Hours ▶ • Submit trade name application(see Selecting a Trade Name [p.224])

Setting Up

Business

Trade > • Notarise the company's Memorandum of Association (DED 'Form
Name 4') at the Dubai Court desk in the DED

Initial > • Go to the Licensing Counter on the first floor; take a ticket and wait
Approval for your number to be called

• Submit all documents and collect the application receipt (cash
payment voucher) that will specify a date

• Return to the Licensing Counter on the specified date to check if
the application received initial approval

• If approved, go to the Cashier and pay the fee

• Return to the Licensing Counter and collect the initial approval
receipt and all documents submitted

• If the department rejects the application, you have 15 days from
the notification date to submit a grievance

⌐ Initial approval is valid 6 months from date of approval. If you fail to
renew the initial approval, it will expire within 10 days of the expiry
date.

Location > **Any bank** Map ref **Various**

Hours > **Various**

• Deposit all capital, then request an undertaking from the bank that
the deposited amount will only be released to the managers upon
proof of company registration

Location > **DED** Map ref **8-H4**

Hours > **Sat – Wed 07:30 – 14:30**

Final > • Go to the Municipality Planning Department Counter (first floor,
Approval DED) to request approval for the business premises

• Submit all required documents at the Licensing Counter; you will
be given an application receipt and a date on which to return

• Return on the specified date to collect the 'fee payment voucher'

• Pay the fee at the Cashier and collect the licence

⌐ You will receive two sealed copies of the licence, one to be used for
inscription in the Commercial Register and the other for registration
with the Dubai Chamber of Commerce (see Registering with the
DCCI [p.247])

Commercial > • Submit all documents and request inscription in the Commercial
Register Register

• Once approval is granted, the company will be entered in the
Commercial Register and have its Memorandum of Association
published in the Ministry bulletin Procedure

5 Related Procedures

• DCCI Membership Registration [p.247]
• Applying for an Establishment Labour Card [p.251]
• Applying for an Establishment Immigration Card [p.253]
• Applying for Representative Cards [p.255]

Setting Up

Business

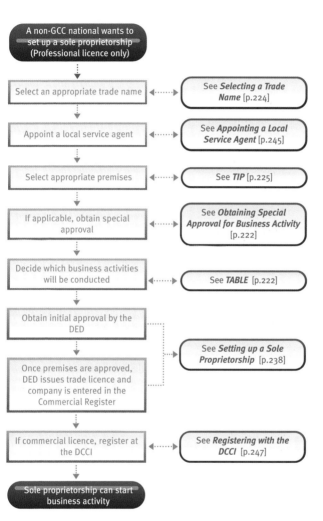

A non-GCC national wants to set up a sole proprietorship (Professional licence only)

Select an appropriate trade name ····▶ See *Selecting a Trade Name* [p.224]

Appoint a local service agent ····▶ See *Appointing a Local Service Agent* [p.245]

Select appropriate premises ····▶ See *TIP* [p.225]

If applicable, obtain special approval ····▶ See *Obtaining Special Approval for Business Activity* [p.222]

Decide which business activities will be conducted ····▶ See *TABLE* [p.222]

Obtain initial approval by the DED

Once premises are approved, DED issues trade licence and company is entered in the Commercial Register ····▶ See *Setting up a Sole Proprietorship* [p.238]

If commercial licence, register at the DCCI ····▶ See *Registering with the DCCI* [p.247]

Sole proprietorship can start business activity

Settingup

Business

Setting up a Sole Proprietorship

1 Overview

A sole proprietorship is the most basic entity form where the owner has a trade licence in his name and is personally held liable for his accounts, i.e. he is responsible for the entity's financial obligations. The proprietor can conduct business in the commercial, professional, industrial, agricultural or real estate industry.

Nationals and GCC nationals are permitted to set up a sole proprietorship with few restrictions. Stricter conditions apply for non-GCC nationals. A non-GCC national setting up a sole proprietorship is restricted in the type of activities he may perform. The entity should be in a service or knowledge-based industry.

Validity ›
- Initial approval is valid six months from approval date
- If you fail to renew the initial approval, it will expire within 10 days of the expiry date

⚠ Since this procedure depends on many variables, and rules and procedures change, we strongly recommend you visit the Corporate Relations Department at the DED for assistance (see [p.215]).

2 Prerequisites

- An appropriate trade name (see Selecting a Trade Name [p.224])
- Appropriate premises
- If applicable, special approval for business activity has been obtained (see Obtaining Special Approval for Business Activity [p.222])

GCC › Nationals
- Must be resident in the UAE
- Must practise the activity on his own

Non-GCC › Nationals
- Must appoint a local service agent (see Appointing a Local Service Agent [p.245])

3 What to Bring

UAE › National
- ☐ Owner's passport with proof of naturalisation (copy)
- ☐ Manager's passport (copy)

GCC › National
- ☐ Owner's passport (copy)
- ☐ Certificate of good conduct from the relevant authorities of his GCC state
- ☐ Local agent's passport (copy)
- ☐ Investor's/manager's passport (copy)

Non-GCC › Nationals
- ☐ Visit visa (copy)
- ☐ If he has a residence permit, a NOC from his sponsor
- ☐ Degree certificate, notarised, legalised and authenticated

Setting Up

Business

□ Work experience certificate if consultancy entity

□ Certificate of good standing from a government body or the body governing the applicant's profession (if applicable)

Initial ❯
pproval

□ Registration and Licensing Application Form ('BR/1') (typed – Arabic and/or English)

□ Trade Name Application Form ('BR/2') (typed)

□ If applying for a professional business licence, the resume of the applicant proving qualifications ('BR/3') (typed)

□ If commercial or industrial activity, approval of the Ministry of Economy & Planning

□ If applicable, no objection certificate from the government authorities according to the type of commercial activity (see Obtaining Special Approval for Business Activity [p.222]

□ If applicant is under 21 years, permission from the court to practise business

Fees ❯

□ Dhs.100 – trade name registration fee

□ Dhs.200 – initial approval fee

□ Dhs.500 – DED express service fee (optional)

Final ❯
pproval

□ Initial approval slip

□ All documents mentioned above

□ Tenancy agreement including plot number (copy) (see Tip [p.223])

□ Sublease no-objection letter from the Department of Real Estate of Dubai Government if the premises will be leased from or granted by Government of Dubai

□ If general trading, contracting or investing in commercial, industrial or agricultural holding & trust company, a bank certificate issued by the applicant's bank in Dubai stating the amount of capital deposited

Fees ❯

□ Dhs.200 – local fee

□ Dhs.300 – wastage fee

□ 5% of tenancy contract – Municipality tax

□ Dhs.500 – registration fee

Local ❯
Agent

□ 'Appointment of National Agent' contract duly authenticated by the notary public ('BR/13') (original & copy)

□ For UAE agents without previous licences, agent's passport and UAE naturalisation identification (copy)

□ Local service agency agreement (original) (see [p.245])

□ If the local service agent is an individual, his passport (copy)

□ If the local service agent is a company, its memorandum of association (original and copy), trade licence (copy), passports and family books of all the members (or proof that the members are UAE Nationals) (copy)

□ Director's passport (copy)

Setting Up

Business

[4] Procedure

Location > DED Licensing Department   Map ref 8-H4

Hours > Sat – Wed 07:30 – 14:30

Initial > • At least one week prior to the proposed start of the permit's
Approval   validity date, go to the Licensing Counter on the first floor of the
           DED. Take a ticket and wait for your number to be called

• Submit required documents and collect the application receipt
  (cash payment voucher) that will specify a pick-up date

• Return to the Licensing Counter on that date and check if the
  application was initially approved

• If it was approved, go to the Cashier and pay the fee

• Return to the Licensing Counter and collect the initial approval
  receipt and all documents submitted

• If the department rejects the application, you have 15 days from
  the notification date to submit a grievance

Initial approval is valid 6 months from date of approval. If you fail
to renew the initial approval, it will expire within 10 days of the
expiry date.

Final > • Go to the Municipality Planning Department Counter (first floor,
Approval   DED) to request approval for the business premises

• Go to the Inspection and Control Counter on the first floor, if there
  are other licences on the proposed premises

• Submit all required documents at the Licensing Counter; you will
  be given an application receipt and a date on which to return

• Return on the specified date to collect the 'fee payment voucher'

• Pay the fee at the Cashier and collect the licence

You will receive two sealed copies of the licence, one to be used for
inscription in the Commercial Register and the other for registration
with the Dubai Chamber of Commerce (see Registering with the
DCCI [p.247])

Commercial > • Submit all documents and request inscription in the Commercial
Register   Register

• Once approval is granted, the company will be entered in the
  Commercial Register and have its Memorandum of Association
  published in the Ministry bulletin

[5] Related Procedures

• Applying for an Establishment Immigration Card [p.253]
• Applying for an Establishment Labour Card [p.251]
• Applying for Immigration and Labour Representative Cards [p.255]

Setting Up

Business

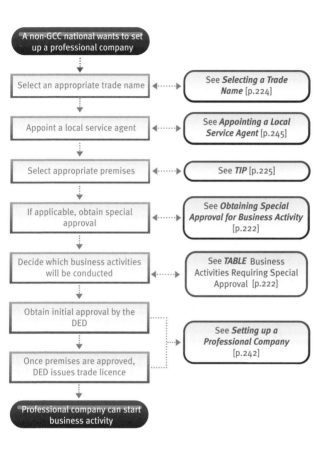

A non-GCC national wants to set up a professional company

↓

Select an appropriate trade name ◀┈┈┈▶ See *Selecting a Trade Name* [p.224]

↓

Appoint a local service agent ◀┈┈┈▶ See *Appointing a Local Service Agent* [p.245]

↓

Select appropriate premises ◀┈┈┈▶ See *TIP* [p.225]

↓

If applicable, obtain special approval ◀┈┈┈▶ See *Obtaining Special Approval for Business Activity* [p.222]

↓

Decide which business activities will be conducted ◀┈┈┈▶ See *TABLE* Business Activities Requiring Special Approval [p.222]

↓

Obtain initial approval by the DED ┈┈┐

↓   ├┈▶ See *Setting up a Professional Company* [p.242]

Once premises are approved, DED issues trade licence ┈┘

↓

Professional company can start business activity

Setting Up

Setting up a Professional Company

1 Overview

Also referred to as a business partnership, professional business company, or consultancy business, this company type falls under the civil code, rather than under commercial law and is unique to the UAE. Such firms may engage in professional or artisan activities but the number of staff members that may be employed is limited and a UAE national must be appointed as a local service agent (see Appointing a Local Service Agent [p.245]).

An important part in applying for the licence is showing evidence of the credentials and qualifications of the employees and partners. According to the DED, 'A professional is a person who independently practices a profession based on investing his intellectual powers and acquired information, which generates an income. In such work, he either depends on his own physical effort or uses the help of some tools and equipment, whether solely or with a maximum number of five workers.'

Business > Activities

These companies usually practise in the following fields:

* Engineering and business consulting
* Graphic and architectural design
* Health care
* IT
* Teaching

Ownership > It may be 100% foreign owned, provided there is a local service agent.

Timing > * Initial approval is valid for 6 months from approval date.

* If you fail to renew the initial approval, it will expire within 10 days of the expiry date.

⚠ Since this procedure depends on many variables, and rules and procedures change, we strongly recommend you visit the Corporate Relations Department at the DED for assistance (see [p.215]).

2 Prerequisites

* Trade name has been selected (see Selecting a Trade Name [p.224])
* Appropriate premises have been selected
* Depending on the activity, additional special approval from the concerned authorities may be necessary (see Obtaining Special Approval for Business Activity [p.222])
* Must appoint a local service agent (see Appointing a Local Service Agent [p.245])

3 What to Bring

Initial approval >
☐ Registration and Licensing Application Form ('BR/1') (typed – Arabic and/or English)

☐ Trade Name Application Form ('BR/2') (typed)

☐ If applying for a professional business licence, the resume of the applicant proving qualifications ('BR/3') (typed)

☐ If commercial and industrial activity, approval of the Ministry of Economy & Planning and the Ministry of Finance & Industry

☐ If established by a company, the company's memorandum of association

☐ If applicable, no objection certificate from the government authorities according to the type of activity (see Obtaining Special Approval for Business Activity [p.222])

Fees >
☐ Dhs.100 – trade name registration fee

☐ Dhs.200 – initial approval fee

☐ Dhs.500 – DED express service fee (optional)

Final approval >
☐ Initial approval slip

☐ All documents mentioned above

☐ Tenancy agreement including plot number (copy)

☐ Sublease no objection letter from the Department of Real Estate of Dubai Government if the premises will be leased from or granted by Government of Dubai

☐ Local Service Agency agreement and documents proving that the agent is a UAE National or the company is fully UAE owned (see Appointing a Local Service Agent [p.245])

Fees >
☐ Dhs.100 – local fee

☐ Dhs.150 – wastage fee

☐ 5% of tenancy contract – Municipality tax

☐ Dhs.500 – registration fee

☐ Dhs.500 – charge per foreign company partner

4 Procedure

Location > DED Licensing Department   Map ref 8-H4

Hours > Sat – Wed 07:30 – 14:30

Initial approval >
• Go to the Licensing Counter on the first floor of the Department; take a ticket and wait for your number to be called

• Submit all documents and collect the application receipt (cash payment voucher) that will specify a date

Setting Up

Business

- Return to the Licensing Counter on the specified date and check if the application received initial approval
- If approved, go to the Cashier and pay the fee
- Return to the Licensing Counter and collect the initial approval receipt and all documents submitted
- If the department rejects the application, you have 15 days from the notification date to submit a grievance

Initial approval is valid for six months from date of approval. If you fail to renew the initial approval, it will expire within ten days of the expiry date.

Final Approval
- Go to the Municipality Planning Department Counter (first floor, DED) to request approval for the business premises
- If there are other licences on the proposed premises, go to the Inspection and Control Counter on the first floor
- Submit all required documents at the Licensing Counter; you will be given an application receipt and a date on which to return
- Return on the specified date to collect the 'fee payment voucher'
- Pay the fee at the Cashier and collect the licence

You will receive two sealed copies of the licence, one to be used for inscription in the Commercial Register and the other for registration with the Dubai Chamber of Commerce (see Registering with the DCCI [p.247])

Commercial Register
- Submit all documents and request inscription in the Commercial Register
- Once approval is granted, the company will be entered in the Commercial Register and have its Memorandum of Association published in the Ministry bulletin

5 Related Procedures

- Applying for an Establishment Immigration Card [p.253]
- Applying for an Establishment Labour Card [p.251]
- Applying for a Representative Card [p.255]

Appointing a Local Service Agent ('Sponsor')

1 Overview

By law, foreign nationals wanting to set up companies such as a sole proprietorship, a branch of a foreign company or a professional company, must find a National agent and sign a local (national) service agency agreement with him. The local agent is usually referred to as a 'sponsor'.

The sponsor will not have any responsibility towards the business but is obliged to assist with all government related procedures such as obtaining government permits, trade licences, visas and labour cards. His signature will be required for most application forms.

**dual/
npany
onsor**

A sponsor may be a UAE national or a company fully owned by UAE nationals. The choice of a sponsor can be of significant importance, especially for a bigger company. Appointing a sponsor who is considered prominent and influential can open many doors that may be difficult for others to open.

Local sponsors may be paid a lump sum and/or a percentage of the profits or turnover.

**ag the
onsor**

There is a lot of trust involved in this system. Before choosing a sponsor, it is highly advisable to first find out about his/her reputation etc.

⚠ It is very difficult to break a local service agency agreement.

alidity › One year, renewed automatically

2 Prerequisites

- The local service agent (sponsor) is a UAE national or a company 100% owned by UAE nationals

3 What to Bring

racts › ☐ Local Service Agent Contract (attested by notary public) (original & copy)

📄 In some cases the DED's 'Appointment Contract of a Local Service Agent' (Form 'BR/13') will be sufficient to make a contract. You can collect it from the DED or download it from www.dubaided.gov.ae. However, if a lot of money is involved and the agreements are more complicated, the owners may have a lawyer draft the contract which is more specific, especially regarding payment and other obligations.

**idual ›
gents**

☐ Passport and UAE naturalisation identification (copy)

**aany ›
ents**

☐ Documents proving that the company is fully UAE owned

☐ Its memorandum of association and articles of association (attested) (original and copy)

☐ Trade licence (copy)

Setting Up

Business

☐ Certificate of registration in the Commercial Register

☐ Passports and family books of all board members or partners (copy)

☐ Letter from the DED certifying that all partners of the selected company are UAE nationals

☐ If company incorporated in Dubai, the Chamber of Commerce (DCCI) certificate (copy)

☐ If company incorporated in another emirate, the memorandum of association (copy)

☐ An authorisation card

4 Procedure

Location › DED Licensing Department   Map ref 8-H4

Hours › Sat – Wed 07:30 – 14:30

• Sign and notarise the contract

Legalising the contract if setting up a Branch or Representative Office of a Foreign Company

• Legalise it by the foreign office of the country from which the parent company originates

• Authenticate it by the UAE Embassy in that country

• Authenticate it by the UAE Ministry of Foreign Affairs

• Translate it into Arabic by a translator registered with the Ministry of Justice and sealed by the notary public of the Dubai Courts Department (copy)

• The contract is ready to be submitted with the other documents required for setting up a company

5 Related Procedures

• Setting Up a Branch of a Foreign Company [p.227]

• Setting Up a Professional Company [p.242]

Registering with the Dubai Chamber of Commerce & Industry (DCCI)

1 Overview

In general, all commercial and industrial businesses in Dubai should be registered with the Dubai Chamber of Commerce and Industry. Companies in the free zones may register to be listed in the Chamber's Directory and use their services.

Validity > One year

2 Prerequisites

- Company has a commercial or industrial trade licence
- Applicant has commercial or industrial premises in Dubai
- Applicant is already operating the business
- Applicant, in the ten years prior to applying for membership, has not been declared bankrupt, or been convicted of theft, swindling, breach of trust, fraud or forgery

3 What to Bring

☐ Licence issued and ratified by the licensing authority (DED, JAFZA, DAFZA, etc (copy)

☐ Valid passport of the owner of the establishment (copy)

ational > ☐ Valid residence permit (copy)

Agent > ☐ Passport of the local agent (copy)

☐ Agency agreement (copy)

☐ Agency contract signed by the foreign company and the local agent (original and true copy)

☐ If the local agent is a company and registered as a member of the Chamber, a copy of the membership certificate with the DCCI

☐ If the local agent is not a registered member with the Chamber, a copy of the company's memorandum of association and professional licence, proving that all partners are Nationals

Sole > orship ☐ Passport of the manager of the establishment, or the authorised signatory

☐ Power of attorney, duly notarised (copy)

☐ Authorised signature cards completed and signed by the licencee, the manager or the local agent

☐ Completed special data form, depending on the company's business activity ('Industrial Firms Data Form', 'Contracting Firms Data Form', 'Hotel Classification Form')

LLC or > sional mpany ☐ Partnership contract (authenticated by the Notary Public at the Dubai Courts) (copy)

Setting Up

Business

☐ If partner is a company, the company memorandum (copy)

☐ If the partner company is a company incorporated in Dubai, the Chamber certificate (copy)

☐ If the partner company is a company incorporated in another emirate, the memorandum of association (copy)

If Partner is a Foreign Company ›

☐ An official certificate from the competent authorities with whom the foreign company is registered, showing that it is registered in that country in accordance with its laws, and stating the legal status of the company, its capital, the names of its officials, their functions and powers

☐ Resolution of foreign company's board of directors, with regard to opening a branch or representative office in Dubai, and the resolution to authorise the company's representative to apply for a licence, the documents having been ratified by the concerned government departments in the country of origin

☐ Passport copy of the company's representative

☐ Identical copy of the foreign company's memorandum of association and articles of association if it is a public or private joint stock company, authenticated by the concerned government department in the country of origin

☐ If company incorporated in the Jebel Ali Free Zone, the certificate of formation (copy)

☐ If company incorporated in another emirate, trade licence and the Chamber certificate (copy)

Branch of a Foreign Company ›

☐ Passport of the manager of the establishment, or the authorised signatory

☐ Notarised power of attorney (copy)

☐ Authorised signature cards completed and signed by the licencee, the manager or the local agent

☐ Completed special data form, depending on the company's business activity

☐ An official certificate from the competent authorities with whom the foreign company is registered, showing that it is registered in that country in accordance with its laws, and stating the legal status of the company, its capital, the names of its officials, their functions and powers

☐ Resolution of foreign company's board of directors, with regard to opening a branch or representative office in Dubai, and the resolution to authorise the company's representative to apply for a licence, the documents having been ratified by the concerned government departments in the country of origin

☐ Passport copy of the company's representative

☐ Identical copy of the foreign company's memorandum of association and articles of association if it is a public or private joint stock company, authenticated by the concerned government departments in the country of origin

Setting Up

Business

☐ Certificate of registration in the foreign companies register at the Ministry of Economy & Planning (copy) (except companies having professional licences and those incorporated in the free zones) (see Setting up a Branch of a Foreign Company [p.227])

4 Procedure

 Location › Dubai Chamber of Commerce   Map ref 8-G4

Hours › Sat – Wed 07:30 – 14:30

Registration › • Collect 'Application for Membership' form from the Chamber of Commerce

• The licencee, the manager or any authorised person may submit the documents at the Chamber of Commerce or at the Department of Economic Development

• The Chamber will make a preliminary check of the paperwork, the credentials and the information

• The annual fee is calculated and a 'Fees Payment Order' will be attached to the application form

• Pay the fee at the Cashier

Membership › • A Certificate of Membership will be issued at the company's request

• The company can also request an English version of the certificate or a 'To Whom It May Concern' certificate that certifies the membership with the Chamber

5 Related Procedures

• Applying for an Establishment Immigration Card [p.253]

• Applying for an Establishment Labour Card [p.251]

• Applying for Immigration and Labour Representative Cards [p.255]

Setting Up

Business

Setting Up

1 Overview

Every company registered with the DED and which has obtained a trade licence, must register with the Immigration Department and the Ministry of Labour. By doing that, the company opens a file at the departments, allowing the company to use their services, such as obtaining work permits for employees and settling any labour related disputes.

Registration must be done as soon as the company receives a trade licence. The authorities will check whether the new business fulfils certain requirements and if it is a working company.

The company must apply for the following cards:

- Establishment immigration card
- Establishment labour card
- Representative card

Main institutions involved		
Establishment Documents		**Page**
Immigration Card	Immigration Department	253
Labour Card	Ministry of Labour	251
Representative Card	Ministry of Labour	255
	Immigration Department	255

Go to these Ministries as early in the morning as possible to avoid the masses.

Prerequisites ▸ • PO Box (see Applying for a PO Box [p.118])

- Company stamp
- Telephone number (see Applying for a Telephone Line [p.82])
- Fax machine

Setting Up

Business

Applying for an Establishment Labour Card

[1] Overview

As soon as a company obtains its trade licence, it must apply for an establishment labour card. This card is issued by the Ministry of Labour and allows a company to hire staff, obtain work permits and apply for visas on the employees' behalf. By holding this card, the company is registered and has a file at the Labour office, with its own establishment number.

Validity > As long as the company exists.

[2] Prerequisites

- Company has received a trade licence
- Company has received an establishment immigration card (see [p.253])

[3] What to Bring

- ☐ Application form in Arabic with company stamp and signed by local partner or national agent (typed) (2 copies)
- ☐ Blank establishment labour card
- ☐ Blank signature authorisation card (2)
- ☐ Passport of the authorised signatories and the owners of the company (all passport details on one A4 sheet) (copy)
- ☐ Trade licence (2 copies & original)
- ☐ If sponsor wants to give authority to other persons to sign, special Ministry of Labour form to give power of attorney to other signatories
- ☐ Passport of sponsor (2 copies)
- ☐ National book of sponsor (2 copies)
- ☐ Service agency agreement (copy)
- ☐ If owner a GCC national, tenancy agreement (attested by notary public)
- ☐ If there are several partners/owners, a letter from the DED listing the names of the partners
- ☐ If applicable, the memorandum of association (copy)
- ☐ An illustrated map of the company location
- ☐ Tenancy contract of the company premises

Fees > ☐ Dhs.200 – signature authorisation card fee
- ☐ Dhs.100 – power of attorney form fee
- ☐ Dhs.1000 – opening a company file fee
- ☐ Dhs.50 – typist fee
- ☐ Dhs.10 – Ministry of Labour envelope

Immigration & Labour

Business

[4] Procedure

Location > Ministry of Labour   Map ref 10-E6

Hours > Sat – Wed 07:30 – 14:00

- Go to a typing office, fill out the relevant documents and pay the fees with e-Dirhams
- An authorised person must sign the forms and seal each with the company stamp
- Submit all documents at the Ministry of Labour
- Collect the card at the same time
- Either the establishment labour card or a rejection will be sent to the PO Box within 10 – 12 days

[5] Related Procedures

- Applying for an Establishment Immigration Card [p.253]
- Applying for Immigration and Labour Representative Cards [p.255]

Web Update

While Dubai's government is committed to cutting back on the red-tape involved in setting up in Dubai, both for individuals and businesses, changes in rules and regulations are inevitable. Therefore, if there have been any changes or additions to the procedures included in this book they will appear on the Explorer website. Just log on to **www.Explorer-Publishing.com** and click on the *Red-Tape* link. This page will tell you if there have been any changes to specific procedures – giving you the heads up before you head off to plough through Dubai's administrative maze!

Applying for an Establishment Immigration Card

1 Overview

Once a company has received the establishment labour card, it must open a file with the immigration department. The Immigration Card which is issued by the Immigration Department allows a company to recruit staff from abroad. Depending on the business activity of the company, it will also allow the company to apply for a 14-day transit visa (visa for a mission), visit visa and/or tourist visa for company clients and other business contacts. Some companies are not granted any visa privileges.

Validity > One, two or three years, renewable

2 Prerequisites

• Company has received the trade licence

3 What to Bring

☐ Completed establishment card application form in Arabic and English with company stamp and signed by local partner or national agent (typed) (2 copies each)

☐ Completed establishment card (2 copies)

☐ Trade licence (2 copies)

☐ Passport of the authorised signatories and the owners of the company (all passport details on one A4 sheet) (copy)

☐ If applicable, local service agent's passport (copy)

☐ If applicable, local service agent agreement (copy)

☐ Power of attorney of authorised signatories, notarised by the Court

☐ If an LLC Company, a memorandum of association or a 'To Whom It May Concern' certificate from the DED listing the partners' names

☐ If applicable, the partnership agreement (copy)

☐ An illustrated map of the company location

Fees > ☐ Dhs.200 – 300 per year – service fee (cash)

Renewal > ☐ All of the above documents

☐ Previous establishment card

Immigration & Labour

Business

[4 Procedure

Location> **Immigration Department**   Map ref 7-F4

Hours> Sat – Wed 07:30 – 14:30

- Go to a typing office, fill out the relevant documents and pay the fees with e-dirhams
- An authorised person must sign the forms and seal each with the company stamp
- Submit all documents at the Immigration Department
- Take a ticket with return date/time
- Collect establishment immigration card upon approval on that day

Renewal> • To renew the card, follow the same procedure

[5 Related Procedures

- Applying for an Establishment Labour Card [p.251]
- Applying for Immigration and Labour Representative Cards [p.253]

Info 'Staffing'

For companies operating outside the free zones, the Ministry of Labour will set a maximum number of expatriate staff that may be hired, according to the size of business and business activity. In some cases, such as banks, the Ministry will state the minimum percentage of employees that must be UAE Nationals. Actually recruiting your staff is a whole other kettle of fish – and there isn't always that many fish in the sea (worth catching). Various agencies can assist with recruitment within the UAE (head-hunting firms are increasing in numbers) or internationally.

Applying for Immigration & Labour Representative Cards

1 Overview

These two cards, sometimes also referred to as 'PRO cards', allow a selected individual to deal on behalf of the company with the Immigration and Labour Departments. Companies usually hire someone who specialises in these procedures. This person is called the PRO (Public Relations Officer).

Validity> Labour representative card: two years

Immigration representative card: one to three years

2 Prerequisites

- The company already has establishment labour and immigration cards
- The representative is employed by the company.

The PRO can work for several companies as long as he has the same sponsor

3 What to Bring

Both> ☐ Trade licence (copy)

☐ Representative's passport (copy)

☐ Representative's labour card (copy)

☐ Passport photographs of the representative (two)

Labour> ☐ Application form

☐ Establishment labour card

Fees> ☐ Dhs.400 – registration fee (e-Dirham)

☐ Dhs.10 – typing fee

ration> ☐ Application form

☐ Establishment immigration card

Fees> ☐ Dhs.200 – annual registration fee

☐ Dhs.100 – urgent fee (optional)

☐ Dhs.10 – typing fee

Immigration & Labour

Business

[4] Procedure

Location > Ministry of Labour   Map ref 10-E6

Hours > Sat – Wed 07:00 – 14:00

- Complete both the application form and representative card at a typist office
- Both the sponsor and representative must sign and stamp the forms
- Submit documents at the Labour Office
- Collect the representative card one week later

Location > Immigration Department   Map ref 7-F4

Hours > Sat – Wed 07:30 – 14:30

- Complete both the application form and representative card at a typist office
- The sponsor must sign and stamp the forms
- Submit documents at the Immigration Department
- Return to collect the representative card

Free Zones > Employees of companies in the free zones have different sponsorship options, depending on the free zone. An employee is sponsored by the Free Zone authority itself. In each case, the free zone authorities will handle the processing of your visa through the Immigration Department and, generally, they seem to be able to process your visa very quickly. Once Immigration has stamped your residence permit in your passport, some free zone authorities will issue a labour card. Both your permit and your labour card are valid for three years.

Info 'Work Permits'

The employer is responsible for all the work permits and related immigration procedures, which unfortunately can be a tedious and lengthy process so you can expect your PRO to be very busy in the beginning. If you are setting up in a free zone, the free zone authority will handle all immigration procedures – this simplifies the setting-up stage dramatically but costs slightly more. The company must cover all costs (visa, medical test, etc) when hiring a employee. But if your new employee happens to already be on a a residence permit (ie. sponsored by their spouse), the costs (and hassle) are lower. So look out for those untapped wives and mothers!

Appointing a Commercial Agent

1 Overview

If a foreign company wants to supply goods and/or services from abroad without establishing a physical presence in Dubai, it can either do so through an appropriately licenced importer on a supply-of-goods arrangement (sale and purchase basis), or through a commercial agent/distributor for its goods and/or services in the UAE. The agent is entitled to statutory exclusive rights to distribute and market specific products and services within a specific territory. The company is not allowed to distribute these products in that territory. If the company does assist in a sale, its commercial agent is entitled to a commission.

Such a commercial agency also covers franchises, distributorships and commission arrangements. The agent must register the agency agreement with the Ministry of Economy & Planning.

Generally, entities established/formed in free zones can only sell goods into the UAE through UAE-based entities that have an appropriate licence to import into the UAE or through a commercial agent/distributor.

It can be difficult to terminate the agency agreement. Although the contract may be limited to a specific timespan, the agreement can be terminated in two ways:

• One can directly seek termination by going to the Commercial Agency Committee at the Ministry of Economy & Planning.

• If you are not satisfied with the committee decision, you can also go directly to court and seek termination of the agency relationship. Note that one is not required to go to the committee before seeking a court decision.

It is very important to be careful in choosing the right agent.

Generally, a commercial agency which is not registered at the Ministry of Economy & Planning will not be recognised and no actions will be entertained by the courts in respect of an unregistered agency.

A foreign company may seek the services of one agent for the whole of the UAE, or may appoint a different agent for each emirate or for each of its products.

Commercial Agent

Business

[2 Prerequisites

- The agent must be a UAE national or a wholly owned UAE entity incorporated in the UAE
- The agent must be listed in the register of commercial agents kept by the UAE Ministry of Economy and Planning

Agency Agreement > Must be in writing, and must include the following:

- The name, nationality and address of the agent and the principal
- If the agent is a commercial company, the company's name, type (legal form), head office and UAE branch addresses, and its capital amount
- Listing of the products, commodities and services covered by the commercial agency
- The territory that the agreement covers
- The date on which the agreement is to come into effect
- The duration of the agency and provisions in the event of default
- The agency agreement must be notarised, legalised by the Foreign Ministry and authenticated by the UAE Embassy in the country in which it is executed

[3 What to Bring

- ☐ Agent's trade licence and commercial register entry certificate (original and copy)
- ☐ Authenticated commercial agency agreement (original and copy)

Fee > ☐ Dhs.400 (registration fee)

Company Agency > ☐ Memorandum of association (certified copy plus one copy)
- ☐ Passport and family book of each partner (copy) or a certificate proving that the company is owned entirely by UAE nationals (original & copy)

Individual Agency > ☐ Passport and family book of the trade agent (copy)

☐ All documents must be translated into Arabic and certified

Commercial Agent

Business

4 Procedure

Location > Ministry of Economy & Planning   Map ref 9-A6

Hours > Sat – Wed 07:30 – 14:30

Commercial Agreement >
- Draft a notarised commercial agency agreement, which includes the information outlined above
- Write the agreement in Arabic or have it translated into Arabic by a translator licenced by the UAE Ministry of Justice

Signing outside the UAE >
- Have commercial agency agreement between agent and principal drafted in English and translated into Arabic by translator licenced by the UAE Ministry of Justice.
- Notarise the agreement here in Dubai, or in the country of the principal, and any documents that give the signatory authorisation to sign on the principal's behalf.
- If notarised in the country of the principal, be sure the agreement is authorised at the UAE embassy in the country of the principal.
- If drafted in Dubai, get it attested at the Ministry of Foreign Affairs.
- Register the agency at the Ministry of Economy & Planning's Commercial Agency Register.
- Submit the above commerical agency agreement, application form and legal documents of agent and principal to the Ministry of Economy & Planning and pay the required fees.
- The Ministry will reply within 15 days of application
- If the registration is accepted, the agent will receive an authenticated certificate confirming the registration
- Details of the registration will be published in the Ministry's Official Gazette
- If registration is not accepted, the Ministry must provide reasons for its refusal

5 Related Procedures

- Obtaining special approval for business activity [p.222]
- Options for Non-nationals & foreign companies [p.226]

Commercial Agent

Business

Free Zone Overview

1 Overview

In a concentrated effort to attract foreign investment, several free trade zones have been established in and around Dubai. Unique laws regarding ownership, taxation, recruitment of labour, and income repatriation apply to these areas. A further advantage of free zones is the assistance they provide in incorporating or setting up companies within them. Such benefits make these zones ideal for companies wishing to establish a distribution, manufacturing, storage or service base for trade outside of the UAE.

The Jebel Ali Free Zone (JAFZA), established in 1985, was the first such entity in the Emirates. Based on its success, other free zones have sprung up around Dubai, including the Airport Free Zone, Internet and Media Cities and Dubai Healthcare City, while Ajman, Fujairah, Hamriya, Sharjah and Abu Dhabi have all incorporated their own versions of this popular model. While each of these follows JAFZA's lead, they also have their own unique base of customers, services and benefits. This makes for a vast amount of flexibility and packages available to those wishing to set up businesses in the area.

Business > Environment

Legally, companies based in free zones are seen as 'offshore', giving them the luxury of full ownership. In other words, no local sponsorship is required. There are many additional benefits, but the most attractive are tax exemption and 100% repatriation of profit and capital. Offshore status also means that companies wishing to trade in Dubai or the Emirates will often have to work through a commercial agent or distributor.

Most free zones are equipped with state-of-the-art facilities, and offer a great deal of administrative support. In some, companies can also purchase lease-hold property on which to build their own offices, warehouses or manufacturing centres.

Licences available at the four main Dubai free zones

	Trade Licences	Service Licences	Industrial Licences	National Industrial Licences
JAFZA	Yes	Yes	Yes	Yes
DAFZA	Yes	Yes	Yes	No
DIC	Yes	Yes	No	No
DMC	Yes	Yes	No	No

Application procedure ›

When setting up a company or office in a free zone, the applicant deals mostly with the free zone authority on the premises. For an administrative charge, they will assist with all government procedures, such as obtaining the necessary permits and visas. This cuts time significantly and saves a good deal of headache.

Company and Office Types ›

The following companies can be set up in the free zones:

- Free zone establishment or company (a company incorporated in and regulated by a free zone)
- Branch of a foreign company
- Branch of a UAE company

A company must apply for a trade licence depending on the type of business activity. Not all free zones offer all types of licences. See the table on [p.260] for a quick overview.

Free Zone Establishment ›

- 100% foreign owned
- Similar to an LLC
- Single shareholder option
- Minimum capital requirement
- Liability is limited to the amount of the paid capital

Free Zones in the UAE

Free Zone	Telephone	Websites
Ajman		
Ajman Free Zone Authority	06 742 5444	www.ajmanfreezone.gov.ae
Dubai		
Dubai Airport Free Zone (DAFZA)	299 5555	www.dafza.gov.ae
Dubai Internet City (DIC)	391 1111	www.dubaiinternetcity.com
Dubai Media City (DMC)	391 4615	www.dubaimediacity.com
Jebel Ali Free Zone (JAFZA)	881 5000	www.jafza.co.ae
Fujairah		
Fujairah Free Zone	09 222 8000	www.fujairahfreezone.com
Sharjah		
Hamriyah Free Zone	06 526 3333	www.hamriyahfz.com
Sharjah Airport International Free Zone	06 557 0000	www.saif-zone.com
Ras Al Khaimah		
Ras Al Khaimah Free Zone (RAK FZ)	07 228 0889	www.rakiftz.com
Umm Al Quwain		
Shk Ahmed Bin Rashid Port & Free Zone	06 765 5882	www.uaefreezones.com

Free Zone

Business

Setting up in Jebel Ali Free Zone (JAFZA)

1 Overview

Laying claim to the largest man-made port in the world, the Jebel Ali Free Zone (JAFZA) is the original free zone established in the UAE. It is also the biggest, with well over 2,200 companies from some 100 countries. Most of the companies in JAFZA are involved with some form of distribution, but a number of manufacturers and a few service providers have chosen to take advantage of the site's facilities and services.

A massive and well-established infrastructure, and an enormous physical area a few minutes south of Dubai allows JAFZA to offer its customers a range of facilities, from individual office units to land sites where companies can construct their own offices, warehouses or manufacturing operations. Customers also have access to on-site staff accommodation, customs and banking, among other services and facilities, making it an attractive option for a diverse array of companies and establishments.

Setting up in the Jebel Ali Free Zone is designed to be a straightforward and relatively simple procedure. Requirements will differ slightly depending on the type of licence required.

Licence Types › Different types of companies will require different licences depending on the nature of their business. It should be noted that companies whose activities fall under different categories are required to carry separate licences for each.

Trading Licence › Allows the import, export, sale, distribution and storage of goods. Distribution of goods within the UAE may have to be made by an agent or distributor (see Appointing a Commercial Agent [p.245])

Industrial Licence › Allows the import of raw materials, manufacture of products and export of the finished goods. Distribution of goods within the UAE may have to be made by an agent or distributor (see Appointing a Commercial Agent [p.245])

Service Licence › Allows the holder to carry out specific services within the free zone as per their parent company, which must be registered in the UAE and have a valid UAE licence.

National Industrial Licence › Allows the import of raw materials, manufacture of products, and export of the finished goods.

Ownership must be at least 51% GCC national, and the value added in the free zone must be a minimum of 40%. This licence gives the holder the same rights as a local or GCC licence. These companies qualify for customs duty exemption on products imported into GCC states.

Free Zone Establishment Free Zone Company ⟩ FZEs and FZCOs are separate legal entities regulated by the free zone authority which can be 100% foreign owned, with limited liability for their owners, and can operate independently from their shareholders. Such companies hold whichever of the above licence(s) are applicable to their business.

Validity ⟩ Licences are valid for one year, and are renewable annually for the extent of the company's lease, provided that certain requirements are met.

To hold any JAFZA licence, a company must have valid registration from either the DED (or equivalent authority) or the JAFZA Authority, or incorporation outside of the UAE. Individual or additional prerequisites are as follows. Companies are also subject to applicable Federal and Municipal laws, as well as the rules and regulations of the free zone.

Trade Licence ⟩ • Company is a free zone establishment, was established outside the UAE or holds a valid licence from the DED

Industrial Licence ⟩ • Company is a free zone establishment or was established outside the UAE

Service Licence ⟩ • Company is already registered in the UAE as a service company
- Service provided must be the same as that named in the parent company's licence
- Provision of services will only be within the free zone

National Industrial Licence ⟩ • Company must be a manufacturing enterprise
- Company must be registered either outside or within the UAE
- Must be at least 51% UAE or GCC owned

☐ At least 25% UAE ownership is required for a certificate of origin issued by the Ministry of Economy & Planning

☐ The UAE value-added input must be at least 40% of the total value of the product

Free Zone Entity ⟩ • Minimum capital requirement: Dhs.1 million for a FZE, and Dhs.500,000 for a FZCO

Charges ⟩ • FZE – Dhs.10,000; FZCO Dhs.15,000
- No licence from DED required
- Any activity, but only in the free zone and/or outside the UAE

Free Zone

Business

3 What to Bring

- ☐ Completed 'Application for Licence' form (downloaded from www.jafza.co.ae/frame-app.htm)
- ☐ One page summary of proposed project
- ☐ Supporting documentation such as company or product brochures (optional)

4 Procedure

Location › JAFZA Sales Department   Map ref 1-B4

Hours › Sat – Wed 07:30 – 14:30

Initial Approval ›
- Submit the application form and one page proposal
- After an initial assessment, JAFZA will give provisional approval and detail which documents will be required next

Legal documents are required. All documents must be notarised by a notary public in the country of origin and attested by the local consulate or a recognised embassy
- JAFZA will review availability of facilities and prepare a proforma lease agreement and possibly a personnel secondment agreement
- Applicant must sign the proforma agreement

FZE/FZCO ›
- Deposit share capital
- JAFZA will issue a certificate of formation and share certificates

Lease Agreement ›
- JAFZA prepares the final lease agreement
- Both parties sign the final agreement
- Applicant pays required licence and rental fees

Fees are contingent on licensing and leasing agreements
- JAFZA prepares and issues the licence

Post Licensing ›
- If required, the free zone will assist with immigration matters
- If construction for factory, storage or other structure is involved, plans must be submitted after licence issued

Free Zone

Business

Setting Up in Dubai Internet City (DIC)

1 Overview

Dubai Technology, E-Commerce & Media Free Zone (TECOM)

Comprising Dubai Internet City (DIC) and Dubai Media City (DMC) (see Setting Up in DMC [s68]) and the Knowledge Village, TECOM has established itself as the hub of a vibrant new regional economy.

Situated 15 minutes from the World Trade Centre on Sheikh Zayed Road, new buildings are being quickly added to catch up with demand for office space.

Dubai Internet City opened in late 2000, and was heralded as the first information technology and telecommunications centre within a free trade zone. Aimed at attracting and supporting information and communications technology, DIC has developed the Middle East's most advanced IT infrastructure, which has drawn IT giants such as Microsoft and IBM, as well as branch offices and smaller companies including local software developers and service providers.

Facilities are geared for service and development companies; hence warehouses and manufacturing facilities are not available. Available office space starts at 600 square feet and optional land leases are available. Additionally, accommodation, retail outlets and restaurants are found (or are soon to be found) within the confines of Internet City.

DIC has gone to great lengths to insure a relatively hassle-free incorporation process.

ompany〉 • Branch of a foreign company
  • Branch of a UAE-based company (including other UAE free zone licensees)
  • Free zone limited liability company (FZ LLC)
  • Established by an individual
  • Established by an entity (company)

2 Prerequisites

Company belongs to one of the following sectors:
  • ASP
  • Consultancy
  • IT Support
  • Sales & Marketing
  • Software Development
  • Web-based

  ☐ Businesses from other related sectors may contact the DIC Commercial Division and explain how the company would fit into the DIC community

Free Zone

Business

[3] What to Bring

Required documents will depend on the type of company to be incorporated

☐ Completed application form collected from the DIC Commercial Division or downloaded from www.dubaiinternetcity.com (typed or hand-written; English/Arabic)

☐ The person signing the application form must be officially authorised to do so and must be able to show proof of this authority

☐ Business proposal with the following points clearly stated:
- Description of the business
- Products/Services
- Role of DIC location
- Marketing
- Target Marketing
- Market segment
- Competition
- Operating procedures
- Personnel
- CV of the owners, if individuals
- Financial data

☐ Company board resolution specifying the establishment of a branch/FZ company (FZ-LLC) in the Dubai Technology Electronic Commerce and Media Free Zone and appointing a manager (notarised)

☐ Manager's passport (copy)

Branch › ☐ Memorandum/articles of association of the company (notarised) (copy)

☐ Specimen signature of the manager (notarised)

☐ If branch of a foreign company, current company registration certificate (copy) or certificate of good standing (original) (authenticated)

☐ If branch of a UAE company, current commercial registration and trade licence (copy)

FZ-LLC › ☐ Proof of minimum capital requirement from a UAE registered bank (Dhs.500,000) (notarised)

☐ Manager's, director's and secretary's signature specimens (notarised) and valid passports (copy)

Free Zone

Business

Individual ❯ ☐ Applicant's personal profile

☐ Banker's reference (original) (notarised)

☐ Business proposal

Multiple ❯ ☐ Current authenticated certificate of company registration (copy) or certificate of good standing (original)

☐ Memorandum and articles of association (authenticated)

☐ Power of attorney to a negotiator or legal representative

☐ Specimen of manager's signature

☐ Manager's valid passport (copy)

4 Procedure

Location ❯ DIC, Commercial/Account Management   Map ref 3- B3

Hours ❯ Sun – Thu 08:00 – 17:00

* Submit the application for review
* If approved, DIC will issue a provisional approval letter listing the required legal documents and a submission deadline
* DIC will also issue a personnel sponsorship agreement (PSA), employment contract, specimen lease agreement, and general terms and conditions of the sponsorship agreement
* Submit all required legal documents
* DIC will review all documents
* Upon approval, DIC issues a final approval letter with the details of the office space, an invoice for the 20% deposit and licence fee, and a sample of the lease agreement
* Applicant pays fee upon acceptance of the PSA
* Upon payment, DIC will issue the lease agreement
* The authorised person has one week to sign the lease agreement and PSA
* DIC issues the licence

Free Zone

Business

Setting Up in Dubai Media City (DMC)

[1] Overview

Next to Dubai Internet City, Dubai Media City has been established to facilitate operation for all manners of company in the media industry. In early 2001, Dubai Media City opened its doors, offering and guaranteeing (within the country's moral code) freedom of expression without censorship for its tenants. Since then, expansion has been rapid, adding several more media companies and facilities to accommodate them.

DMC offers clients access to a global interconnected network supporting print, television, radio, film and web-based media ventures within an attractive complex of inspired architecture featuring landscaped lakes and dining facilities. Additional free zone benefits of full foreign ownership and tax exemptions are also included as benefits of incorporating within Media City.

Target > Companies in the following fields are encouraged to become 'Media Companies City Partners': broadcasting, communication, music, new media, post-production, production and publishing.

Company Options Within DMC:

• Branch of a UAE or non-UAE company

• New company: free zone establishment-limited liability company (FZE-LLC)

• Media business centre office (open or private serviced offices with administrative support) as a freelancer or a company

[2] Prerequisites

• Company activity belongs to any type of media discipline (i.e. communication, broadcasting, music, production, publishing, or new media)

• Company is not trading in goods (companies needing storage can rent a warehouse in Dubai)

[3] What to Bring

☐ As always, all documents, especially copies, should be notarised and attested

Company > ☐ Completed application and partner registration forms Branch downloaded from www.dubaimediacity.com

☐ Business plan/company profile/planned business proposal

☐ Partners' and manager's passports (copy)

☐ Banker's reference

☐ Power of attorney (if required)

☐ Certificate of registration of the company and the trade licence

☐ Memorandum & articles of association

☐ Board resolution calling for establishment at Dubai Media City

Newly › Incorporated company ☐ Completed application and partner registration forms downloaded from www.dubaimediacity.com

☐ Business plan/company profile/planned business proposal

☐ Partners' and manager's passports (copy)

☐ Banker's reference

☐ Power of attorney (if required)

4 Procedure

Location › DMC Commercial/Account Management   Map ref 3-A3

Hours › Sun – Thu 08:00 – 17:00

• Submit the application forms and attach all relevant documents listed above

• Book office space in one of the commercial buildings, or lease land for development

• Make necessary payments to secure office space within three days of the booking date

• Sign the lease agreement, and submit along with two post-dated cheques for the rent (the first dated as per the commencement date on the lease agreement for the first eight months of occupancy; the second post-dated for the remaining four months)

Info New Free Zones

Knowledge Village and Dubai International Financial Centre

There are a number of licensing options for educational facilities that want to set up in Knowledge Village, Dubai's educational free zone. You can set up a Free Zone Limited Liability Company (FZ LLC), a Branch of a Local or Foreign Company or you can apply for a freelance permit. For more information visit www.kv.ae.

Dubai International Financial Centre (DIFC), an onshore capital market and financial free zone hopes to attract international business and will consider licence applications from financial institutions in banking services, capital markets, asset management & fund registration, reinsurance, Islamic Finance and back office operations. For more information visit www.difc.ae.

Free Zone

Business

Made with hand luggage in mind

Don't be fooled by its diminutive size, this perfectly pocket proportioned visitors' guide is packed with insider info on travel essentials, shopping, sports and spas, exploring, dining out and nightlife.

Business

Accountants - Chartered

AF Ferguson & Co.	331 8856
AGN MAK Chartered Certified Accountants	228 3008
Ernst & Young	331 4035
Grant Thornton	268 8070
Griffin Nagda & Company	222 2537
Kant & Clients Auditors & Chartered Acountants	221 2168
Pricewaterhouse Coopers	304 3100
Spicer & Pegler	331 3399
Tri Hospitality Consulting	345 4241

Airports

Abu Dhabi International Airport	02 575 7500
Al Ain International Airport	03 785 5555
DNATA Export Office	211 1111
Dubai Cargo Village	211 1111
Dubai International Airport	224 5555
Fujairah International Airport	09 222 6222
Ras al Khaimah International Airport	07 244 8111
Sharjah International Airport	06 558 1111

Business Councils

American Business Council	331 4735
Australian Business in the Gulf (ABIG)	395 4423
British Business Group	397 0303
Canadian Business Council	359 2625
Denmark Business Council	222 7699
French Business Council	335 2362
German Business Council	359 9930
Iranian Business Council	344 4717
Pakistan Business Council	337 2875
South African Business Group	050 653 2469
Swedish Business Council	337 1410
Swiss Business Council	321 1438

Commercial Banks
@ ...E-Dirham available

ABN AMRO Bank	351 2200
Abu Dhabi Commercial Bank @	345 0000
Abu Dhabi National Bank	02 666 6800
Al Ahli Bank	222 4175
Algemene Bank Nederland	351 2200
Arab Bank for Investment & Foreign Trade @	221 2100
Arab Bank Ltd.	222 8845
Bank Banorab	228 4655
Bank Melli Iran	226 8207
Bank of Sharjah	282 7278
Bank Pariba	222 5200

Commercial Banks (Contd.)

Bank Saderat Iran	222 1161
Banque Du Caire S.A.E.	222 5175
Banque Indosuez	331 4211
Banque Libannaise Pour Le Commerce	222 2291
Barclays Bank Plc	335 1555
Citibank	800 4000
Dubai Commercial Bank @	352 3355
Emirates Bank International	225 6256
Habib Bank AG Zurich	221 4535
Habib Bank Limited	226 8171
HSBC Bank Middle East	353 5000
Lloyds TSB Bank Plc	342 2000
Mashreq Bank @	222 9131
Middle East Bank	800 4644
National Bank of Dubai @	222 2111
National Bank of Ras Al Khaimah	222 6291
National Bank of Sharjah @	06 568 1000
Royal Bank of Canada	222 5226
Standard Chartered	800 4949
Standard Chartered Grindlays	508 8111
Union Bank Ltd.	355 2020
Union National Bank @	800 2600
United Arab Bank	222 0181
Wardly Middle East Ltd.	222 1126

Courier Services

Aramex International	282 2578
DHL International	800 4004
Federal Express	265 5333
Memo Express	336 4400
Overseas Courier Services	262 5757
TNT Skypack International	285 3939
UPS Worldwide	800 4774

Hotels

Airport Hotel	282 3464
Al Bustan Rotana Hotel	282 0000
Al Khaleej Holiday Hotel	227 6565
Al Khaleej Palace Hotel	223 1000
Al Maha Resort	303 4224
Ambassador Hotel	393 9444
Astoria Hotel	353 4300
Burj Al Arab	301 7777
Capitol Hotel	346 0111
Century Hotel	352 0900
City Centre Hotel	294 1222
Comfort Inn	222 7393
Crowne Plaza	331 1111
Dubai Grand	263 2555
Dubai International Airport Hotel	282 4780

Business Directory

Directory

Hotels	(Contd.)
Dubai Marine Beach Resort	346 1111
Dubai Palm Hotel	271 0021
Dubai Park Hotel	399 2222
Dusit Dubai	343 3333
Emirates Towers Hotel	330 0000
Fairmont Hotel	332 5555
Four Point Sheraton	397 7444
Hatta Fort Hotel	852 3211
Hilton Dubai Creek	227 1111
Hilton Dubai Jumeirah	399 1111
Holiday Inn Bur Dubai	336 6000
Holiday Inn Downtown	228 8889
Hyatt Regency Hotel	209 1234
Imperial Suites Hotel	351 5100
Inter-Continental Dubai	222 7171
Jebel Ali Hotel & Golf Resort	883 6000
Jumeirah Beach Club	344 5333
Jumeirah Beach Hotel	348 0000
Jumeira Rotana Hotel	345 5888
JW Marriott Hotel	262 4444
Le Meridien Dubai	282 4040
Le Meridien Beach Resort	399 5555
Le Meridien Mina Seyahi	399 3333
London Crown Hotel	351 8888
Lotus Hotel	222 1111
Marco Polo Hotel	272 0000
Metropolitan Hotel	343 0000
Metropolitan Palace Hotel	227 0000
Metropolitan Resort	399 5000
Oasis Beach Hotel	399 4444
Palm Beach Rotana Inn	393 1999
Ramada Continental	266 2666
Ramada Hotel	351 9999
Regent Palace Hotel	396 3888
Renaissance Hotel	262 5555
Ritz-Carlton Dubai	399 4000
Royal Mirage	399 9999
Rydges Plaza Hotel	398 2222
Sea Shell Inn	393 4777
Sheraton Deira	268 8888
Sheraton Dubai & Towers	228 1111
Sheraton Jumeira Beach Resort	399 5533
Towers Rotana Hotel	343 8000
World Trade Centre Hotel	331 4000

Insurance Companies	
Alliance	605 1111
Axa Insurance	800 2924
Eagle Star International Life	397 4444
Nasco Karaoglan Group	352 3133
National General Insurance Co.	222 2772
New India Assurance Co.	352 5563
Norwich Union Insurance (Gulf)	324 3434

Insurance Companies	(Contd.)
Northern Assurance Co.	331 8400
Oman Insurance Co.	262 4000
Royal International Insurance Holdings	336 6551
Sedgewick Forbes Middle East	331 3265
United Insurance Brokers (UIB)	294 0842

Legal Consultants	
Afridi & Angell	331 0900
Allen & Overy	332 3190
Al Owais & Manfield	221 9000
Al Tamimi & Co	331 7090
Barahim	228 4399
Clifford Chance	331 4333
Clyde & Co	331 1102
Denton Wilde Sapte	331 0220
Emirates Advocates	330 4343
Hadef Al Dhahiri & Associates	**332 3222**
Hill Taylor Dickinson	331 7788
James Berry & Associates	351 1020
Key & Dixon	359 0096
Nabulsi Legal Consultants	222 3004
Naji Beidoun & Associates	222 5151
Simmons & Simmons	02 627 5568
Stockwell & Associates	228 3194
Towry Law Group	335 3137
Trench & Associates	355 3146

Ports	
Dubai Ports Authority	345 1545
Jebel Ali Terminal	881 5000
Khor Fakkan Port	09 238 5324
Mina Saqr	07 266 8444
Mina Zayed Seaport Authority	02 673 0600
Port Fujairah	09 222 8800
Port Khaled	06 528 1666
Port Rashid Terminal	345 1545
Sharjah Ports Authority	06 528 2216
Umm al-Qaiwain Port	06 765 5882

Trade Centres & Commissions	
American Business Council	331 4735
Australian Trade Commission	331 3444
British Embassy - Commercial Section	397 1070
Canadian Trade Commission	352 1717
Cyprus Trade Centre	228 2411
Danish Trade Centre	222 7699
Egyptian Trade Centre	222 1098
Export Promotion Council of Norway	353 3833
French Trade Commission	222 4250

Business Directory

Directory

Directory

Trade Centres & Commissions

German Office of Foreign Trade	352 0413
Hong Kong Trade Development	223 3499
Indian State Trading Corporation	227 1270
Indian Trade Centre	393 5208
Italian Trade Commission	331 4951
Japan External Trade Organisation	332 8264
Korean Trade Centre	222 0643
Malaysian Govt. Trade Centre	331 9994
Philippine Embassy - Commercial Section	223 6526
Polish Trade Centre	223 5837
Romanian Trade Representation	394 0580
Singapore Trade Centre	222 9789
Spanish Commercial Office	331 3565
Sultanate of Oman Office	397 1000
Taiwan Trade Centre	396 7814
Thailand Trade Centre	228 4553
Trade Representative of the Netherlands	352 8700
USA Consulate General - Commercial Section	331 3584

Cars

Driving Institutes

Al Hamriya Driving School	269 9259
Dubai Driving School	271 7654
Emirates Driving Institute	263 1100

New Cars

Alpha Romeo	Gargash Motors	266 4669
Audi	Al Nabooda Automobiles	285 1091
BMW	AGMC	339 1212
Cadillac	Liberty Automobiles	282 4440
Chrysler	Trading Enterprises	295 4246
Chevrolet	Al Yousuf Motors	339 5555
Daewoo	Al Yousuf Motors	339 5555
Dodge	Trading Enterprises	295 4246
Ferrari	Al Tayer Motors	282 5000
Fiat	Al Ghandi Auto	266 6511
Ford	Al Tayer Motors	282 5000
Galloper	Al Habtoor Motors	269 1110
GMC	Liberty Automobiles	282 4440
Honda	Trading Enterprises	295 4246
Isuzu	Genavco Llc	396 1000
Hyundai	Juma Al Majid	269 0893
Jaguar	Al Tayer Group	282 5000
Jeep	Trading Enterprises	295 4246
Kia	Al Majed Motors	268 6460
Land Rover	Al Tayer Group	282 5000
Lexus	Al Futtaim Motors	228 2261
Mazda	Galadari Automobiles	299 4848

New Cars (Contd.)

Mercedes	Gargash Enterprises	269 9777
Mitsubishi	Al Habtoor Motors	269 1110
Nissan	Arabian Automobiles	295 1234
Opel	Liberty Automobiles	282 4440
Porsche	Al Nabooda Automobiles	285 1091
Rolls Royce	Al Habtoor Motors	269 1110
Skoda	Autostar Trading	269 7100
Toyota	Al Futtaim Motors	228 2261
Volkswagen	Al Nabooda Automobiles	285 1091
Volvo	Trading Enterprises	295 4246

Used Cars

4 x 4 Motors	Opp Al Bustan Rotana	282 3050
Autoplus	Sheikh Zayed Road	339 5400
Boston Cars	Aweer	333 1010
Car Store, The	Sheikh Zayed Road	343 5245
House of Cars	Sheikh Zayed Road	343 5060
Motor World	Nr. Ports & Customs	333 2206
Off Road Motors	Jct 3, Sheikh Zayed Rd	338 4866
Quality Cars	Trading Enterprises	295 4246

Education

Nurseries & Pre-Schools

De La Salle Montessori International	398 6218
Dubai Infants School	337 1463
French Children's Nursery House	349 6868
Jumeirah Infants Nursery School	349 9065
Kids' Island Nursery	394 2578
Ladybird Nursery	344 1011
Little Land	394 4471
Little Star Nursery	398 2004
Palms	394 7017
Safa Kindergarten	344 3878
Super Kids Nursery	**288 1949**
Tiny Home Montessori Nursery	**349 3201**
Yellow Brick Road Nursery	282 8290

Primary & Secondary Schools

American School of Dubai	344 0824
Cambridge High School	282 4646
Deira Private School	282 4082
Dubai College	399 9111
Dubai English Speaking School	337 1457
Emirates International School	348 9804
English College	394 3465
International School of Choueifat	399 9444
Jebel Ali Primary School	884 6485
Jumeira English Speaking School	394 5515
Jumeira Primary School	394 3500
School of Research Science	298 8776

Embassies

Embassies/Consulates	
Algeria	02 444 8949
Argentina	02 443 6838
Australia	331 3444
Austria	02 626 7755
Bahrain	02 665 7500
Bangladesh	272 7553
Belgium	02 631 9449
Brazil	02 666 5352
Canada	352 1717
China	398 4357
Denmark	222 7699
Egypt	397 1122
Finland	02 632 8927
France	332 9040
Germany	397 2333
India	397 1222
Iran	344 4717
Italy	331 4167
Japan	02 443 5696
Jordan	397 0500
Kuwait	222 1900
Lebanon	397 7450
Lithuania	344 1644
Malaysia	335 5528
Morocco	02 443 3963
Netherlands	352 8700
Norway	353 3833
Oman	02 446 3333
Pakistan	397 0412
Palestine	397 2363
Panama	226 3366
People's Republic of China	398 3167
Philippines	02 634 5664
Poland	02 446 5200
Qatar	398 4456
Romania	394 0580
Russia	02 672 1797
Saudi Arabia	266 3383
Slovakia	02 623 1674
Somalia	02 666 9700
South Africa	397 5222
South Korea	02 443 5337
Spain	02 226 9544
Sri Lanka	02 642 6666
Sudan	02 666 6788
Sweden	345 7716
Switzerland	329 0999
Syria	266 3354
Thailand	349 2863
Tunisia	02 681 1331
Turkey	331 4788

Embassies/Consulates	(Contd.)
UK	397 1070
USA	331 3115
Uzbekistan	394 7400
Yemen	397 0213

UAE Embassies Abroad	
Algeria	00213 2154 9677
Australia	00612 62 86 8802
Austria	0043 1 368 1455/56
Bahrain	00973 72 3737
Bangladesh	008802 98 2277
Belgium	00322 640 6000
Brazil	0055 61 248 0717
Canada	**001** 613 565 7272
Egypt	0020 2 360 9722
France	0033 1 4553 9404
Germany	0049 228 26 7070
India	0091 11 687 2822
Indonesia	0062 21 520 6518
Iran	0098 21 878 8515
Italy	0039 6 3630 6100
Japan	081 3 5489 0183
Jordan	00962 6 593 4780
Korea	0082 2 790 3235
Kuwait	00965 252 6356
Lebanon	00961 1 85 7000
Libya	00218 21 483 2595
Malaysia	0060 3 4253 5221
Mauritania	00222 29 1098
Morocco	00212 37 70 2035
Oman	00968 60 0302
Pakistan	0092 51 227 9052
Pakistan - Consulate	0092 21 587 3819
Peoples' Republic of China	0086 10 8451 4416
Philippines	0063 2 818 9763
Qatar	00974 483 8880
Russia - CIS	007 095 237 4060
Saudi Arabia	00966 1 482 6803
South Africa	0027 12 342 7736
Spain	0034 91 570 1001
Sudan	0249 11 47 1094
Switzerland - Mission	0041 22 918 0000
Syria	00963 11 333 0308
Tunisia	00216 1 78 2737
Turkey	0090 312 447 6861
Turkey – Consulate	0090 212 27 8062
UK	0044 20 7581 1281
UK – Consulate	0044 20 7589 3434
USA	001 202 243 2400
Yemen	00967 1 24778

Embassy Directory

Directory

UAE Tourist Offices Abroad

Australia	0061 2 9956 6620
France	0033 1 4495 8500
Germany	0049 69 710 0020
Hong Kong	00852 2827 5221
India	0091 22 283 3497
Italy	0039 02 8691 3952
Japan	0081 3 3379 9311
Kenya	00254 2 246909
Russia	0070 95 248 7430
South Africa	0027 11 784 6708
Sweden	0046 8 411 1135
UK	0044 207 839 0580
USA, California	001 310 752 4488
USA, Pennsylvania	001 215 751 9750

Government Offices

Free Zones

Ajman Free Zone Authority	06 742 5444
Dubai Airport Free Zone Authority	299 5555
Fujairah Free Zone Authority	09 222 8000
Hamriya Free Zone Authority – Sharjah	06 526 3333
Jebel Ali Free Zone Authority	881 5000
RAK Free Zone	07 228 0889
Sharjah Airport Free Zone Authority	06 557 0000
Umm Al Quwain Ahmed Bin Rashid Free Zone Authority	06 765 5882

Government Departments in Dubai

Department of Civil Aviation	224 5333
Department of Economic Development	222 9922
Department of Health & Medical Services	337 0031
Department of HH the Ruler's Affairs & Protocol Affairs	353 1060
Department of Ports & Customs	345 9575
Department of Tourism and Commerce Marketing	351 1600
Development Board	228 8866
Dubai Chamber of Commerce & Industry	228 0000
Dubai Courts	334 7777
Dubai Drydocks	345 0626
Dubai Duty Free	206 6444
Dubai Electricity & Water Authority	334 8888
Dubai Government Workshop	334 2999
Dubai Municipality	221 5555
Dubai Police Headquarters	229 2222
Dubai Ports Authority	881 5000

Government Departments in Dubai	(Contd.)
H.H. The Ruler's Court	353 3333
Lands Department	222 2253
Legal Advisors Office	353 1073
Real Estate Department	352 2997
UAE Radio & TV - Dubai	336 9999

Government Websites

Dubai e-Government	www.dubai.ae
e-Dirham (Ministry of Finance)	www.e-dirham.gov.ae

Dubai Government Departments & Related Organisations

Department of Civil Defence	www.dcd.gov.ae
Department of Tourism & Commerce Marketing	www.dubaitourism.com
Dubai Chamber of Commerce & Industry	www.dcci.gov.ae
Dubai Civil Aviation	www.dubaiairport.gov.ae
Dubai Court	www.dubaicourts.gov.ae
Dubai Department of Economic Development	www.dubaided.gov.ae
Dubai Department of Health & Medical Services	www.dohms.gov.ae
Dubai Electricity & Water Authority (DEWA)	www.dewa.gov.ae
Dubai Municipality	www.dm.gov.ae
Dubai Naturalisation & Residence Department	www.dnrd.gov.ae
Dubai Police	www.dubaipolice.gov.ae
Dubai Ports and Customs	www.dxbcustoms.gov.ae
Dubai Ports Authority	www.dpa.co.ae
Dubai Traffic Police	www.dxbtraffic.gov.ae
Dubai Transport Corporation	www.dubaitransport.gov.ae
Emirates Internet & Multimedia	www.emirates.net.ae
Emirates Post	www.emiratespostuae.com
Etisalat	www.etisalat.ae/e4me.co.ae
Real Estate Department	www.realestate-dubai.gov.ae

Federal Government Departments & Organisations

General	www.uae.gov.ae
Ministry of Economy	www.economy.gov.ae
Ministry of Finance	www.fedfin.gov.ae
Ministry of Health	www.moh.gov.ae
Ministry of Information	www.uaeinteract.com
Ministry of Labour	www.mol.gov.ae

Free Zones

Jebel Ali Free Zone Authority	www.jafza.co.ae
Dubai Internet City	www.dubaiinternetcity.com
Dubai Media City	www.dubaimediacity.com
Dubai Airport Free Zone	www.dubaiairportfreezone.co.ae

Government Directory

Directory

Ministries

Federal National Council	282 4531
Federation of UAE Chambers of Commerce & Industry	221 2977
General Secreteriat of UAE Municipalities	223 7785
Ministry of Agriculture & Fisheries	295 8161
Ministry of Communications	295 3330
Ministry of Defence	353 2330
Ministry of Economy & Commerce	295 4000
Ministry of Education & Youth	299 4100
Ministry of Electricity & Water	262 2000
Ministry of Finance & Industry	393 9000
Ministry of Foreign Affairs	222 1144
Ministry of Health	396 6000
Ministry of Information & Culture	261 5500
Ministry of Interior	398 0000
Ministry of Justice, Islamic Affairs & Endowments	282 5999
Ministry of Labour & Social Affairs	269 1666
Ministry of Planning	228 5219
Ministry of Public Works & Housing	269 3900
Ministry of State for Cabinet	396 7555
Ministry of Youth and Sports	269 1680
Protocol Department	253 1086
State Audit Institution	228 6000
UAE Central Bank	393 9777

Personal Affairs

Alcohol/Liquor Stores

A&E	
Al Karama	334 8056
Bur Dubai	352 4521
Deira	222 2666
Jumeira	344 0327
Mirdif	**2882715**
MMI	
Al Karama	335 1722
Al Wasl	394 1678
Bur Dubai	393 5738
Deira	222 2342
Jumeira	334 0223
Ramada	352 3091

Death-Related

Hindu Temple	353 5334
Holy Trinity Church	337 0247
St. Mary's Church	337 0087

Hospitals

Al Amal Hospital	344 4010
Al Baraha Hospital Emergency	271 0000
Al Baraha Hospital (Kuwait) Preventive Medicine	273 1161
Al Maktoum Hospital	222 1211
Al Wasl Hospital Emergency	324 1111
American Hospital Emergency	336 7777
Belhoul Intern Hospital Centre	345 4000
Dubai Hospital Emergency	271 4444
International Pvt Hospital Emergency	221 2484
Iranian Hospital Emergency	344 0250
Rashid Hospital Emergency	337 4000
Welcare Hospital Emergency	282 7788

Real Estate Agents

Alpha Properties	228 8588
Arenco Real Estate	337 2402
Asteco	269 3155
Better Homes	344 7714
Cluttons	334 8585
Emaar Properties	884 5000
Real Estate Specialists	331 2662
Rocky Real Estate	353 2000
Union Properties	294 9490

Recruitment Agencies

BAC	336 0350
Clarendon Parker	331 7092
Job Hunt	355 8507
Kershaw Leonard	343 4606
Nadia	331 3401
Seekers	351 2666
SOS	396 5600
Talent	334 0999

Personal Life Directory

Directory

Relocation Companies	
In Touch Consultants	332 8807
Real Estate Specialists	331 2662
Resco Relocation Consultants	339 3334

Removal Companies	
Allied Pickfords	334 5567
Crown Worldwide Movers	289 5152
Gulf Agency Company (GAC)	345 7555
TNT (UAE) LLC	800 2222

Telephone Codes	
Abu Dhabi	02
Ajman	06
Al Ain	03
Dubai	04
Hatta	04
Fujairah	09
Jebel Ali	04
Sharjah	06
Umm Al Quwain	06
Ras al Khaimah	07
Mobile Telephones	050
Dubai number from outside the UAE	+971 4 ...
Mobile number from outside the UAE	+971 50...

Veterinary Clinics	
Al Safa Veterinary Clinic	344 2498
Dr Matt's Clinic	349 9549
European Veterinary Clinic	343 9591
Jumeirah Veterinary Clinic	394 2276
Modern Veterinary Clinic	395 3131
Veterinary Hospital	348 3799

Personal Life Directory

Directory

Further Reading

If you want to read more about Dubai, the UAE and the Middle East region in general, there are plenty of books to choose from. Explorer Publishing also publishes the Dubai Explorer and Abu Dhabi Explorer as well as expat guides to Oman, Kuwait, Bahrain and Qatar. It also produces a range of regional activity guides, such as the UAE Off-Road explorer and the OmanTrekking Explorer.

TimeOut and Lonely Planet also produce guide books to Dubai and the region, and for a different perspective, read any of Wilfred Thesiger's books on his experiences in the deserts of the

Web Update

While Dubai's government is committed to cutting back on the red-tape involved in setting up in Dubai, both for individuals and businesses, changes in rules and regulations are inevitable. Therefore, if there have been any changes or additions to the procedures included in this book they will appear on the Explorer website. Just log on to **www.explorer-publishing.com** and click on the **Red-Tape** link. This page will tell you if there have been any changes to specific procedures – giving you the heads up before you head off to plough through Dubai's administrative maze!

Middle East.

Expat life – sorted!

Whether you have just arrived in Dubai, are thinking of moving here or have been a resident for years the all new **Dubai Explorer** is a must-own. With help and advice on everything from where to live, what school to pick, what spas to visit, what restaurants to dine in and what sports to take up, if you don't already have this book then stop reading now and run down to the shop to buy it. Be smart and don't miss out on the best book in town!

Dubai Chamber of Commerce & Industry (DCCI)

PO Box ▶	1457	Map ref ▶	8-G4
Tel ▶	228 0000	Fax ▶	202 8544
Location ▶	Beniyas Road, next to the Sheraton Dubai Hotel, Deira Creek Side		
Timings ▶	Sat-Wed 07:30- 14:30, Thu 07:30-12:00 (Attestation)		
Web ▶	www.dcci.gov.ae		

Branches	Details	Map ref
Jebel Ali Branch	881 8333 Main Gate - Entrance No.1, Jebel Ali Free Zone Sat- Wed 08:00-14:00, Thu 08:00-12:00	1-D3

Dubai Court

PO Box ▶	4700, Dubai	Map ref ▶	8-G6
Tel ▶	334 7777	Fax ▶	334 4477
Location ▶	Bur Dubai, near Al Maktoum Bridge		
Timings ▶	Sat-Wed 07:30- 13;30		
Web ▶	www.dubaicourts.gov.ae (Arabic only)		

Branches	Details	Map ref
Notary Public	334 7863 Next to main entrance 07:30-14:30, 17:30-20:15	8-G6

Government & Municipality Offices

Directory

Dubai Department of Economic Development (DDED)

PO Box ▶	13223, Dubai	Map ref ▶	8-H4
Tel ▶	222 9922	Fax ▶	222 5577
Location ▶	Opposite Sheraton Dubai Hotel		
Timings ▶	Sat-Wed 07:30-14:30		
Web ▶	www.dubaided.gov.ae		

Dubai Electricity & Water Authority (DEWA)

PO Box ▶	564, Dubai	Map ref ▶	7-D8
Tel ▶	324 4444	Fax ▶	324 9345 (Billing Dept.)
Location ▶	Za'abeel East, near Wafi Mall		
Timings ▶	Sat-Thu 07:30-21:00		
Web ▶	www.dewa.gov.ae		

Branches	Details	Map ref
Al Rashidiya	285 0622 Nr. Rashidiya police station Sat-Thu 07:30-20:00	6-E7
Al Satwa	398 5560 Power Station - opp Port Rashid Sat-Thu 07:30-20:00	7-B1
Al Qusais	261 3719 Nr. Union Co-op Society Sat-Wed 07:30-14:00	6-F5
Ayal Nasser	271 7864 Nr. Hyatt Regency Sat-Thu 07:30-20:00	8-H1
Burj Nahar	271 4777 Deira Water Tank Sat-Thu 07:30-20:00	9-B3
Hatta	852 3410 Hatta Sat-Thu 06:30-14:30	n/a
Jebel Ali (Complaints Centre)	883 6423 Jebel Ali Free Zone 24 hours, 7 days a week	1-C4
Jumeira	343 1666 Al Wasl Rd, behind Al Mazaya Centre Sat-Wed 07:30-14:00	5-B3
Safia	266 2445 Nr. Choithrams Supermarket Sat-Wed 07:30-14:00	9-D5

Government & Municipality Offices

Directory

Dubai Municipality (DM)

PO Box ▶	67, Dubai	Map ref ▶	8-H3
Tel ▶	221 5555	Fax ▶	224 6666
Location ▶	Baniyas Rd, near InterContinental Hotel, Deira		
Timings ▶	Sat-Wed 07:30-14:30		
Web ▶	www.dm.gov.ae		

Branches	Details	Map ref
Burial & Graveyard Services Unit	264 3355 Al Qusais Sat- Wed, 07:30-14:30	5-C8
Emergency Office	223 2323 Baniyas Rd 24 hours, 7 days a week	8-H3
Fees & Revenues Section	206 3274 Dubai Muncipality Bldg Sat- Wed, 07:30-14:30	8-H3
Legal Affairs Dept.	206 3331 Dubai Muncipality Bldg Sat- Wed, 07:30-14:30	8-H3
Public Relations Section	206 4678 Dubai Muncipality Bldg Sat- Wed, 07:30-14:30	8-H3
Public Transport (Inquiries)	286 1616 Dubai Muncipality Bldg Sat- Wed, 07:30-14:30	8-H3
Rent Committee	221 5555 Dubai Muncipality Bldg Sat- Wed, 07:30-14:30	8-H3
Used Car Exhibitions Complex	333 3800 Al Awir Sat- Wed, 09:00-20:00	5-B7
Veterinary Services Section	285 7335 1.5 km after Mushriff Park Sat-Wed 07:30-14:30	6-G9

Dubai Police

PO Box ▶ 1493, Dubai
Tel ▶ 269 2222, 269 4848
Location ▶ Near Al Mulla Plaza, Al Qusais
Timings ▶ 24 hrs
Web ▶ www.dubaipolice.gov.ae

Map ref ▶ 10-E7
Fax ▶ 221 5158

Branches	Details	Map ref
Air Wing	282 1111 Cargo Area 24 hours	9-B6
Airport	224 5555 Airport, Terminal 1 24 hrs	9-B9
Al Muraqqabat	266 0555 Muraqqabat 24 hrs	9-B4
Al Rashidiya	333 3800 Rashidiya 24 hrs	5-B7
Al Rafaa	393 7777 Nr. Peninsula Hotel 24 hrs	8-F1
Bur Dubai	398 1111 Trade Centre r/a 24 hrs	7-B4
Criminal Investigation Department (CID)	229 2222 Dubai Police H.Q, Al Qusais 24 hrs	10-E7
General Ports & Airport Department	206 6599 Nr Airlines Office, Departures Dubai International Airport	6-E5
Hatta	852 1111 Hatta 24 hrs	n/a
Jebel Ali	881 4849 Jebel Ali 24 hrs	n/a
Nad Al Sheba	336 3535 Nr. Horse Club 24 hrs	4-H6
Naif	228 6999 Naif Road 24 hrs	8-H2
Rashidiya	285 3000 Rashidiya 24 hrs	6-E7

Dubai Police

Directory

Dubai Traffic Police

PO Box ▶	1493, Dubai	Map ref ▶	10-E7
Tel ▶	269 2222, 229 2222	Fax ▶	various
Location ▶	Al Qusais, near Al Mulla Plaza		
Timings ▶	Sat-Wed, 07:00-14:30		
Web ▶	www.dxbtraffic.gov.ae		

Branches	Details	Map ref
Bur Dubai Traffic Police	347 2222 Junction 4, Sheikh Zayed Rd Sat-Wed 07:00-14:30	3-D4
Driving License Offices		
Al Safa Union Coop.	394 5007 Jumeira Sat-Wed 08:30-13:30 16:30-21:30	4-G3
Al Tawar Union Coop.	263 4857 Al Qusais Sat- Wed 08:30-13:30 17:00-20:30	10-F9
Jumeira Plaza	342 0737 Jumeira Sat-Wed 09:00-14:00 17:30-21:00	5-B2

External Traffic Police Desks		
Branches	**Details**	**Map ref**
Al Awir Used Car Showroom	333 3800 Ras Al Khor Sat-Wed 10:00-17:00	5-B7
Ducamz (Dubai Customs Free Zone)	333 5000 Al Awir Road Sat-Wed 07:30-21:00	5-B8
EPPCO Al Qusais	267 3940 New Sharjah Road Sat-Wed 07:00-21:00; Thu 07:00-14:00	6-H5
EPPCO Bur Dubai	347 6620 Junction 4, Sheikh Zayed Rd Sat-Wed 07:00-21:00; Thu 07:00-14:00	3-D4
Honda (Trading Enterprises)	295 4246 Deira, near DNATA Sat-Wed 09:00-13:00, 17:00-19:00	9-A6
Hyundai (Juma Al Majid)	266 5153 Deira, near DNATA Sat-Wed 09:00-13:00, 17:00-20:00	9-A6
Mazda (Galadari)	299 4848 Dubai - Sharjah Road Sat-Wed 09:30-13:00, 17:00-19:00	10-E6
Mitsubishi (Al Habtoor Motors)	269 1110 Deira, near DNATA Sat-Wed 09:00-13:00, 17:00-20:00	9-A6
Nissan (Arabian Automobiles)	295 1234 Deira, near DNATA Sat-Wed 09:30-13:00, 17:00-19:00	9-A6
Toyota (Al Futtaim)	295 4231 City Centre Sat-Wed 09:00-13:00, 17:00-19:00	8-H6

DUbai Traffic Police

Directory

Emirates Post

PO Box ▶	8888, Dubai	Map ref ▶	8-E5
Tel ▶	337 1500	Fax ▶	337 4444
Location ▶	Zabeel Road, Karama		
Timings ▶	Sat-Thu 08:00-20:00, Public Holidays 08:00-12:00		
Web ▶	www.emiratespost.co.ae		

Branches	Details	Map ref
Abu Hail	269 4301 Hamriya, in front of Dubai Hospital Sat-Thu 08:00-14:00	9-D2
Airport	216 4994 Near Gate 18 and Dubai Duty Free 24 hours, 7 days a week	9-B9
Airport Free Zone	299 6130 In the Free Zone Food Court Sat-Thu 08:00-14:00	9-D8
Al Musalla	359 6699 Bur Dubai in front of Dubai Museum, behind Dubai Court Sat-Thu 08:00-14:00	8-F2
Al Quoz	338 8482 Behind Al Waha mall, bes. Emirates Post warehouse Sat-Thu 08:00-14:00	4-F4
Al Qusais	261 3307 Beside Civil Defence Sat-Thu 08:00-14:00	6-G5
Al Ras	225 1298 Deira, behind Public Library Sat-Thu 8am-2pm	8-F1
Al Rashidiya	285 1655 In front of Rashidiya market and police Sat-Thu 08:00-20:00	6-E7
Al Riqqa	295 8978 Deira, Ministry of Agriculture, beside Clock Tower r/a Sat-Thu 08:00-20:00	9-A6
Al Sanaweya	223 3656 Nr. Dubai Muncipality Sat-Thu 08:00-14:00	8-H3
Al Tawar	261 2687 Tawar 2 Kasit Mosque, Al Tawar Clinic Sat-Thu 08:00-14:00	10-E9

Branches	Details	Map ref
Deira	2221952 Beniyas Road, Sheikha Latifa bld., Behind Emirates Bank Sat-Thu 08:00-20:00 Fri- 17:00-20:30	8-H3
Deira Main Office	262 2222 Deira, Nr Abu Hail Centre Sat-Thu 08:00-20:00	10-E5
DNATA	295 5949 Inside Deira DNATA bld. Sat-Thu 08:00-14:00	9-A6
Hor Al Anz	262 9334 Beside Hor al Anz mosque Sat-Thu 08:00-20:00	9-C4
Jebel Ali	881 6988 Jebel Ali Free Zone Next to Gate 2 Sat-Thu 08:00-14:00	1-D3
Jumeira	344 2706 Al Wasl Road, beside Driving Institute Sat -Thu 08:00-20:00	4-H3
Masood	852 3662 Beside Masood police and hospital Sat-Thu 08:00-14:00	Off Map
Ramool	286 2782 In front Al Mawakeb school, Nr Empost office Sat-Thu 08:00-14:00	6-E5
Satwa	344 0364 Beside Etehat Coop Sat-Thu 08:00-20:00	7-A3
Trade Centre	331 3306 Dubai Trade Centre 3rd floor Sat-Thu 08:00-14:00	7-A4

Emirates Post

Directory

Etisalat

PO Box ▶ 300, Dubai   Map ref ▶   8-H3
Tel ▶ 101   Fax ▶   105
Location ▶ Beniyas Rd., opposite Creek Sheraton
Timings ▶ Sat-Wed 07:00-15:00, 17:00-19:00, Thu 08:00-13:00
Web ▶ www.etisalat.co.ae   Home Website
www.emirates.net.ae

Branches	Details	Map ref
Al Baraha	271 3131 Al Baraha Business Centre Sat-Wed 07:00-15:00 17:00-19:00	N/A
Al Khaleej	355 3333 Al Mankhool Rd., Bur Dubai Sat-Wed 09:00-16:00 Thu 09:00-13:00	8-E2
Al Wasl	343 2000 Sheikh Zayed Rd., Jct.1 Sat-Wed 07-15, 17-19 Thu 08:00-13:00	5- A3
Jebel Ali	881 6216 Jebel Ali Free Zone Sat-Wed 08:00-16:00 Thu 08:00-13:00	1-D3

Immigration & Naturalisation Department (IND)

PO Box ▶ 4333, Dubai   Map ref ▶   7-B4
Tel ▶ 398 0000   Fax ▶   398 1119
Location ▶ Al Karama, Trade Centre R/A
Timings ▶ Sat-Wed 07:30-14:30
Web ▶ www.dnrd.gov.ae

Branches	Details	Map ref
Dubai Airport	206 6666 Airport Road 24 hrs	9-B8
Dubai Airport Free Zone	202 7506 Al Quds road Sat- Thurs 07:30-14:30	9-D8
Hamriah Port	269 1042 Hamriah Port Area Sat- Thurs 07:30-14:30	10-F2

Branches	Details	Map ref
Hatta	852 1718 Hatta 24 hrs	Off Map
Jebel Ali Port	881 5000 Jebel Ali Sat -Thu 07:30-14:30	1-B4
Rashid Port	345 1545 Port Rashid Area Sat-Thu 07:00-16:00	7-C1

Ministry of Economy and Commerce

PO Box ▶	3625, Dubai	**Map ref ▶**	9-A5
Tel ▶	295 4000	**Fax ▶**	295 1991
Location ▶	Nr. Dnata		
Timings ▶	Sat - Wed 07:30-14:00		
Web ▶	www.economy.gov.ae		

Ministry of Health/Dubai Dept. of Health & Medical Services

PO Box ▶	4409, Dubai	**Map ref ▶**	7-C4
Tel ▶	396 6000	**Fax ▶**	Various
Location ▶	Opposite Bur Juman Centre on Trade Centre Rd, Karama		
Timings ▶	Sat-Wed 08:30-14:30		
Web ▶	www.moh.gov.ae www.dohms.gov.ae		

Ministry of Labour & Social Affairs

PO Box ▶	4409, Dubai	**Map ref ▶**	10-E6
Tel ▶	269 1666	**Fax ▶**	269 5865
Location ▶	Dubai-Shj Road, Nr. Al Mulla Plaza		
Timings ▶	Sat-Wed 08:30-14:30		
Web ▶	N/A		

Ministries

Directory

Even women will love it!

With multiple street names, bad directions and road rage, it's easy to loose your cool on Dubai's roads. At least with the Dubai Street Map Explorer in your glove compartment you won't loose your way too!

	A	B	C	D
1	The Palm Jebel Ali (u/c)		Jebel Ali Harbour	
2	*Jebel Ali Hotel* / *Jebel Ali Golf*			
3	53		JEBEL ALI PORT	Etisalat Emirates Post
4	← Abu Dhabi / Interchange No.9	DEWA / Immigration & Naturalisation Dept. / Interchange No.8	Sheikh Zayed Rd	11
5		JEBEL ALI		77
6				Emirates Ring Rd
7			311	
8				
9				

	E	F	G	H	
1			*Arabian Gulf*		

Sheraton Jumeirah Beach Hotel

Hilton Dubai Jumeirah Hotel
Oasis Beach Resort
Ritz Carlton Hotel

Jumeirah Beach Residence (u/c)
MARSA DUBAI

E1 11

Interchange No.6

Sheikh Zayed Rd
Ibn Battuta Mall

Jumeirah Lake Towers(u/c)

Interchange No.7

The Gardens

Jumeirah Islands(u/c)

JEBEL ALI VILLAGE

JEBEL ALI INDUSTRIAL AREA

The Gardens View

Lost City(u/c)

Emirates Ring Rd

E1 311

Green Community

DUBAI INVESTMENT PARK

E1 77

DUBAI INVESTMENT PARK 2

1100m

	A	B	C	D
1				Arabian Gulf
2	Le Royal Meridien Beach Resort & Spa — Metropolitan Resort & Beach Club — Le Meridien Mina Siyahi	The Palm Jumeirah (u/c) — One & Only Royal Mirage		Jumeirah Beach Hotel — Burj Al Arab — Mina A' Salam
3	Marina Towers — Dubai Media City — Interchange No.5 — Emirates Golf Club — The Meadows	Dubai Pearl — Dubai Internet City — Knowledge Village — The Greens	Al Sufouh Rd — AL SUFOUH — Sheikh Zayed Road	Madinat Jumeirah — Wild Wadi Water Park — Police Training Collage — UMM AL SHEIF — Interchange No.4
4	The Lakes — EMIRATES HILLS — The Springs	Jebel Ali Racecourse	AL BARSHA'A	Mall of the Emirates — Diamond & Gold Park — Bur Dubai Traffic Dept. — Tasjeel
5		Al Khail Rd		
6				
7		Emirates Ring Rd — Dubai Autodrome		
8			Arabian Ranches	
9				DUBAI LAND

3

Maps

	E	F	G	H	
1		The World (u/c)			
		Arabian Gulf			
2		Dubai Offshore Sailing Club		Jumeirah Beach Club	
		Jumeira Rd		*Jumeirah Beach Park* 94	
3	UMM SUQEIM	*Al Manara Rd*	Dubai Traffic Police	Emirates Post	
	Al Wasl Rd	02	AL SAFA	Safa Park AL WASL	
	AL MANARA	Interchange No 3 11	*Sheikh Zayed Road Oasis Centre*	Australian Embassy	
				Metropolitan	
4	AL QUOZ IND AREA	Emirates Post	AL QUOZ		
				Al Khail Rd	
5			44	Dubai Camel Racecourse	
	Al Khail Rd			AL MARQADH	
6				Dubai Police	
				Dubai Equestrian Centre	
7					
8		DUBAI LAND			
9	Global Village	*Emirates Ring Rd*	311		
	E	F	G	H	

	A	B	C	D
1			Arabian Gulf	
2	Town Centre — Mercato — Dubai Zoo — JUMEIRA	Beach Centre — The Village — Palm Strip — Jumeira Centre — Traffic Police — Iranian Hospital	Dubai Drydock — AL MINA — Al Mina Rd — HUDHEIBA	PORT RASHID — Shindagha Market — AL RAFFA
3	Al Wasl Rd — Al Safa St — DEWA — Mazaya Centre — Shangri-La — Interchange No.1 — Dusit Dubai — Etisalat	Al Satwa Rd — SATWA — DIFC — Emirates Towers	Hana Centre — AL JAFILIYA — Immigration Dept. — Karama Souk	Golden Sands Area — BurJuman Centre — AL KARAMA — Za'abeel Rd — GPO
4	Dubai Mall (u/c)	ZA'ABEEL	Lamcy Plaza — Movenpick — Wafi City — Al Wasl Hospital — Al Wasl Club	Maktoum — OUD METHA — Creek Park — Dubai Creek — Al Garhoud Bridge
5	Business Bay (u/c)	Dubai Wildlife & Waterbird Sanctuary	JADDAF	
6	BuKadra I/C — Nad Al Sheba Racecourse		RAS AL KHOR	Festival City (u/c)
7	NAD AL SHEBA — Dubai - Al Ain Rd	RAS AL KHOR IND AREA	Ras Al Khor Rd	Nad Al Hamar Rd
8			Used Car Complex	NADD AL HAMAR
9	← Al Ain	Emirates Ring Rd	DEWA	Hatta / Oman →

7 **8**

	E	F	G	H

1

Shindagha Tunnel

The Palm Deira (u/c)

2

Hyatt Regency

Al Khaleej Rd

HAMRIYA PORT

Mamzar Beach Park

3

Murshid Bazaar

NAIF

MUTEENA

Al Ghurair Centre

RIGGA

ABU HAIL

HOR AL ANZ

AL MAMZAR

Mamzar Beach

Al Shabab Club

Al Taawun Shopping Mall

Al Taawun Rd

4

Bridge

Deira City Centre

Sofitel

Cargo Village

Airport Rd

Abu Hail Centre

Al Qiadah Interchange

Terminal 2

Al Mulla Plaza

Al Ahli Club

Al Ittehad Rd

Sharjah

5

Terminal 1

9

10

Al Bustan Centre

AL GARHOUD

Emirates Post

DUBAI INTL AIRPORT

DEWA

Al Quds Rd

Al Nahda Rd

AL QUSAIS

Emirates Post

AL QUSAIS IND AREA

Tasjeel

Cemetery

6

UMM RAMOOL

AL TWAR

7

Emirates Post
DEWA
Dubai Police

AL RASHIDIYA

Emirates Rd

8

MIRDIF

Al Khawaneej Rd

AL MIZHAR

6

Maps

9

AL WARQAA

AL WARQAA

Mushrif Park

Dubai Municipality •
Veterinary Section

1100m

	E	F	G	H

	A	B	C	D
1			**AL MINA**	Dubai Ports & Customs Authority
			Al Mina Rd DEWA	D4 92
2	*Al Diyafa St* Dune Centre	*Sri Lanka* HUDHEIBA	Mankhool Rd	Kuwait St D4 90
		Hana Centre	**AL MANKHOOL**	
3	Emirates Post	**AL JAFILIYA** *China*	*Qatar*	
4	Trade Centre R/A DWTC *USA, Italy Japan, Swiss*	Immigration Dept. Dubai Police *Za'abeel Park(u/c)* **AL KIFAF**	Trade Centre Rd Al Adhid Rd	Ministry of Health D4 77 **AL KARAMA**
5	Emirates Post D4 84		D4 75	Karama Souk Za'abeel Rd Lamcy Plaza *Malaysia*
6	*2nd Za'abeel Rd*	**ZA'ABEEL**		American Hospital **OUD METHA**
7	D4 73			
8		E1 66 Oud Metha Rd Al Wasl Club	Al Wasl Hospital	Wafi City DEWA HQ Grand Cineplex
9			**JADDAF**	*Grand Hyatt*

350m

	E	F	G	H	
1	Etisalat **BUR DUBAI** Dubai Police	**Norway** AL RAS Ministry of Finance & Industry Hindu Temple	*Shindagha Tunnel* **Deira Old Souk**	DEWA	**1**
2	**Khaleej Centre** **Al Ain Centre**	*Textile Souk* **AL RAFFA** Emirates Post **Musalla Tower**	Gold Souk **NAIF** Baniyas Squre [85]	Dubai Police	**2**
3	Golden Sands Area **Netherlands Canada** Citibank **BurJuman Centre**	**Egypt Pakistan India Oman Jordan** Lebanon [88]	**Britain Saudi Arabia Kuwait** Inter-Cont.	**RIGGA** Maktoum Hospital Emirates Post Al Ghurair Centre	**3**
4	[79]	[84]	**Sheraton Tower** NBD DCCI	Ministry of Forign Affairs **MURAQQABAT** **Hilton Dubai Creek**	**4**
5	Central Post Office Dubai Central Laboratory *Umm Hurair Rd*	Dubai TV	Dhow wharfage [85] Maktoum Bridge	**Marriott Apts** Emirates Ministry of Agriculture Clock Tower	**5**
6	St. Mary's Church Holy Trinity Church	Rashid Hospital Dubai Courts [81]		Ministry of Economy & Commerce Dnata [74]	**6**
7	Dubai Healthcare City (u/c)	*Creek Park*		**Deira City Centre**	**7**
8	*Children's City*		*Dubai Creek Golf & Yacht Club*	**Millinium Airport** Dubai Tennis Stadium [70]	**8**
9	*Wonderland*	Al Garhoud Bridge	Emirates Training Centre	**Al Bustan Rotana Hotel** **AL GARHOUD**	**9**
	E	F	G	H	

Khalid Bin Waleed Rd

Al-Seef Rd

Baniyas Rd

Al makhtoum Rd

Baniyas Rd

Dubai Creek

8

Maps

	A	B	C	D
1	*Hyatt Regency*			
2	**AL BARAHA**	*Al Khaleej Rd* Baraha Hospital Dubai Hospital	92 Emirates Post	**CORNICHE DEIRA**
3	*har Bin Al Khattab Rd* **MUTEENA**	*Reef Mall*	*Abu Bakar Al Siddiq Rd*	**ABU HAIL** *Abu Hail Rd*
4	*Renaissance* *Salahuddin Rd* Dubai Police	Dubai Police Emirates Post	82 **HOR AL ANZ**	*Hamriya Shopping Centre*
5	Post *Hamrian Centre*	*JW Marriott* 80		DEWA 91
6		**AL KHABAISI** 11 Dubai Flower Centre		*Abu Hail Centre* Al Qiadah Interchange
7	89	Cargo Village		*Al Quds St* Dubai Traffic Dept
8	*Airport Rd* Civil Aviation Dept			Airport Free Zone
9	*Le Meridien*	Emirates Post Terminal 1	**DUBAI INTL AIRPORT**	Emirates Post Terminal 2

350m

The Palm
Deira (u/c)

**HAMRIYA
PORT**

AL MAMZAR

Al Wuheida Rd

Mamzar
Beach

Al Shabab
Club

Emirates
Post

Al Ittehad Rd

Ministry of
Labour

Al Mulla
Plaza

Dubai
Police

Al Ahli
Club

AL NAHDA

Baghdad St

Al Bustan
Centre

AL TWAR

Al Nahda Rd

Damascus St

Dubai Traffic
Police

Emirates Post

AL QUSAIS

10

Maps

Index

Index